SEVEN DAYS TO DISASTER

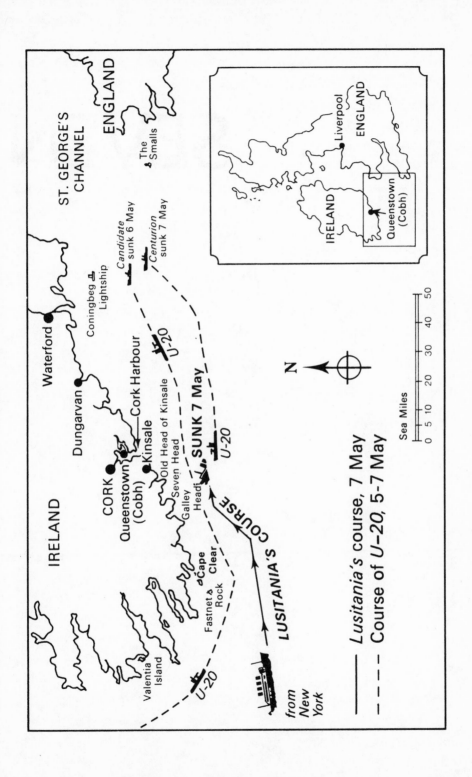

IRELAND

ST. GEORGE'S CHANNEL

ENGLAND

Waterford

Dungarvan

CORK
Queenstown
(Cobh)

Cork Harbour

Kinsale

Old Head of Kinsale

Seven Head

Galley Head

**SUNK 7 May**

U-20

Coningbeg
Lightship

*Candidate*
sunk 6 May

*Centurion*
sunk 7 May

The Smalls

ENGLAND

U-20

Fastnet
Rock

Cape
Clear

Valentia
Island

U-20

*LUSITANIA'S* COURSE

from
New
York

N

*Lusitania's* course, 7 May
Course of *U-20,* 5-7 May

Sea Miles

0  5 10   20   30   40   50

IRELAND

Liverpool

ENGLAND

Queenstown
(Cobh)

# SEVEN

# DAYS
# TO DISASTER

## The Sinking of the
## LUSITANIA

DES HICKEY and GUS SMITH

G. P. PUTNAM'S SONS
NEW YORK

First American Edition 1981

Library of Congress Cataloging in Publication Data

Hickey, Des.
  Seven days to disaster.

  Bibliography: p.
  Includes index.
  1. Lusitania (Steamship)   I. Smith, Gus.
II. Title.
D592.L8H53   1981     940.4'514     81-19892
ISBN 0-399-12699-6             AACR2

PRINTED IN THE UNITED STATES OF AMERICA

To the memory of
Albert Bestic,
Junior Third Officer
on the *Lusitania*

# AUTHORS' NOTE

THE STORY OF the voyage of the *Lusitania* that follows is
entirely factual. Eye-witnesses and survivors have substanti-
ated our account of the event in authors' interviews. We have
also drawn on contemporary reports, depositions and statements, and followed hitherto unexplored avenues of research.

In this respect we are particularly grateful to Alan Bestic
for the account of the voyage written by his father, the late
Albert Bestic; Professor M. A. Ricklin for his memoir of
Charles Voegele of the *U-20*; Dr. John de Courcy Ireland of
the Maritime Institute of Ireland for his interview with
Raimund Weisbach, torpedo officer of the *U-20*; Annelotte
Weisbach-Zerning and Christian-Rainer Weisbach for their
accounts; Quest Research and Information Services for their
inquiries into the career of Detective-Inspector William Pierpoint; Len Chappell of the Canadian Broadcasting Services,
Toronto, for the interview with Otto Rikowsky of the *U-20*;
and Frederick Smyth for the account of the significant
*Candidate* incident.

Many others who co-operated in our researches are listed in
the acknowledgements. They have all helped to recreate the
story of a voyage that changed the course of history.

DES HICKEY and GUS SMITH

*May 1981*

# CONTENTS

# PART I

# New York

## 30 April – 1 May, 1915

*For what is comfort, and more than*
*comfort—luxury—and the certainty*
*of safety—we come to an understanding*
*of the significance, which is assurance,*
*certified by this hallmark: Cunard.*

William Ewart Gladstone

# 1

# EMBARKATION

ALL THAT MORNING the passengers filed up the gangways of the *Lusitania*, the porters following with their baggage.

By nine am on Saturday, 1 May 1915 Pier 54 at the foot of New York's 14th Street was noisy with the farewells of more than a thousand passengers and those who had gathered to see them off. A war was raging on the other side of the Atlantic, and many of those boarding the liner were women on their way to join their soldier husbands, or doctors and nurses who had volunteered to work with the Red Cross in the field.

The *Lusitania* was a favourite with travellers. Her appointments were so superb she merited the epithet 'a floating palace'. The 197 Americans booked to sail that morning might have chosen instead to join the *New York* which was scheduled to leave her pier at midday; she had room for another 300 passengers. But the *Lusitania* was the fastest and smartest liner on the Atlantic; compared to the *New York* her great speed at full steam would save them two days. Since her maiden voyage in 1907, when she captured the world's attention with an average speed of 23 knots, she had made 201 crossings. She could accommodate 2,198 passengers and 920 crew, yet this morning there was room for almost another thousand passengers. Thus few of those walking up the gangways can have given serious thought to the dangers of the voyage or taken heed of the German warning in the morning papers. Junior Third Officer Albert Bestic was standing at the head of one of the gangways when a woman stepped on board

with her three children. She told him she had been approached on the quayside by men with foreign accents who
had warned her not to sail that day. 'Do you think there's any
truth in what those men are saying?' she asked. 'That the ship
is going to be torpedoed?'

'I don't, madam,' the Third Officer assured her. 'I believe
it's bluff. There's no submarine that can catch the *Lusitania*.'

In the early morning drizzle the great liner towered above
the green-painted sheds of the pier, her mastheads rising 216
feet into the sky, her 790-foot length extending beyond the
wharf into the Hudson River. The four giant funnels,
scarlet and black paintwork glistening from the rain, gave
an assurance of power and speed against the threat of
destruction.

The woman smiled gratefully at Bestic. 'Thank you. I'm
sure everything will be all right. It's just when one has
children . . .'

The *Lusitania*'s gangways were like bridges to Liverpool;
once they were crossed the passengers believed that all would
be well. Bestic heard the laughter and conversation that rose
to conceal the pain of separation. He noticed that an unusual
number of bouquets of flowers had been sent on board.

As they made their way towards the gangway in the wake of
the porters Surgeon-Major Frank Warren Pearl and his family
were handed leaflets by men on the quayside warning them
not to travel. Alice Lines, the young family nurse, turned to
Mrs. Pearl. 'Did you get this leaflet?' she asked.

'Take no notice, dear,' Amy Pearl reassured her. 'It's just
propaganda.'

The Pearl family were en route for London where the
Surgeon-Major was to report to the United States Embassy.
During the Spanish-American War he had served as a surgeon
in the United States Army, and since the spring of 1914 he and
his wife and three children had spent most of their time
travelling. They had holidayed in England at Folkestone,
where their third child was born and where they had recruited
Nurse Alice Lines. The outbreak of war in August found them

in Stockholm where Pearl secured passports for Petrograd, hoping to apply his military experience in Russia. But when threats of bombardment halted their journey at Helsingfors they decided to stay in Denmark at a seaside hotel. A few days later Pearl crossed to England, with a view to putting down their son Stuart's name for Eton. Returning by way of Belgium and Germany he was arrested at Lübeck by two German officers. The fair-haired, blue-eyed, young American wearing well-cut English tweeds and carrying a copy of the London *Times* was, to all appearances, an Englishman.

Amy Pearl had no idea what had become of her husband. As she waited in the hotel at Skager, she confided her worries to Alice Lines. Then, one evening, she was handed a telegram from Lübeck: COME AT ONCE. IN TROUBLE. WARREN. She signed an open cheque for Alice Lines to pay for any expenses while she was away, and travelled alone to Lübeck. Here she too was arrested and taken to a police court on suspicion of spying.

For three hours she was questioned, and then released. Only when she demanded to see the American Consul was she escorted to the city prison and allowed to speak to her husband. Pearl told his wife his captors regarded his reasons for travelling through Germany as unlikely; they were convinced he was a spy. He asked her to return to Denmark to plead with the American Ambassador for his freedom.

Two weeks later Warren Pearl was released and ordered to leave by steamer that evening for Copenhagen where he was reunited with his family. Alice Lines engaged a Danish girl, Greta Lorenson, to help her look after the three children: Stuart, nearly five; Amy, two; and Susan, born in Folkestone early that year. Mrs Pearl was expecting a fourth child and wanted it to be born in America, so they decided to return home. They travelled to the United States on board a German steamer, with Alice Lines posing as an American girl for fear of being recognised as English. The baby was born in New York and christened Audrey and the Pearls moved into an apartment on Fifth Avenue. Now, on the evening of 30 April,

Alice Lines completed the packing for the family. She filled large trunks with the couple's clothes, laying them neatly on trays which she covered with tissue paper and placed, one on top of the other, until each trunk was full. Then, the family having invited her to attend, she joined their farewell dinner party in a private room at the Plaza Hotel. Next morning she took a cab to the Cunard pier with Greta and the children.

Major and Mrs Pearl shared one of the Regal Suites, the nurses and children being given adjoining cabins, each with a bathroom and toilet. Greta took the three older children; Alice improvised a cot in her cabin for Audrey. To the Pearls, first-class travel was their right—it was, after all, the only civilised way to cross the Atlantic. Even Greta, whose brother, a ship's petty officer, had been drowned on the *Titanic*, was disarmed by the splendours of the Cunarder, and her eagerness to see Europe again made her indifferent to danger. So lively were the crowds on deck that Alice Lines found it difficult to believe she was on a British ship sailing to wartime Europe. In the sunshine that chased away the early morning drizzle she walked with Stuart around the deck. Across the Hudson she could see the ensigns flying from the sterns of the German ships interned at Hoboken.

The sight gave her a sudden chill.

The impresario Charles Frohman took a cab from his permanent suite at the Knickerbocker Hotel on the corner of Broadway and 42nd Street in a mood as gloomy as the weather. His felt hat tilted over bushy eyebrows, he carried the manuscript of a play tucked in his inside pocket. Just before leaving the hotel he had received a telegram from his friend, the actor John Drew. It read: I'LL NEVER FORGIVE YOU IF YOU GET BLOWN UP BY A SUBMARINE. On his way to the Cunard pier he stopped off at his office in the Empire Theatre to dictate a note to the playwright Porter Emerson Browne. It said simply, 'Goodbye. Keep me posted'. Earlier, an actress who had called to wish him *bon voyage* found him staring at a notebook he always carried with him. 'Isn't it strange,' he sighed. 'My little book is full — there's no room for anything more in it!'

His friend the actor, Paul Potter, said he would try to meet Frohman at the pier. In case they missed each other Frohman wrote a note to him and left it at the hotel:

Saturday a.m., 1 May 1915

Dear Paul: We had a fine time this winter. I hope all will go well with you. And I think luck is coming to you. I hope another *Trilby*. It's fine of you to come to the steamer with all these dark, sad conditions.

But Potter was there, waiting at the Pier. As they went aboard he asked, 'Aren't you afraid of the U-boats, C.F.?'

The impresario smiled. 'No, my dear Paul, only of the IOU's.'

Once aboard, leaning heavily on a stick because of his crippling arthritis and looking older than his forty-seven years, Frohman walked slowly along the promenade deck with Paul and the playwrights Charles Klein and Justus Miles Forman. They all wanted to discuss the warning in the morning paper, but he scoffed at their fears. During a visit to Philadelphia to see a production of one of his shows he had received an anonymous letter warning him that the *Lusitania* was to be destroyed. Friends had urged him to transfer to an American liner, but he ignored their anxiety. He would sail, as he had planned, on the *Lusitania*.

It had been a trying morning for Frohman. The New York papers had got wind of a rumour that he had secretly married his leading actress Maude Adams, and before leaving the Knickerbocker he and his manager had parried reporters' telephone calls. Theatre had been Maude's life since her mother first carried her on stage at the age of nine months, but it was Frohman who groomed her and taught her to make the most of the delicate features and caressing voice which gave her an irresistible charm. He cast her in J. M. Barrie's *The Little Minister* at the age of twenty, and she earned 50,000 dollars in her first year with him.

Frohman himself had been fascinated by the theatre from an early age. But his first job at the age of fourteen, when his parents moved to New York from Sandusky, Ohio, was with the *New York Graphic* as a night clerk. The *Graphic* sent him to Philadelphia in 1876 to sell their daily newspaper to the crowds then thronging the Centennial Exposition; young Frohman took charge of the newsboys, hustled the bundles of papers from the New York trains, rushed them to the news-stands and even sold them himself on the streets. When he moved to the *New York Tribune* he worked by day and sold tickets by night at a theatre in Brooklyn. At seventeen he followed his brother Daniel into management. Three years later in Boston he went to the opening of *Shenandoah*. He had fifty cents in his pocket, but before the night was out he had bought the road rights to the play. That was the start of his success.

Yet by 1915, having produced more than 700 shows, em-ploying an average of 700 actors a season and paying salaries totalling 25,000 dollars a week, Charles Frohman was an enigma not only to the public and the actors he managed, but even to his family. 'Charlie does things differently,' they said. He lived a life of total privacy and encouraged his stars to do the same. Although a member of the world's most exposed profession, he avoided fashionable restaurants and public places and was never known to go on stage to take a curtain call. At the end of a performance he returned to his office. Nobody knew what time he went home to bed. Once when he was trapped in an elevator, he sat patiently on the floor for hours smoking a cigar. 'Boys,' he remarked to the mechanics who released him, 'that's the first vacation I've had in years.'

Edna May, John Drew, Ethel Barrymore and Nat Goodwin were his principal American stars; George du Maurier, Marie Tempest, Seymour Hicks and Ellaline Terriss were among his stars in England. 'Frohman takes America to England and brings England back to America', was a saying in the profession. Five years earlier he had founded a repertory theatre in London at the Duke of York's. His journey this May was at the invitation of his friend James Barrie whose burlesque, *Rosy Rapture, the Pride of the Beauty Chorus*, with music by the promising young Jerome Kern, had opened at the theatre in St. Martin's Lane.

Ten years earlier other producers had dismissed Barrie's script for *Peter Pan* as theatrical madness. Frohman saw its possibilities at once.

Theatre producers in New York were mostly showmen who gambled on Broadway strictly for financial gains — a successful show could and did make their fortunes. But Frohman cherished a deep love for the stage: indeed, there were few better off-stage actors when the occasion demanded. He could choke with emotion over a trifle or could cry at a moment's notice. Backstage on the opening night of *A Celebrated Case* he had urged his partner, David Belasco, 'Take the next call — go on — act your damnedest. Put your hand on your heart. Cry — they expect it!' And he added, 'I guess they think *I'm* in the box office counting the filthy lucre.'

In a curious way Frohman envied the players on whom he lavished his attention. He would pore over proofs of their photographs and designs for their costumes for hours, coach them in their parts, advise them on their choice of hotel, and caution them to remain secluded during their tours. He spoilt them as a father would spoil his children with gifts of toys, books, flowers and gaily-coloured boxes of candy. Yet his ego was such that he once ordered thousands of envelopes to be destroyed because they had been printed bearing the photograph of one of his stars, but not him.

Although he shaped his actors' lives with an almost hypnotic power some rebelled at what they considered his lightweight taste — he detested Ibsen and most other modern European playwrights, yet he had an unerring sense of what would work on the stage. By casting Maude Adams as *Peter Pan* he made theatrical history and a fortune for the actress, Barrie and himself.

Frohman usually travelled to his 'London playmarket' or his 'Paris playmarket', as he called them, in the autumn; this year

Barrie had persuaded him to travel in the spring to see Gaby Deslys starring in *Rosy Rapture* at St. Martin's Lane. The impresario seldom maintained an interest in a play after he had seen a couple of performances, but now the anticipation of a new production in London was enough to bring colour to his cheeks.

The famous mine-owner and politician David Alfred Thomas and his daughter Margaret (Lady Mackworth) were among the first of the saloon passengers to board the liner. A Welshman, Thomas hated to be away from his home in Monmouthshire during what he considered the two most perfect weeks of the year, the second and third weeks of May. Llanwern, his solid redbrick house set among beech and elm trees, was never far from his thoughts. His needs were simple — so much so that a Labour politician once observed. 'There goes Thomas — with the income of a duke and the tastes of a peasant.'

He had been inspecting his mining interests in Pennsylvania, launching a new barge service on the Mississippi, planning extensions of Canada's railroad system. At fifty-nine he was remarkably energetic. His American friends reckoned he would have been more at home in the States than in the modest confines of Wales, but it was in the South Wales coalfields that 'D.A.' had made his fortune, undeterred by the spectre of poverty and near-starvation, and determined to introduce his own remedies for the ills of the people. As a Liberal MP he served his constituency for twenty years, and was disappointed that front bench appointments eluded him. To the Welsh nationalists, however, he was a formidable opponent. Their parochialism repelled him and he regarded their hopes of 'Wales for the Welsh' as senseless. Lloyd George so respected his local power and influence that he remarked during a visit to South Wales, 'There's no room for two kings here.'

Thomas adored his daughter, now in her early thirties. 'Margaret and I are not like father and daughter,' he would say. 'We're buddies.'

Margaret Mackworth, who was equally fond of her mother Sybil, had arrived in New York three weeks earlier to find her father waiting at the docks to greet her. Her voyage had not been pleasant. As a precaution against submarines even the lighting of cigars was forbidden at night and the ship's lights were switched off for fear of attack. Ten days at sea had left her sick and miserable. It took the spirit of New York to revitalise her. She soon forgot the journey and the war and revelled in American hospitality and warmth. With a generous allowance from her father she bought fine clothes in the smart shops on Fifth Avenue.

Margaret Thomas had led a sheltered childhood in Wales among a small circle of family and friends. She married, unsuccessfully, a neighbour, Sir Humphrey Mackworth, twelve years her senior. Their interests were at odds: he had a passion for fox-hunting — she loved books and considered hunting uncivilised. Soon tiring of her empty life in a household run by three maids, a cook, a housemaid and a parlourmaid, she looked for more rewarding interests. Within four months of her marriage she had joined the Pankhurst movement, the Women's Social and Political Union, espousing the cause of votes for women. She invited Mrs. Pankhurst to speak at the first meeting in Newport: she, unable to come, sent her daughter Sylvia instead. Sir Humphrey refused to allow her inside the house.

As her local suffrage branch became more aggressive, Lady Mackworth grew more daring. She burned Post Office mails, a militant strategy adopted by the movement. Not surprisingly, she was arrested and charged. As her trial drew near it became clear that she would be given the option of a fine or a prison sentence. She discussed the options with her husband. He was strongly opposed to her going to prison, but she insisted that it would do her cause no service if she paid her fine. She was found guilty and sentenced to a month in the county jail at Usk. As a suffragette she was allowed to wear her own clothes and keep some books in her cell. She refused to eat the prison food and drank only water. The experience marked her and on her release she vowed, 'I shall campaign for the suffrage cause until the franchise is granted to women.'

Among the many children Margaret Mackworth noticed running about the first-class promenade deck were the Cromptons. The six childrens' ages ranged from six months to twelve years. Mrs. Crompton had come aboard hugging the youngest in her arms. Her husband Paul was an Englishman living in Philadelphia, a partner in the firm of Alfred Booth and Company and a director of the Booth Steamship Company. He planned to see Alfred Booth as soon as they reached Liverpool.

Cunard advertised the *Lusitania* not only for its speed and luxury, but also for the safety it afforded mothers and their children. That morning 129 children, including 39 infants, were taken aboard.

Wearing a wide-brimmed stetson, an outsize velvet bow tie and a long, loose-fitting overcoat the Sage of East Aurora looked every inch an eccentric. Elbert Hubbard was author, publisher and lecturer. Through his magazines *The Philistine* and *The Fra*, printed unconventionally and filled with his rambling, homespun philosophy, he had become known as 'Fra Albertus'. But his real income came from the de luxe editions of the classics which he published from his shop in East Aurora, New York.

With his wife Alice, the flowing-haired Hubbard was travelling to Europe to report on the war — about which he had definite, if odd, notions:

In Germany no private individual can operate an automobile. All the oil and 'petrol' have been seized to incinerate the dead. No slab marks their resting place. No records of the slain are kept. In Germany today no bands play in the public parks; all savings banks are closed; commercial banks pay, or not, as the War Minister orders; all insurance companies, both life and

fire, are bankrupt; colleges are turned into hospitals —
all students are at the front; factories are closed;
laboratories are memories.

As for the Kaiser, 'he has a withered hand and a running ear,
a shrunken soul and a mind reeking with egomania. He is
swollen like a drowned pup with a pride that stinks.'

Hubbard's attack on the Kaiser was the most savage to
appear in an American publication. He claimed his heart was
with the Germany of science, invention, music and education,
not with the Germany represented by an Emperor who had
caused crepe to be worn by millions. Clutching a battered
briefcase, 'The Man Who Lifted The Lid Off Hell' told
reporters that the German warning was directed as much at
himself as at the *Lusitania*.

'To be torpedoed,' he said, 'would be a good advertisement.
If they sink the ship it might be a good thing for me. I would
drown with her, and that's about the only way I could succeed
in my ambition to get into the Hall of Fame.' In 1912 he had
written of the drowning of a couple aboard the *Titanic* as 'a
glorious privilege'. Barring accidents, Hubbard boasted, he
would live to be a hundred. 'All disease is indecent. There are
just two respectable ways to die: one is of old age, the other is
by accident.'

He would not have been on board the *Lusitania* that
morning but for the sympathy of President Wilson. In 1913 he
had been fined 100 dollars on a charge of misusing the mails
by publishing objectionable matter in his magazines; it was a
modest fine, but the conviction automatically deprived him of
his rights of citizenship. President Taft had denied him a
pardon, saying his petition was premature, but in 1915
Hubbard went to the White House to complain that, although
he wanted to visit Europe to write about the war, he could not
obtain a passport because of his conviction. A sympathetic
Woodrow Wilson signed a pardon.

Two days before leaving East Aurora the Sage wrote to J. M.
Shumate of St. Louis:

Saturday of this week, May 1, I board the *Lusitania* to sail to Europe. The foreign authorities have been kind to me. I will be given an opportunity to observe conditions as they are. Abroad I will represent myself and I will edit my copy. I intend to store all in my bean and in that way to elude the censor. When I get back — if I do — I will give it to the readers of *The Fra* and *The Philistine* straight. I aim to be a reporter — not a war correspondent. (Raus mit Der Puttees.) I'll write about what I see, only that. I will return 20 June (perhaps).

The wealthiest passenger on board the *Lusitania* was Alfred Gwynne Vanderbilt. The heir to the world's biggest fortune strolled along the promenade deck, more sporting than businesslike in a charcoal-grey pin-stripe suit with a blue polka-dot bow tie and a wide tweed cap.

Slightly built, Alfred Gwynne at thirty-eight was the handsomest of the fourth generation of Vanderbilts. At Yale he had been voted 'the greatest social light' in his class. His Grand Tour on graduation in 1899 was a world trip which ended abruptly in China when news was cabled to him of his father's death in New York. He chartered trains and steamers to reach home, but when he arrived at the 70-room mock renaissance palace above the cliffs at Newport, Rhode Island, his father's remains had been buried for four weeks. The family had waited patiently for his return before gathering in the great marble and mahogany library to hear the lawyer read the will.

Even though he had whittled his vast wealth away by giving freely to charities, the fortune of Cornelius Vanderbilt II was valued at 72,500,000 dollars. The lawyer announced that four of his five children would share a twenty million dollar trust fund, each of them receiving an outright five million dollars. The family's most treasured heirloom was the gold medal with which Congress had honoured Commodore Cornelius Vanderbilt, the founder of the family fortune, for his gift of the SS *Vanderbilt* during the Civil War. This was bequeathed to Alfred Gwynne, confirming him as head of the Cornelius Vanderbilt line. With the medal went the residual estate of 42,575,000 dollars.

Alfred's brother Cornelius, 'Neily' to the family, was left a mere half million in cash and a million dollars in a trust fund. The charities of Cornelius Vanderbilt II may have extended far beyond the knowledge of the other Vanderbilts, yet, despite such generosity, he had cut off his son for marrying against his wishes. Embarrassed by this snub to his brother, Alfred decided to make the inheritance equal by giving Neily six million dollars.

A few weeks later the heir to the Vanderbilt millions was perched dutifully at a clerk's desk in the offices of the New York Central Railroad, in which his father had been a major stockholder, working from nine to five, with an hour's lunch break, for a nominal salary of 1,200 dollars a year. For a good-looking millionaire of twenty-two, with membership of a dozen exclusive clubs and an avid interest in polo ponies, dedication to clerking was not to last. In 1901 Alfred Gwynne married the heiress Elsie French, whom a social reporter described as 'tall and divinely fair, with a wealth of titian-coloured hair, and a brilliant complexion that outdoor life in sun and sea only tends to beautify'.

Their wedding cake was baked in the form of a trolley so that when the bride gave the ribbons a gentle tug the cake advanced towards her; she then cut it into slices to be divided among the guests whose aggregate wealth totalled an estimated thousand million dollars. Each slice contained an item of precious jewellery so that everybody had a keepsake of the occasion.

Within seven years Elsie had obtained a divorce from her husband on the grounds of his misconduct with Mary Agnes O'Brien Ruiz, the wife of a Cuban attaché in Washington. Alfred closed his house at Oakland Farm, Newport, and moved into the Hotel Plaza. Elsie, taking the name of Mrs. French Vanderbilt, went to live at her brother's house, maintaining custody of their son, William Vanderbilt III.

Alfred's second marriage, to Margaret Smith Hollins McKim, heiress to the Bromo Seltzer drug fortune, came as no surprise. When Mrs. McKim obtained a Reno divorce from her English doctor husband in 1911, on the grounds of 'drunkenness and cruelty', she and Alfred married at the registry office in Reigate and sailed away on a Mediterranean cruise. Their first child, Alfred Gwynne II, was born in Surrey, their second, George Washington III, at Newport, Rhode Island.

Since 1908, when Elsie divorced him, Alfred had spent as much time in England as in America. He and Margaret crossed the Atlantic two or three times a year, but after the birth of George at the beginning of the war Margaret had not left America, preferring to spend her days in the Vanderbilt Hotel which Alfred had built on the site of the old Vanderbilt home on Park Avenue and 34th Street.

Vanderbilt was sailing without his wife on the *Lusitania* for a London meeting with his fellow-directors of the International Horse Show Association. At their country home at Oakland Farm, the Vanderbilts trained horses for road coaching and horse shows, and each summer Alfred drove a coach between London and Brighton.

The night before sailing Vanderbilt took his wife and another couple to the Empire on Broadway to see *A Celebrated Case*, Charles Frohman's and David Belasco's first co-production for some years. While the Vanderbilts were at the theatre, nursemaids tucked up Alfred and George in bed and Ronald Denyer, the valet, packed his master's suitcases and trunks for the voyage to England. Denyer would travel on the *Lusitania*, as would Vanderbilt's close friend Charles Williamson, whose name had been linked with that of Mary Ruiz.

A year previously Mary Ruiz had committed suicide in London. The details of the inquest were not made public; the only two reporters present were said to have been paid 15,000 dollars each to 'spike' their copy. The coroner's verdict was that Mrs. Ruiz had taken her own life 'while of unsound mind'. Subsequent attempts by the Press to secure the records of the proceedings were blocked by the deputy coroner who declared, 'Coroners need not allow themselves to be bothered by newspapers which have failed to obtain the facts at the inquest'. Hush money was said to have been lavished 'on persons associated with Mrs. Ruiz' and others 'who might be in a position to reveal the true facts'. Williamson closed up Mrs. Ruiz' house in Grosvenor Square, took charge of her belongings and sacked the servants. Mary Ruiz may have killed herself because of her infatuation for Vanderbilt. But the millionaire would never discuss the matter.

Close friends protected him from inquisitive reporters. Along with Williamson, his bachelor friend Thomas Slidell was also on board on his way to France. In the autumn of 1907 Alfred Vanderbilt and 'Tommy' Slidell had sailed down river in the Vanderbilt yacht, past clanging buoys and ships blowing impatient sirens, to welcome the *Lusitania* on her maiden voyage.

Slidell refrained from criticising his friend's society life, but praised him to others for the generosity he had shown to the Red Cross. The newspapers of the day, however, were interested only in Vanderbilt the playboy 'with more money to spend than he knows what to do with'. They followed the fortunes of Viscount, one of his six famous greys. Vanderbilt had spotted the horse on a cab stand in New York and Viscount was to discover the delights of being owned by a millionaire. He was taken to Oakland Farm where Vanderbilt supervised the training of his coaching horses in the belief that, 'Under the master's eye the mare grows fat.'

So preoccupied was the millionaire with his horses that he seldom found time for a plunge in the farm's white marble swimming pool; indeed, he had never learned to swim.

His fad was coaching, his weakness womanising. Newport folk knew that he and his men friends frequently drove out of Oakland on wild trips and returned with mixed company. It was accepted that he had lost interest in the business which his forefathers had built up and his father had entrusted to him.

Even his second marriage had not tamed him.

When the reporters on the promenade deck questioned him about the German warning, he fingered the red carnation in his buttonhole, and remarked, 'Why should we be afraid of German submarines? This ship can outdistance any submarine afloat'.

# 2

# PREMONITIONS

THE TALL FIGURE of Charles Sumner was jostled on the quayside by a group of reporters who questioned him on the passengers' safety in view of the German warning. Sumner, a blunt Bostonian who ran the Cunard Line's New York office, assured them that no bookings had been cancelled. 'There's no risk to anyone, I can assure you, gentlemen,' Sumner said. 'Everybody's safe on this crossing.' In his concern to see the liner sail from her pier he had not bothered to notify his chairman, Alfred Booth, in Liverpool of the warning. If he had checked with his office clerks they could have given him a list of cancellations.

Edward Bowen, a wealthy Boston shoe dealer, had telephoned that morning to have his name taken off the list of saloon passengers. He could not explain his premonition that some disaster lay in wait for the *Lusitania*. He discussed these misgivings with his wife, and together they decided he should cancel his booking. Al Woods, a New York theatrical manager and his business friend Walter Moore, also cancelled. Woods had booked a stateroom adjoining the playwright Charles Klein's, but decided that morning not to travel. He and Moore were uneasy at the news of German submarine attacks. They had another, yet more compelling, reason for not making the trip; both of them had been booked to sail on the *Titanic* on her maiden voyage, and only a last-minute business appointment in London had prevented them leaving in time to catch the liner. John McFadden, a millionaire stockbroker from Philadelphia, had also cancelled that morning because of a premonition about the liner's fate. And one man walked off the liner when he found his favourite cabin had been given to another passenger.

A few passengers had made bookings in defiance of explicit warnings. Sam Abramovitz, from Albany in New York State, had received a telegram signed 'German Consul' three days before the sailing which read: DO NOT TAKE LUSITANIA. THIS WILL BE SUNK. George Morris, a saloon passenger from Toronto, had laughed at the concern of a New York friend. 'I'll feel safer,' he declared, 'crossing to England on the *Lusitania* than crossing Broadway at 34th Street.' Charles Lauriat, a Boston bookseller on his way to his London office, shrugged off his earlier doubts. When buying a first-class ticket he had asked if the liner would be escorted safely through the war zone. 'Yes, sir,' he was told. 'Every precaution will be taken.'

On three of the *Lusitania*'s previous voyages Dowie, the ship's black cat and stokers' mascot, had attempted to jump ship. On Friday night he scurried down a hawser onto the dockside and disappeared into the darkness, succeeding at his fourth attempt. Some of the superstitious firemen and stokers, scared by what seemed a clear warning, jumped ship before daybreak.

The thin face of the diminutive scenic designer, Oliver Bernard, was not so much anxious as gloomy as he climbed the first-class gangway. Over an early breakfast at the Knickerbocker Hotel he had read in the *New York Tribune* the warning from the German Embassy. He was not unduly perturbed. Just another bluff to embarrass the American Government and cause consternation in England, he thought. He was certain the British Admiralty had taken heed of the warning.

His gloom stemmed from his rejection at the start of the war by the British Army, the Royal Flying Corps and the Royal Naval Air Force on the grounds of poor hearing. Ashamed to be a non-combatant, he had quit his designing job at the

Royal Opera House, Covent Garden, and gone to Boston where he had previously worked in opera. He disliked having to explain his situation to American friends who laughed at him for believing he might be of use in the war and instead encouraged him to settle in America. A surgeon friend persuaded him to illustrate in colour some of his operations.

A few months before the outbreak of war he had gone to Berlin for a production of *The Ring* at Charlottenburg. On his way out of a café a German officer had followed him to the door, deliberately treading on his heels. At the Palais de Danse a group of young men had tried to start a quarrel, and on a train a young man had informed him, 'Germany will soon show your Mr. Churchill how to trim his Navy.' At the Opera House they had received him with an icy politeness which 'could not conceal their contempt for the Engländer from Covent Garden'.

Bernard chafed at being out of England in wartime. He believed he understood his country's plight and after a few months in Boston he decided to sail for home, determined to try again for the services. Friends lavished presents and advice on him and invited him to settle in Boston when the war was over. The millionaire William Lindsey's parting words were, 'Keep an eye on my little girl, Oliver.' Lesley Lindsey had married a young Englishman and was making her honeymoon trip on the *Lusitania*. Bernard wondered how one kept an eye on a newly-married couple with youth, good looks, riches in abundance and the world — subject to the conditions of war — at their feet.

Before returning to his room at the Knickerbocker on Friday night he called in at a party given by friends on Riverside Drive. The conversation among the guests convinced him that few people in America, apart from those who saw it as a means of increasing their wealth, had the faintest idea of what the war meant to those who were engaged in it.

Bernard's jaundiced view of the wealthy was explained by his background. Born to a London theatrical couple, he had been placed in charge of an aunt in London's Waterloo area

B

because he would have 'encumbered them on their travels'. He could remember his nurse telling another on Brighton sands, 'When he was shown to his mother for the first time she said, "Very nice, but please take him away".'

His parents had passed out of his life when a Manchester couple offered to care for him at the age of thirteen. He moved north, only to realise that his most important task in Manchester would be to escape from it. Determined to become a designer, he set himself the drudgery of learning to draw from sight and from memory, working by candlelight at the dressing table in his bedroom with only a pencil. He found work in a city theatre as property boy and paint-room assistant, earning starvation wages and living on cheese and an occasional eccles cake, which accounted, or so he was convinced, for his present slight, undernourished figure.

Unable to save enough money for his rail fare to London, he made his escape through the Manchester Ship Canal as a cabin boy on a Norwegian barque. He had sailed twice to Montreal before he escaped from his 'floating slum' and finally arrived in London to begin his apprenticeship to a scenic artist.

After London Bernard found New York in 'the throes of a spectacular disease'. Monuments to commercial energy climbed faster and higher. The Flatiron, Singer, Metropolitan and Woolworth buildings created sunless chasms swarming with greedy people whose preoccupation was the dollar. On board the *Lusitania* he decided the sight of overfed saloon passengers wearing fur collars and expensive shoes would make him seasick. He was returning to England with nothing more than the hope of some type of active service—a hope which made him restless and impatient for the voyage to begin.

Marie de Page, the special envoy in the United States of Belgium's King Albert and Queen Elizabeth, was equally anxious to return home. Her seventeen-year-old son Lucien had joined the army and she wanted to see him again before he went to the trenches. A woman of charm and intelligence,

Madame de Page had spent two months touring American cities, appealing for help for her war-torn country with such conviction that she collected pledges for more than 100,000 dollars for the Belgian Red Cross. Her husband, Antoine de Page, was Surgeon-General to the Belgian Army and director of the 'Queen's Hospital' at La Panne; here Marie de Page visited wounded soldiers from both sides, talking to them and writing letters home for them.

'Why do you bother?' a young German soldier asked her. 'I'm your enemy.'

'No, you're not,' she told him. 'To me you're just a wounded man who needs help.'

On Friday afternoon she had addressed a meeting of the Special Relief Society. She told her wealthy listeners of Belgium's plight. As she spoke her thoughts must have turned many times to her young son, Lucien.

It's like a day at the races, Julia Sullivan thought. She and her husband Flor stood at the ship's rail watching the passengers embarking by three gangways, one for third class, another for second, and a special gangway, just beneath where they stood, for saloon. Flor, who had worked at New York's Stuyvesant Club, knew many of the millionaires and wealthy industrialists by sight.

For eight years, since leaving her native County Cork, Julia had worked for the Branders on Long Island, 'the nicest old couple God ever brought together and left childless'. They accepted her as one of the family, taking her with them on vacations to Florida and the Great Lakes. When she met the big, handsome Flor Sullivan from Kerry the Branders found him his job at the Stuyvesant. Julia would make excuses to call at the club just to admire her fiancé in his bartender's smart white uniform with blue facings.

When the Branders died within three months of each other Flor and Julia married and moved into New York. Flor's father had written from Ireland to ask his son to come home to the family farm, but the young couple kept putting off the journey. However, when the old farmer died they had no choice but to return or lose the farm. The expensive furniture the Branders had left them was packed in crates and loaded on board the *Lusitania*. Flor's friend John McCubbin the purser promised them that if they came on board early he would give them the best second-class cabin and table.

Avis Dolphin had travelled overnight from St. Thomas, Ontario, with Nurse Hilda Ellis and the nurse's friend Sarah Smith. Avis was twelve. Ten years earlier she and her parents and baby brother had emigrated to Canada from England. Her father had been invalided out of the Army, but within a year he died from tuberculosis. Just before his death another daughter was born, so Avis's mother ran a small nursing home to support herself and her young family. She dearly wanted Avis to have an English education, and when Nurse Ellis told her she was going home on leave she decided to send Avis to an English school. As the three travellers from St. Thomas rode in a taxi-cab through the city to Pier 54 Avis was surprised to notice that American mail boxes were not red, but blue. Even more surprising was her first glimpse of the liner they would travel in: the *Lusitania* was the biggest she had ever seen!

George Hook's children were equally surprised by the great liner. Hook was a widower in his mid-forties. His wife had died eighteen months earlier and he decided he could make as good a living in his native England as in Toronto, where he worked at a metal plant. He sold his house and took his twelve-year-old daughter Elsie and eleven-year-old son Frank to New York, where they stayed for a week. After the comparative calm of Toronto they found the big city noisy and dirty. Elsie was tall for her age, but extremely shy, while Frank was small but adventurous. Both of them were excited to be sailing on 'the big ship'. George Hook had paid half-fare for his daughter, although she was a year over age. As they walked up the third-class gangway he whispered to her, 'Duck down, Elsie! Make yourself as small as possible.'

The Cunarder was preparing to sail from a city in which the citizens gave little thought to German submarines. That weekend the weather had changed dramatically. A fortnight earlier the city had been submerged in a snowfall and New Yorkers had huddled into furs and heavy coats, expecting the winter to stretch on for weeks to come. Then, unexpectedly, midsummer weather burst upon the city. East Side families from tenement rooms crowded fire excapes and front steps, determined to catch the faintest breath of wind, and even when it rained they stayed out of doors. Downtown electric fans were switched on, straw hats donned and vests discarded, and at lunchtime office workers crowded into the soda emporiums.

Passengers arriving in the city the night before the sailing could have chosen to see the longest running play in town, *Daddy Long-Legs*, or three Shaw plays, opera, melodrama, Gilbert and Sullivan, burlesque, vaudeville or even a 'water spectacle' at the Hippodrome. D. W. Griffith's new movie, *The Birth of a Nation*, with 18,000 actors and 3,000 horses, was packing the Liberty Cinema on 42nd Street, where a new cooling system had been installed in expectation of a long summer run.

In contrast to a London subdued by a wartime blackout, Broadway's lights dazzled its pleasure-seeking crowds. Americans followed the newspaper accounts of a conflict thousands of miles across the Atlantic with detachment. They shared the wish of their pacifist President for neutrality. So far they trusted him. When a German torpedo sank the cargo and passenger steamer *Falaba* in St. George's Channel on 28 March, killing an American citizen, Leon Thresher, the majority of Americans did not share the alarm of their newsmen nor the views of editorial writers who described the incident as 'cold-blooded', 'cowardly' and 'atrocious'. The *Falaba* sinking was not designed by the Germans to provoke the United States. President Wilson regarded it as an isolated incident and made no formal protest to Berlin.

That Friday evening before the *Lusitania* sailed William

Jennings Bryan, the Secretary of State, and a man of religious fervour, made a surprise appearance to preach temperance at Carnegie Hall, persuading several hundreds among the audience of two thousand gathered under the banner of the National Abstainers' Society to sign pledges to stay off alcohol for the rest of their lives. He might have been better engaged, according to some commentators in Washington, discussing with his President the new submarine threat by Germany to transatlantic shipping. But Bryan was probably unaware that the *Lusitania* was due to sail the next morning or that the Germans would publish an advertisement warning travellers on Allied ships of the risks involved.

The previous evening an anonymous caller, presumably a newspaper employee, had delivered an envelope to the British Embassy in Washington containing a proof copy of the German advertisement with an accompanying note:

> Above notice will appear in a
> local paper on Saturday, 1 May,
> and in about forty other papers
> the same day and two ensuing
> Saturdays. The information
> may have no value, but am send-
> it because I wish Allies to win.
> No signature because it might cost
> me my job.

> Signed (patriotically) 1776

# 3

# THE WARNING

ALONE IN HIS DAY CABIN William Turner was breakfasting on his favourite grilled kippers and two boiled eggs.

The previous night he had dined at his favourite restaurant on 14th Street, close by Union Square and a short cab ride from the Cunard pier. Turner, like many ships' Masters of other nationalities, made his way almost instinctively to Lüchow's baroque dining-rooms with their stags' heads, gilt-framed paintings and a model of the four-masted *Great Republic* destroyed by fire before her maiden voyage from New York.

Turner always chose a table beneath the Wagner murals in the Niebelungen Room from where he could see the eight-piece orchestra which Victor Herbert had brought from Vienna. The expansive August Lüchow, an emigrant from Hanover, had started his restaurant thirty years earlier. He would come bustling, despite his great girth, between the tables, stroking his handlebar moustache and encouraging his friend 'Herr Kapitän' to choose prime beef and red cabbage and follow it with sliced pancakes, the Emperor Franz Josef's favourite dessert.

August Lüchow took care not to discuss the war with Turner; he talked about food and wine and the celebrated writers, musicians and theatre people who thronged his restaurant. For Turner it was just as an American writer had put it, 'I took a walk and got as far as Lüchow's.' He insisted on maintaining his peacetime habits during the war; he was after all nearly sixty and he didn't intend to change his ways.

One of New York's German agents overheard him remark that he would follow his 'usual track' home to Liverpool 'regardless of the submarines'.

Turner ate with a trencherman's relish that Friday evening. It had been a tiring day. He had made a deposition in the afternoon before a notary to be read during court proceedings in which the White Star Line would seek to limit their liability in the sinking of the *Titanic* three years earlier to 97,000 dollars. He made his statement on behalf of his employers, but his answers were typically brusque. He said he knew little about the construction of ships. 'I'm only interested in them,' he said, 'as long as they keep afloat.' The stenographer waited, pencil poised for the notary's next question, but Turner surprised her by adding, 'If they sink, I get out.'

Did the crew members in the crow's nest of the *Lusitania* use binoculars? the notary asked him.

'Certainly not. Might as well give them soda bottles.'

At the notary's request he described the particular features of the *Lusitania*'s bulkheads. He explained how the hull below the draught line, more than 32 feet deep, was divided into 175 watertight compartments by means of ten transverse bulk-heads with watertight doors. Longitudinal watertight compartments were used to store coal, a common practice on ships, but what Turner omitted to mention was that when the *Lusitania* was filled with the 6,000 tons of coal needed to drive her across the Atlantic the watertight hatches could not be closed.

The *Lusitania* was an uncommonly tall liner. In an effort to please Cunard, who needed increased accommodation, and the Admiralty, who were paying an annual subsidy of $360,000, Leonard Peskett had designed a 'floating hotel' taller than any previous ship. After the initial tank tests the beam had to be increased by ten feet to 88 feet. Nevertheless, with her watertight compartments the *Lusitania* was reckoned to be unsinkable.

Turner told the notary he had learned nothing from the sinking of the *Titanic*. 'Not even one lesson?' the notary pressed him.

'I didn't learn the slightest thing from that accident. It could happen again.'

At four o'clock he walked up the steps of the neo-classic Custom House to the Marine Division. Before the acting Deputy Collector John Farrell, he swore the Master's oath that the manifest he was presenting contained a full and true account of all the goods, wares and merchandise laden on board the *Lusitania*.

Farrell examined the single-page manifest which Turner handed him. It was his duty to ascertain whether or not arms and ammunition were included in a ship's cargo. He glanced down the list to see if the clerk had made any telltale marks in red ink at the side. There was none. The list included pork, beef, bacon, lard, dressed skins, rolls of cloth, woollen samples, cotton clothing, tobacco, furs and aircraft and machine parts. Neither Turner nor Farrell apparently noticed that the manifest had been completed by the Cunard office in the name of Captain Dow, the *Lusitania*'s former Commodore. Customs staff had supplied a supplementary sheet which stated that the cargo was 'as per manifest attached'. Farrell seemed satisfied that the manifest had passed through the customary routines and bore the markings of the clerk whose job it was to examine such papers.

Dinner at Lüchow's over, Turner picked up his bowler hat, thanked the maitre d'hotel and bade 'Augy' Lüchow goodnight. A cab took him to the Harris Theatre on 42nd Street, just west of Broadway. The curtain had just come down on Henry Arthur Jones's play *The Lie* in which Mercedes Desmore had a part. She was his only relative in New York and whenever he was in town he called to see her. She greeted him warmly in her dressing room. Turner told her he hoped her play would still be running when he returned. She sighed as she remembered he was due to sail next morning for Liverpool. 'Will it really be safe?' she asked him.

'Don't worry,' he reassured her, 'the Germans won't catch us. We're too fast for them.' A photographer took their picture together. It was said afterwards that the pair showed 'an unusually close resemblance'.

Back aboard ship next morning Turner poured himself
another cup of tea and propped his favourite newspaper, the
*New York Tribune*, against the teapot. On its front page the
*Tribune* drew attention to an advertisement published in a
number of newspapers that day from the German Embassy.
Turner leafed through the pages to the shipping columns.
Here were advertisements for holiday trips up the Hudson and
the Cunard sailing schedule, which announced that the
*Lusitania*, 'the fastest and largest steamer in Atlantic service',
would sail to Liverpool on 1 May and again on 29 May. Beside
this was a black-bordered announcement:

## NOTICE!

Travellers intending to embark on the Atlantic voyage
are reminded that a state of war exists between Germany
and her allies and Great Britain and her allies; that the
zone of war includes the waters adjacent to the British
Isles; that, in accordance with formal notice given by the
Imperial German Government, vessels flying the flag of
Great Britain, or any of her allies, are liable to
destruction in those waters and that travellers sailing in
the war zone on ships of Great Britain or her allies do so
at their own risk.

Imperial German Embassy,
Washington, DC, 22 April 1915.

The *Tribune* correspondent quoted the statement of a
senior official at the State Department that he didn't think the
advertisement would 'affect the existing situation' between the
two nations. Germany would be held to account for the death
of any American on an Allied passenger ship. Turner also read
in his *Tribune* that a British steamer carrying coal had been
sent to the bottom off the coast of Scotland by a German
submarine. There was news too of fierce fighting in the
Dardanelles, of bombings of German towns, of attacks by
Allied warships on German submarine bases.

Turner folded the newspaper and laid it aside. He was about to go to the bridge when a message was handed him with the news that the Anchor Line steamer *Cameronia* had been requisitioned by the Admiralty. Forty-one first- and second-class passengers and crew were to be transferred to the *Lusitania*. Another 300 third-class passengers from the *Cameronia* were also entitled to be transferred. But as this would cause a further delay of at least five hours they would have to wait until the following Friday to sail on the *Transylvania*.

Slipping on his gold-braided jacket Turner stepped onto the bridge, impatient at the delay caused by this transfer of passengers and baggage. He looked down on the people thronging the decks and crowding the dockside. After almost twenty years as a ship's Master the scene still made his pulses quicken.

From his vantage point six storeys high he was not to know that some of his passengers were being questioned about the German warning, while more reporters on the pier had been firing questions at Charles Sumner. Would the *Lusitania* sail? Would the passengers transfer to another ship?

'The voyage will be attended by no risk whatsoever,' Sumner said. 'The *Lusitania* has a speed of 25 knots and she is provided with unusually positioned, watertight bulkheads.' He was prepared to make light of the German warning before the Press, not wishing to have his sailing cancelled or refunds made to his passengers. He had been shown a batch of mysterious telegrams which had been telephoned through to the Marconi room on board the liner. They were addressed to some of the liner's most important passengers, including Alfred Gwynne Vanderbilt and Charles Frohman. Some were signed with fictitious names, others with the word *Morte*.

Sumner was angry. If the passengers concerned were to see these telegrams they might be alarmed. From now on he expected that any method the Germans could devise would be used to prevent passengers travelling on Cunard ships. He went to his office and locked the telegrams in his desk.

Reporters had intercepted Secretary of State William Jennings Bryan as he was returning to Washington after his temperance meeting in Carnegie Hall to read him a copy of the German advertisement. Bryan refused to comment. When it was brought to the notice of Bernhard Dernburg (special representative of the Kaiser) at the Ritz-Carlton Hotel he issued a statement through his secretary: 'I believe the advertisement is a warning by Germany in a sincere effort to prevent injury to travellers of neutral countries.' But reporters who tried to contact Ambassador Count von Bernstorff next morning at the Embassy in Washington were told he was out of town.

The Chancery occupied the ground floor of the house with the Ambassador's quarters upstairs. The reporters suspected von Bernstorff might be keeping out of sight on the upper floors, and they were persistent in calling and telephoning. At length the Embassy staff issued a statement: 'The public notice in the papers is intended merely to remind neutral travellers of their danger; it does not indicate any new naval operation by the German fleet.' The staff believed they had acted in accordance with instructions from Berlin. After all, the season of summer travel was beginning and surely it was an act of friendship to warn travellers to avoid the passenger ships of Germany's enemies in the war zone? Since the outbreak of war the German Consular offices throughout the United States had made use of the advertising columns of the newspapers to inform German reservists where to register and where to draw passage money for their travel to the front line.

Shortly after eleven am Captain Turner was summoned unexpectedly to the British Consulate. It was usual for the Consul to deliver sailing orders direct to the Cunarders, but none had been received by Turner that morning. He left the bridge, obviously displeased at being called away during the delayed sailing preparations. Ramming on his bowler hat he strode down the third-class gangway, unnoticed by most of the passengers crowding the entrances.

As well as having responsibility for civilian counter-intelligence, Sir Courtenay Bennett also held the position of senior naval officer in New York. Turner surmised there might be two reasons for the Consul's call: either Sir Courtenay wanted to talk to him privately about a change of sailing orders or the German warning meant the sailing was to be cancelled. Unlike Captain Dow, he was not on familiar terms with the Consul or the Embassy staff. He regarded them as diplomats with no particular love for the sea. He was greeted by Bennett. 'Is something the matter, Sir Courtenay?' Turner asked, taking a chair opposite the Consul's desk. 'Is it about the German warning?' To his relief the Consul replied, 'Not really. We regard the warning as serious, but, of course, it will not affect your sailing. I sent for you about your course instructions. In fact we've not received them, so you may assume that you will take the same course as on your last sailing.'

Whatever other instructions Bennett may have given him that morning, apart from his code and wireless signals, Turner was never to reveal.

He was about to leave the office when the Consul remarked that he had just received news of an attack by a German submarine on an American vessel off the Irish coast. It did not seem to have occurred to Sir Courtenay Bennett or Charles Sumner that they should perhaps transfer some of the *Lusitania*'s passengers to the *New York*, on board which a handful of passengers had the run of the ship and the services of a full crew.

Turner walked out of the Consulate, determined, once the decision to sail had been made for him, to put on a brave front. Like other British captains he had been given special instructions in the previous November regarding trade routes in wartime. In January he had been advised to keep a sharp lookout for submarines and display the ensign of a neutral country while in the vicinity of the British Isles. In March instructions had been issued to the Masters of homebound vessels passing up the Irish and English Channels to keep a mid-channel course. On 15 April there had been a warning that German

submarines were operating chiefly off headlands and land-
falls, and all vessels were advised to give prominent headlands
a wide berth.

'Captain,' a woman called as Turner returned aboard,
'what about the German warning?'

'There is no danger, madam,' he said firmly. 'We are
sailing.'

# 4

# A SCRATCH CREW

SALOON PASSENGERS hoping for an invitation to dine at the Captain's table during the voyage would probably be disappointed. This was a privilege seldom accorded even to the most distinguished travellers. Captain Turner preferred to eat alone on the bridge. Although courteous, he lacked any refinement. His gruff manners were scarcely suited to the role of host, and he had been known to describe his well-to-do passengers as 'bloody monkeys'. In his place Staff Captain Anderson was chosen by Cunard to socialise with the passengers. His manners were more polished than his Master's, and he was respected by his fellow officers who believed him capable of taking full command.

Like Turner, the genial Anderson had listened to criticism levelled against the British crew. A number of them had made use of the westward voyage to evade conscription; there was nothing he could do when they jumped ship in New York. Naval reserve men had been called up and passenger liners like the *Lusitania* were left with scratch crews. Yet Anderson believed his men were as competent as most sailors at that time. Turner had convinced him that the oldtime seamen who could reef, splice and steer had gone with the sailing ships. Any green hands on board were down among the coal trimmers in the stokeholds. 'Does it need nautical training,' Turner asked, 'to push a barrow of coal?'

Both men were apparently satisfied that all hands knew their stations and their lifeboat duties. With a scratch crew, Turner was grateful to have a Chief Engineer of long

47

experience. The veteran, walrus-moustached Archibald Bryce came from a seagoing family: his father had been an engineer on one of Cunard's first paddle steamers, and he knew every component of the gleaming machinery in the boiler rooms. Turner felt at home with him.

Turner was a Liverpudlian, born in Clarence Street, Everton. He was given his first taste of sailing at the age of eight by his ship's Captain father and developed a boy's passion for the sea. At thirteen, although a promising student, he persuaded his parents to allow him leave the Liverpool College in Shaw Street to serve his time before the mast as a deck boy. His first ship was the windjammer *White Star*. His second, the *Queen of Nations*, was captained by his father; she lost her sails in a gale and sprang a leak homeward-bound off Cape Horn. To save her his father jettisoned the cargo and the *Queen* limped to the Falkland Islands for repairs. Aboard the *War Spirit* young Will Turner watched crew men die from yellow fever. Homeward bound from St. John, New Brunswick, the *War Spirit*'s deck load was washed away and she became waterlogged. For four days the ship drifted until the crew were rescued by a steamer and towed to a Spanish port.

When he joined Cunard in 1878 as Third Officer of the *Cherbourg* Turner was twenty-two. Steaming out of the Huskisson Dock in heavy fog the *Cherbourg* collided with a barque, sinking her and drowning the pilot and four of the crew. Turner jumped into a boat and rescued a man and a boy from the sinking craft's main cross-tree. Seven years later, on an icy February day, he made another rescue, plunging into Liverpool's Alexandra Dock to save a boy who had fallen into the water; for this he was awarded the Humane Society's silver medal.

He was Chief Officer on the *Umbria* when she carried troops safely to South Africa during the Boer War, a voyage which won him the Transport Medal. In 1903, at the age of forty-seven, having almost abandoned hope of achieving his life's ambition, he was awarded his first Cunard command. He took the bridge on the *Aleppo*, on which he had served as Third

Officer some years earlier. He was promoted in turn to command the *Carpathia*, the *Ivernia* and the *Caronia*. He saw the *Lusitania* through her early crossings to New York, and made her the fastest liner on the Atlantic, a record he surpassed when captaining the *Mauretania*. In May 1914, he was given the *Aquitania*, the deepest and broadest of Cunard's mammoth liners, on her maiden voyage. Later, when Captain Dow complained of wartime strain, Alfred Booth decided to give Turner command of the *Lusitania* again.

Will Turner was far happier standing on the bridge, delighting in his ship's performance as she cleaved the Atlantic, than presiding at the Captain's table or wasting time in boardroom talk. It was his seamanship, not his manners, that had earned him his reputation. Snobbery among the cabin passengers irked him, socialising bored him, and it was unlikely that any wealthy passenger would bequeath him a legacy of 50,000 dollars, as one grateful American dowager had done for a captain on the *Lucania*.

Turner was reticent about his private life. Occasionally he talked to Anderson or Bryce about his sons Percy and Norman serving in the war, but he never spoke about his marriage. Relations with his wife were breaking down, but he tried not to let this personal crisis interfere with his judgement as a sea captain.

In recent years, when his ship sailed into Liverpool, a vivacious young woman was waiting to greet this rather lonely man.

Turner had first met Mabel Every seven years earlier when she was in her early twenties. Although she cheerfully described herself as 'plain and ordinary' Mabel Every was tall and slender and an amusing and natural story-teller, qualities that appealed to Turner who retailed his own anecdotes with a dry relish. The youngest of seven, she had a romantic turn of mind, though she was not married. Her father, a captain in the Indian Army, survived the Indian Mutiny, the Siege of Lucknow and the Crimean War; on his retirement he entered the prison service and for some years was Governor of the penal settlement at Gibraltar. He later became Governor of Dartmoor Prison, where his wife died soon after giving birth to Mabel.

Mabel became a student nurse with a reputation for pranks. She once threw an orange through a bathroom window of the doctors' quarters and it struck one of the consultants who happened to be taking a bath. 'Don't think I don't know who did it,' the doctor said later — and produced the offending orange from behind his back.

With no money of her own, Mabel set about earning her living, and after a spell at nursing she arrived in Liverpool to look after Captain Turner. The tough, sea-faring man enjoyed his domestic life. After an ocean voyage he liked nothing better than to potter in his garden, his dog and cat never far from his heels, or sit in a deckchair on summer afternoons.

From the first moment he had seen the *Lusitania* as a boy on holiday in Scotland his heart went out to her in admiration. Albert Bestic had stood on the banks of the Clyde watching the splendid liner sweep past. If I could sail on a ship like that, he thought, I'd go to sea.

Albert grew up in Dublin and was apprenticed to sail at eighteen, bringing with him his schoolboy's athletic prowess. After four years before the mast, he signed on the *Denbigh Castle*, a three-master out of Cardiff. One misty day in the Atlantic, with a strong westerly wind straining the canvas, he heard the lookout yell, 'Steamer right ahead!' He clambered with the crew onto the bulwarks for a better view.

'There she is!' the bosun shouted, 'and she looks like one of the big 'uns, too!'

A blur in the mist rushing towards them took the shape, as though sketched by a lightning artist, of an Atlantic liner. Albert caught a glimpse of four towering red and black smokestacks, tier upon tier of portholes, fluttering handkerchiefs, a roaring stem wave and the name *Lusitania* fastened in gold letters on her bow. Once again he felt that curious thrill he had experienced as a boy on the Clyde. Mesmerised, he remained standing on the bulwarks long after she had vanished in a welter of mist and spray. Then her wash came, a wall of water that mounted the deck rail and sent him sprawling.

Until the outbreak of war, the Cunard Line had employed only officers with 'square-rig' tickets as Master, so Albert did not make an application to them. Now times had changed. Some Cunard officers had been called to the Royal Navy and the crew numbers were diminishing. When he first applied at the age of twenty-three he was surprised to be told, 'Join the *Lusitania* at nine am tomorrow morning at the Landing Stage'. He could scarcely believe that his boyhood ambition was near fulfilment.

Lying alongside her pier the *Lusitania* looked colossal; she dwarfed every other ship anchored in the Mersey. A deckhand took Albert by lift to the officers' quarters situated just abaft the bridge and knocked at a door marked 'Chief Officer'. Albert was introduced to John Piper, a tall, thin officer with greying hair and a brusque manner. 'Come along to the wardroom. I'll introduce you to whoever's there.' He ushered Albert into a comfortable room and introduced him to four of the ship's officers. Captain Anderson put him at ease with a hearty handshake and a broad smile. At first glance First Officer Jones had a somewhat grim expression. Second Officer Hefford seemed likeable, while Senior Third Officer Lewis was, like Albert himself, small, sturdy and good-humoured. They were all 'pukka Cunard men' with Masters' certificates who had worked their way up from cargo ships.

Albert quickly adapted to the routine of a big passenger liner. Second Officer Hefford gave him sound advice and he listened to yarns in the wardroom about the passengers. 'There's one thing you must be careful of,' he was warned. 'You mustn't talk to passengers, especially women.'

'What if they talk to you?' Bestic asked.

'Answer politely, of course. But if they want to go on talking — make an excuse that duty calls.'

Leslie Morton and his brother John had been crewmen on the steamer *Naid*, now berthed in Brooklyn. With two shipmates they had crossed over to Manhattan Island to see the *Lusitania* at the Cunard pier. They were astonished by her size. As they stood on the quayside Chief Officer Piper noticed them and walked down the gangway. 'What do you boys want?'

Leslie had cabled home for their fares and had been surprised and pleased to receive seventy-five pounds, enough to pay for two third-class tickets on the *Lusitania*'s next sailing.

'We're going to sail on your ship,' he said truthfully. He told him they had been paid off a full-rigged ship and were going home to England to take their examinations. 'Why pay your fares?' asked Piper. 'We've lost ten of our deckhands this trip. I could use you four boys.'

Morton said they had other friends from the *Naid* who might want to join too. Piper asked them to be on the pier next morning. 'We sail in forty-eight hours.'

The quartet returned to the *Naid* and recruited four more seamen. That night they dressed in as many singlets, shirts, jerseys and oilskins as they could and walked off the ship. With their fare money the Mortons decided they would all have a night on the town before joining the *Lusitania*. In a Broadway bar Leslie sampled his first alcoholic drink, a Manhattan Cocktail with a cherry on a stick. After three or four drinks his head began to swirl. He came to lying on the sidewalk, gazing up at a large policeman.

Chief Officer Piper met the eight seamen at the *Lusitania*'s gangway and signed them on as deckhands, dividing them between port and starboard watches. Leslie found himself a bunk, three decks down in the fo'c'sle — not quite the Cunard luxury he had expected. He climbed the companionway again and began his job of washing down the decks. He and John had squandered all their money in one night on the town. Now this was their only way home.

Neither George Wynne nor his father heard the noisy farewells that morning. They were too busy working in the kitchens on

C deck preparing the first lunch of the voyage. George, a small, wiry lad of seventeen, owed his job on the *Lusitania* to his friend Charlie Westbury, a second cook. As a boy he had wandered through the Liverpool docks looking wistfully at the great liners. He got a job with a catering firm at half-a-crown a week. But with Charlie's help he had found work in the *Lusitania*'s kitchens. His hours were from six in the morning until ten at night, with two hours off in the afternoon; but he was happy: all he had ever wanted to do was work on a big ship. He had also found a job for his unemployed father. His mother would have preferred her husband to have found work near home on a Liverpool building site, but at least he was with George and she was content.

Out of his weekly earnings of eighteen dollars George sent his mother about two and one-half dollars. Sometimes he missed his home at Oakes Street, not far from Lime Street Station, but the spacious kitchens of the *Lusitania* proved a noisy, fascinating and exciting world inhabited by chefs, cooks, bakers, butchers, assistants and scullions. He had an ambition to be a chef, but he reckoned his chances were slim; the chefs he knew were French, Italian or Greek, never English. Still, he had won promotion to assistant cook in first class, away from the second- and third-class kitchens, which were linked together. Wearing a singlet and regulation check trousers, he peeled vegetables and thought himself slightly superior to be working in a saloon kitchen.

His thirty-seven-year-old father, Joseph Wynne, suffered from acute bronchitis. The warm atmosphere of the ship's kitchens was healthier for him than a damp building site. George was pleased to have his father beside him, even in a scullion's job, but he sensed he was homesick. It was George Wynne's sixth round trip across the Atlantic and his father's first. 'Cheer up, Dad,' he told him. 'We'll be home in Liverpool inside a week.'

Hurrying along the ship's corridors, knocking on the doors of suites and saloon cabins, William Holton, his dark hair neatly brushed and wearing his bellboy's beige uniform with gold braiding, delivered the 'bon voyage' telegrams Chief Purser McCubbin had handed him to the more important first-class passengers. Holton had scrubbed himself clean after a rough day spent raking ashes from the stokehold, a dirty job which had been meted out as punishment. He was a Liverpool boy of sixteen, about to make his fourteenth crossing of the Atlantic on the *Lusitania*. When his mother was widowed she had sent him and his elder brother to a boarding school while she set about earning a living. He left school at fourteen and found a clerking job in Liverpool. During his lunch break he would hurry down to the Pier Head, no matter what the weather, to stare at the great liners. His family had connections with the sea and now he too was filled with a longing for ocean travel.

One afternoon he plucked up enough courage to walk into the White Star Line office to ask for a job. He was taken on as a ship's bellboy, but he couldn't bring himself to break the news to his mother until the time came for him to be fitted for his uniform. She accepted his decision because it seemed inevitable: if he wanted to go to sea, this job was a good start.

By the time he joined the *Lusitania* he had acquired an air rifle. He had taken it aboard, and with another boy had gone down in one of the lifts to the lazarette, a storeroom aft. As the large, open-fronted lift clanked its way to the bottom Holton and his companion took turns in shooting pellets at the rats that scurried to their hiding places.

'Look at them!' exclaimed Holton. 'They're as big as bloody cats!'

A crewman, hearing the shots, surprised the boys with the rifle and hauled them before the officer of the day. Their punishment, while the liner was tied up at Pier 54, was raking ashes in the stokehold.

Another Liverpool boy, John O'Connell, was at nineteen the youngest fireman in the stokehold. Six of the twenty-five boilers were cold that Saturday morning and would remain that way. On his final inspection of the boiler room Archibald

Bryce made certain the firemen were busy stoking the boilers in use.

O'Connell had signed on the *Lusitania* for her westward voyage with experience in the stokeholds of the *Alsatian* and the *Celtic*. One of four children, his mother had died when he was seven and his docker father when he was ten. His grand-mother could not afford to feed and clothe the children in the prevailing poverty of the time so John and his two older sisters were sent to the workhouse and imprisoned behind a ten-foot wall. Although John could not actually remember being frightened there he was glad, when he reached his teens, to return to his grandmother, who showed him a rough kindness. Soon there were eight of them living in the tiny two-storey house in Bootle: John, his three sisters, two aunts, an uncle and his grandmother. During his years in Elm Street he could not remember sleeping in a bed.

At thirteen John left school and went to work as a baker's delivery boy for a dollar and a quarter a week. But of this he only saw three pence — the rest he dutifully handed to his grandmother so that she could pay the weekly rent of one dollar and sixpence. Clearly a lad of spirit, he was sacked for locking up the manager in the bread shop, and moved on to a tobacco factory, where he extracted the nicotine from tobacco plants for four twenty-five a week.

John's first sea job was as a trimmer on board the *Celtic*, a passenger ship plying between Liverpool and New York. He worked in the stokehold, wheeling coal in barrows to the furnaces, and was paid twenty-four dollars a month. When the war began, he approached the Second Engineer just as the *Lusitania* was about to sail from the Pier Head and asked for a job.

'Come on then,' said the engineer to the youngster. 'You almost left it too late.'

Like other crewmen he brought his own blankets, clothes, knife, fork and spoon on board but, unlike some of the others, no smuggled bottles of beer. He didn't drink or smoke, and had no time for seamen who 'tanked up' in the Scotland Road pubs before sailing.

He found the job of feeding the liner's furnaces filthy and exhausting. The men who went through this grim routine in a subterranean world of blinding coal dust and blistering heat were known as the 'dirty gang'. He had spent the previous evening strolling down brilliantly-lit Broadway, mingling with the crowds and studying the billboards of the theatres and the picture palaces. During the day he had worked on board the *Lusitania*, clearing one of the fires of clinkers with a heavy steel poker, known as a 'jumbo', which reached deep into the furnace. With a short-handled hammer he broke up the clinkers after which the ashes and fragments were shovelled by trimmers into barrows and emptied down the 'blower', a metal receptacle at the side of the ship, into the Hudson River. 'Burning down' was a process which the *Lusitania* dared not undertake at sea. German submarine commanders stalking their prey had learned to take advantage of a ship which had to cut speed to 'shoot the ashes'; thus if the *Lusitania*'s furnaces were not burning at full blast her engines would lose power and she would become an easy target.

John returned to the liner on Friday night with a present for the Liverpool girl he loved, Nora Hanaway. On Saturday morning, wearing his regulation singlet, trousers and heavy boots, he descended by a succession of steep ladders to join his watch in the engine room. He recognised Chief Engineer Bryce inspecting the boilers and checking the water levels with his assistant engineers. The furnaces were burning at full capacity, and the coal, bunkered the night before, was being dumped on the plates ready for use. Under the eye of an experienced overseer, responsible to the engineer on duty in the adjacent engine room, the firemen began stoking up the furnaces. O'Connell pushed over the draught lever on his furnace; if he forgot to do this a searing flame would shoot across the stokehold. He threw a dozen shovelfuls of coal on the fire and slammed the door tight.

Captain Turner was confident that the *Lusitania*, in spite of her reduced speed, could outrun the German U-boats operating off the Irish coast. He had no say in Cunard's decision to reduce the liner's top speed from 26 to 21 knots or her cruising speed from 24 to 18 knots. The crew had been reduced and one of the four boiler rooms shut off to save coal.

From his vantage point on the bridge wing that morning he could see the rows of lifeboats, symbols of Cunard's concern for the passengers' safety. Even if his great ship was struck by a German torpedo she would probably not sink because of her many watertight bulkheads; or if she did sink there would be enough time to get the passengers away in the lifeboats. While commanding the *Transylvania* in January he was pursued off the Irish coast by a German U-boat. He gave orders to increase speed and within an hour the liner was running at 18 knots. A British cruiser came alongside and flashed warning signals to the *Transylvania*, advising her to hug the shore and douse her lights. He brought her safely into Queenstown.

No steamer cruising at the *Lusitania*'s speed had been torpedoed. There was no reason, he told himself, why he should not be in Liverpool at the appointed time, early on the morning of the following Saturday, 8 May.

# 5

# 'EVERY PRECAUTION'

WAS THE *LUSITANIA*, which at noon still lay at Pier 54, armed to defend herself?

The question had been asked two years earlier by the *New York Tribune* when the liner had gone into dry dock at Liverpool to have her turbines replaced. The *Tribune* had suggested that the *Lusitania* was being refitted with high-power rifles in conformity with Britain's policy of arming passenger ships. Yet when she returned that August to New York the newspaper could report no trace of guns.

If the *Lusitania* was equipped with armaments she was, in effect, a warship and as such subject to U-boat attack without notice. If unarmed she was entitled under existing law to be warned in time so that the lifeboats could be lowered to allow her passengers to get safely away. Admittedly she had been built at John Brown's shipyard on the Clyde with provision for equipping her as an armed cruiser in wartime; plans were published in 1907 showing where guns might be mounted. At the outbreak of war in August 1914, the British Government ordered nine liners to be requisitioned for conversion to armed merchant cruisers. A month later the Admiralty informed Cunard that the *Lusitania* would not be included among the nine; instead, she would continue to provide a fast passenger service between Liverpool and New York.

The decision pleased Alfred Booth, scion of a wealthy Liverpool trading family, chairman of Cunard, and a fiercely independent figure in shipping circles. He claimed to know all his Captains, officers and senior office staff by name and

58

prided himself on his loyalty to them. Though relieved that the *Lusitania* would remain in service, he was unhappy to learn that in future all Cunard ships would be under the direction of the Admiralty; Captains would be subject to Admiralty instructions on the sailing courses they should follow, and both the War Office and the Admiralty could call on the company at any time for cargo space. Booth knew that this could involve Cunard in the transportation of contraband. But he made no protest. His country was at war.

The *Lusitania* and her sister ship the *Mauretania* had been a special joy to Booth since their launching, and he involved himself deeply in their running. The 31,550-ton *Lusitania* was the most powerful and magnificent ship in the world, fitted with a new type of turbine engine to restore Britain's supremacy of the north Atlantic and regain the Blue Riband held for ten years by the record-breaking Germans. To pay for this ship and the *Mauretania* Cunard had borrowed $12,480,000 from the Government.

On the evening of 7 September 1907, Booth had been among the 200,000 people lining the banks of the Mersey as the *Lusitania* prepared for her maiden voyage. All that day, as the 3,000 passengers embarked and thousands of pieces of luggage and items of mail were loaded on board, sightseers crowded the Pier Head, the Liverpool waterfront and the shores of Seacombe and New Brighton across the river. In the gathering dusk, as a sudden blast from her siren sent seagulls screaming into the air, the liner's electrical installations were switched on at the command of Captain J. B. Watt. To those who lived in gaslit homes and streets the thousand glittering lights transformed the *Lusitania* into a magical floating palace. The crowds yelled themselves hoarse with patriotic fervour as the great liner moved slowly down river into the darkness.

At Queenstown in Ireland the next morning 200 passengers had to remain ashore because the steamship agents had ignored the company's advice to discontinue bookings. When the *Lusitania* steamed up river to her Manhattan berth on the following Friday morning she had completed the voyage at an average speed of 23.01 knots. News of her arrival at Sandy Hook had come ticking over the tape machines in Wall Street early that morning. At the Battery squads of mounted police held back the straw-hatted, parasol-waving crowds. The liner's sheer size and splendour and the excitement generated by her arrival acted like a magnet on New Yorkers. The comparisons quoted were on a giant scale: the *Lusitania* could dwarf the Great Pyramid, the Capitol in Washington, St. Peter's in Rome, or the Houses of Parliament. 'She is more beautiful than Solomon's temple,' an American admirer wrote, 'and big enough to hold all his wives.' She was equipped with a nursery, a hospital, a swimming pool and such 'wondrous innovations' as lifts, telephones, kennels for dogs and private bathrooms in first-class which were larger than third-class cabins. If life in third-class was slightly austere the first-class passengers moved in a world of Doric columns and candelabra, inlaid mahogany tables and damask sofas in their regal suites, which had separate rooms for valets and maids.

On the first crossing the *Lusitania* burned a railway yard of coal. Her passengers and crew consumed 40,000 eggs, 4,000 pounds of fish, two tons of bacon, 4,000 pounds of coffee, 500 pounds of grapes, 1,000 lemons, 25,000 pounds of meat, 11,870 quarts of milk, 2,675 quarts of cream and 30,000 loaves of bread. Alfred Booth worried about the economy of the liner. The maiden voyage had cost $120,000. But *Lusitania* fever gripped the public and their enthusiasm found its justification with the liner's second voyage from Liverpool on 5 October when she crossed the Atlantic in four days, 19 hours and 52 minutes at an average speed of 23.93 knots. For the very first time the journey to New York had taken less than five days. The *Lusitania* was now the undisputed Queen of the Atlantic.

Alfred Booth always invited William Turner and the other Cunard Captains to call to see him in his room in the Cunard building overlooking the Pier Head 'as soon as possible' after a voyage.

'Captains of the service,' he pointed out, 'are not generally aware that I am always anxious to see them privately as well as in the committee room when they are in port.' Few company chairmen set such an example as Booth. He worked long hours, engaged in prodigious correspondence, and imposed his own strict discipline on employees. When one of his Captains asked permission to bring his wife on a voyage Booth agreed, and then in the same letter demanded his resignation.

After the sinking of the *Titanic* in the spring of 1912 he sent a circular letter to his Captains emphasising that two types of accident should never happen to a capable ship's Master: collision in the open sea in clear weather and stranding when making land in any weather. He cautioned them to beware of the 'folly or stupidity' of other ships' Masters and to steer clear of their vessels. 'If your ship is lost or damaged it will be poor compensation to us, and to you, to know that you are technically free from blame.'

Turner answered one such letter with the assurance, 'It will always be my endeavour to take every precaution necessary for the well-being and safety of the ship and those entrusted to my care.'

It was at this period that Booth took the unusual step of creating the position on Cunard liners of Staff Captain at a salary of $1500 a year. He stressed, however, that it was the Captain and not the Staff Captain who remained in 'supreme command' of the ship. The Captain 'must be consulted on all matters when required'.

Cunard problems in New York were more complex. His manager Charles Sumner wrote of 'deteriorating relations' between the company and the British Consul-General, Sir Courtenay Bennett, who believed the Cunard offices harboured German spies.

Cunard's New York operation had proved troublesome since the war. On a number of occasions Booth was told of allegations that some of the staff held pro-German sympathies. He reserved judgement in the matter, uncertain whether there was any foundation in the claims. Certainly Sumner did not see eye to eye with Sir Courtenay, an important figure in British counter-intelligence in New York. Nor were relations harmonious between Sumner and Captain Guy Gaunt, the Washington-based British naval attaché who kept a room in Cunard's New York office.

Opinions varied about the capabilities of the ebullient Consul-General, but there was no doubting his patriotism. As the tempo of the war increased and the German submarine menace grew more threatening Sir Courtenay became increasingly edgy. He was furious at allegations made in *The Fatherland* (a German-American weekly which served the large German community) that the *Lusitania* and other Cunarders were being used by the Admiralty to transport arms and munitions to Britain. He believed that German sympathisers in the Cunard building posed a threat to his country and that every British vessel in the port was under surveillance by German agents. And he decided that Charles Sumner (though the latter could trace his ancestry back to sixteenth-century Oxfordshire) was anti-British.

He reported these suspicions to his superiors at the Foreign Office. 'Sumner must be in the pay of the Germans,' he told Sir Eyre Crowe, the titular head of British Intelligence. 'He refuses to ship munitions in any Cunard passenger ships. Worse, he sees neither the logic nor the necessity of shipping Government supplies in bottoms of registry, even when these bottoms are under control of the Admiralty.' He found Sumner 'very offensive and extremely rude'.

He directed his agents to investigate Cunard staff and report any suspected German sympathisers. The shadow of suspicion fell on a number of staff with foreign-sounding names, among them the American-born Herman Winter, Sumner's assistant manager, who reacted strongly to the allegations. 'It's a damned lie,' he told Sumner angrily.

Winter was fortunate in having an ally in the Cunard chairman who was resentful of any suspicions directed against his staff. Booth was not impressed by Sir Courtenay Bennett nor by the British Ambassador Sir Cecil Spring-Rice. He referred to them in correspondence as 'those gentlemen' and expressed the hope that the Consul-General would soon be removed from New York.

Captain Guy Gaunt was diplomatic in his dealings with Alfred Booth, although he shared the Consul-General's suspicions of both Sumner and Winter, and wanted Winter sacked. He had noticed 'tremendous friction' between Sir Courtenay and the Cunard staff, although if there was cause for complaint against the company there was also something to be said in their favour because of the Consul-General's 'excessive stupidity and gullibility'.

Sir Courtenay, however, was not so wide of the mark in his accusations. He had been given new information that Cunarders were being closely scrutinised by German agents operating in the port of New York. From the start of the war the port had been a hive of German and British espionage activity with the intelligence services of both countries engaged in a battle of wits in which money was no object. German agents had kept a close watch on the *Lusitania* since her arrival at Pier 54, and Sir Courtenay feared for her safety.

Franz von Papen, the new German military attaché, had cabled Berlin that 'every munitions factory in the United States is working overtime on Allied orders. The ports are filled with transports loading munitions for France, Russia and England. Steps must be taken to stop it.' He was determined to cut supplies to the Allies and in Captain Karl Boy-Ed, the young naval attaché who had established a network of German spies in New York, he had an able accomplice. He was encouraged by a message from the German General Staff on Berlin's Wilhelmstrasse promising funds and authorising sabotage in factories supplying munitions of war; railway embankments and bridges must not be destroyed, however, and the German Embassy must in no circumstances be compromised.

The tall, slim attaché with the close-cropped hair seemed an ideal choice to play the dangerous Jekyll-and-Hyde role of diplomat and secret agent. Then aged thirty-five, von Papen was a Westphalian aristocrat, a Junker, and, like his father, an officer of the War Academy. In building up a network of agents he used the name of a Wall Street merchant firm, G. Amsinck & Co., as a front for his activities. When sabotage orders arrived from Berlin he consulted with Count Johann Heinrich von Bernstorff, the German Ambassador, whose melancholy looks made him a distinctive figure at diplomatic receptions. Born in London, where his father was Ambassador, von Bernstorff had arrived in the United States as Ambassador in 1908. By the outbreak of war he was familiar with all shades of opinion. His function as he saw it was to counter Allied propaganda as best he could.

Captain Franz Kleist von Rintelen, a young naval reserve officer, arrived in New York on a false Swiss passport as a special agent. He took a cab to the German Club where he was to hand over the 'Most Secret' code to the two attachés. It seemed to him that neither von Papen nor Boy-Ed were particularly pleased to see him. Von Papen seemed 'an all-round dilettante'; Boy-Ed had 'superior opinions'. But he knew that both diplomats had been instructed by Berlin to co-operate with him.

A week later von Rintelen met Bernstorff at the Ritz-Carlton in Madison Avenue. The Ambassador came quickly to the point. 'What is the exact nature of your work?' he enquired. Von Rintelen replied that his work had 'a purely military character which lay in the general direction of sabotage'. Bernstorff seemed perturbed.

Von Rintelen travelled to Washington where von Papen tried to dissuade him from his mission, telling him it would be impossible to carry out the sabotage he envisaged. But von Rintelen told him emphatically that he would obey only the orders from Berlin. He strode out of the office shouting, 'I shall do exactly as my superiors tell me!'

Dining with his Ambassador that evening von Papen expressed his concern at the turn of events. Von Rintelen, he advised, should be recalled before he did irreparable damage to the German cause in America. The German High Command, however, did not agree. They wanted positive results; they wanted them quickly; and Captain von Rintelen was the man to achieve them.

Von Rintelen moved into a small hotel on 57th Street, and began to lead a double life. In the evening he changed into white tie and tails and cultivated influential people, using his own name to avoid the attentions of the Secret Service. By day he dressed unobtrusively and sauntered through the sprawling docks area, observing the Allied transports taking munitions on board. Watching the ships steaming down the Hudson for Europe, he determined to send them, by whatever means he could, to the bottom of the ocean.

Taking a leaf out of von Papen's book, he rented an office in the financial district and registered a bogus import-export firm. It was to his newly-furnished office as director of the firm that a young chemist, Walter Scheele, called. Dr. Scheele, a graduate of Bonn, whose Swedish grandfather had discovered chlorine gas and whose father had died in the discovery of prussic acid, had been sent to the United States to report on the chemistry of warfare. He had set up a business front as a drug-store owner in Brooklyn.

Scheele took a piece of lead tubing the size of a large cigar from his pocket and laid it on the desk. Von Rintelen picked up the tubing and examined it. The inside was hollow and into the middle of the tube a circular disc of copper had been pressed and soldered, dividing it into two chambers. The chemist explained that one of the chambers would be filled with pitric acid, the other with sulphuric acid. A plug of wax would make both ends of the tube airtight. By regulating the thickness of the disc it was possible to determine when the acids should come together, whether within hours or days; when they met an intense flame would shoot out from both ends of the tube, the lead casing would melt without trace,

C

while the flame ignited any ordinary substance such as coal or wood.

Von Rintelen was fascinated. After a demonstration in a suburban wood he wrote Scheele a company cheque for the use of his invention.

Scheele's fire bombs, however, could not be manufactured on American soil. After considerable soul-searching von Rintelen decided on the *Friedrich der Grosse*, the flagship of the German High Seas Fleet which lay interned at Hoboken, as a place of manufacture. The steamer would be a haven of safety from the New York Police bomb squad which had been formed to capture Germans working against Allied shipping.

He then recruited German reservists and Irish workers from the docks to plant the detonators. He was prepared to use this form of sabotage if it was the only way to stop munitions reaching the Allies. He had already selected a ship on which to plant incendiaries, the steamer *Phoebus*, bound for Archangel with a cargo of explosives.

It was left to Captain Boy-Ed to discover if the *Lusitania* was armed. If it could be proved to the satisfaction of the Americans that there were guns on board, the liner could be interned as a warship. The first man he approached was Paul Koenig, the security chief of the Hamburg-Amerika Line. Koenig, who had charge of the German liners interned at Hoboken, was a shadowy figure. To those few Germans who claimed to know him Koenig was just the name on his forged passport. His other alias was believed to be Timothy Trebitsch Lincoln. His real name was Ignacz Trebitsch and he was said to be Hungarian-born.

Koenig's investigative work was carried on behind the locked doors of three rooms at number 11, Broadway, in the same building as the German Consulate and the offices of the Hamburg-Amerika Line. The rooms were on the eighth floor, their plain varnished panels giving no indication as to their use. Koenig was known as 'Stemler' to his agents, who included Heinz Hardenberg, Carl Thummel, and one Gustav Stahl.

One of his most mercenary agents, Stahl had worked his

passage to America in August 1914, on board a Belgian steamer. He had left Frankfurt and his wife in a hurry, having, it was said, pushed a policeman over a bridge into the Main. In Hoboken he found a job in a delicatessen and later took a room in downtown Manhattan at 20 Leroy Street which he shared with Adolph Mittelacher, another emigrant who worked as a barman. Stahl confided in Mittelacher about his work for the German Consulate and told him that Heinz Hardenberg, another resident, had made special trips as an agent to England for which he had been paid by the Consulate. Mittelacher learned that Stahl's contact at the Consulate was a man named 'Stemler', and that the 'big fish' as far as the Germans were concerned was the *Lusitania*.

One German who claimed to have seen guns on board the liner was Curt Thummel, alias Chester Williams, alias Charles Thorne. He had arrived in New York as a steward on board the *Lusitania* on 24 April when Staff Captain Anderson had given him his discharge papers. While staying at Leroy Street, Thummel wrote a detailed description of the liner for Captain Boy-Ed, claiming he knew the exact location of four guns.

Among the crew of the *Lusitania* that first morning in May was Neal Leach. Only a few days before the liner was due to sail Staff Captain Anderson had given him a job as a steward. He was twenty-five years old and the son of an English judge in Jamaica. Having studied law in England, he squandered the $500 sent by his father to pay the fees for his final examination and crossed to Germany where he worked as a private tutor to a wine merchant's family. He picked up the German language quickly and was soon able to converse fluently.

In March 1915, Leach sailed for America. He took lodgings in New York city with George and Josephine Weir at 132 West 16th Street, a boarding house popular with seamen and patronised by German agents who found the Weirs devoted to the German cause. On the voyage from Germany he had become friendly with Heinz Hardenberg, a German of his own age who had escaped from England at the outbreak of war. At the Weirs he met Hardenberg's younger brother, Hans, and Adolph Mittelacher.

It was at West 16th Street that Leach joined in a party given by the Weirs the night before he joined the *Lusitania*. He danced and sang with the boarders. Josephine Weir warned him, 'Don't sail tomorrow, Neal. It's too dangerous.' He knew the Weirs were German sympathisers, but he assured her he had no fears. 'They'll never trap the *Lusitania*. She's faster than any U-boat.'

At Leroy Street he had been introduced by Heinz Hardenberg to Gustav Stahl and the agent made a strong impression on him. Stahl would claim later that Leach called at the rooming house on Leroy Street on the evening of the party and asked him to help carry his trunk, which contained his belongings, to the *Lusitania*. According to Stahl they collected the trunk from a bar close to the boarding house and took it by cab to the docks. Neither the watchman at the crew entrance nor the seaman stationed at the gangway asked for their passes. They boarded the liner and carried the trunk down three flights of stairs to the 'gloria', the stewards' quarters, where they selected a bunk and lifted the trunk onto it.

Stahl was to say they spent thirty minutes on board the *Lusitania*. He alleged they walked the length of the deck on the water side and back again. It was then that he saw 'two guns mounted, fastened with screws and covered with leather', close to the main mast.

The two men left the *Lusitania* by the same route by which they had come on board. According to Stahl, nobody challenged them.

Through his network of agents the tireless Captain Guy Gaunt learned that von Rintelen was meeting Dr. Scheele, who was also in the pay of von Papen. He suspected they were manufacturing incendiaries that could be smuggled on board ships to cause fires and explosions.

Knowing how desperate his enemies were to halt the export

of munitions to Europe, he was concerned that they might become reckless in their efforts to disable British steamers. The *Lusitania* was an obvious target for the saboteurs.

Ambassador Bernstorff had protested to the United States Government that guns had been seen on board the *Lusitania* and demanded that the liner be interned immediately. But when detectives searched the vessel they found nothing. The Germans, Gaunt observed, were losing the propaganda war. Their apparent failure to prove that the *Lusitania* carried armaments suggested to Gaunt that they might attempt other methods to put her out of commission. Smuggling explosives on board a liner, he had to admit, was not difficult. Crew members greedy for money were not above accepting bribes, and then jumping ship. He conveyed these fears to the Secret Service; he also asked Sir Courtenay Bennett, without much success, to insist that Cunard allow only bona fide passengers on board the *Lusitania* on sailing day.

# 6

# THE WAR ZONE

THREE DAYS BEFORE the *Lusitania* was due to sail
Captain Gaunt had cabled Captain William Reginald Hall,
the director of British Naval Intelligence, about the sinister
German warning to passengers boarding the liner. Hall shared
Gaunt's fears of a possible plot to sink her. From Room 40 in
the old Admiralty building in Whitehall he cabled his naval
attaché in Washington: 'We must be ever more vigilant.'

Hall was able to read von Papen's wireless messages as they
were transmitted from Washington to Berlin, and noted the
names of von Rintelen, Boy-Ed and Koenig; but these
messages gave little information, certainly nothing sufficient
for him to take action. He knew that Ambassador Bernstorff
and the German Embassy staff were working to keep
American opinion in their favour, but he needed to unmask
agents such as von Papen and von Rintelen to swing American
sympathy away from Germany.

Hall was emerging in the espionage war as a figure of
authority. The dapper naval officer had retired from the sea
at forty-five for reasons of health and seemed well-chosen to
head the Intelligence Division. He persuaded the Post Office
to allow him to set up an unofficial censorship to open the
Atlantic mails which were channelled to and from Europe
through the main sorting office at London's Mount Pleasant.
What began as an unlawful tampering with the mails, for
which he could have been prosecuted, eventually became a
Government project for which Winston Churchill promised
money and support. When Prime Minister Asquith finally

gave official consent to this undemocratic wartime weapon at a special cabinet meeting at 10 Downing Street Hall found himself with two and a half million dollars to run his new department.

He developed the system of intercepting naval wireless signals. From February 1915, a chain of wireless stations set up around the English and Irish coasts enabled him to read every German signal transmitted. He even planted a spy in the United States Embassy in London to intercept coded messages between the State Department in Washington and Berlin. In addition, Captain Gaunt fed him information from New York on the date and place of arrival and departure of each ship and details of their cargoes.

In November 1914, the British had proclaimed the North Sea a war zone and instructed their armed merchant ships to disregard the Cruiser Rules and attack German submarines. In February 1915, Count von Bernstorff presented to the State Department in Washington his country's proclamation of a war zone in the waters surrounding Great Britain and Ireland:

> On and after the 18 February 1915 every enemy merchant ship found in the said war zone will be destroyed without it being always possible to avert the dangers threatening the crews and passengers on that account. Even neutral ships are exposed to dangers in the war zone, as in the misuse of neutral flags ordered on 31 January by the British Government and of the accidents of naval war, mistakes will not always be avoided and they may be struck by attacks directed at enemy ships.

The State Department protested to Germany, describing the German decision as 'a wanton act unparalleled in naval warfare'. On 18 February the Kaiser admitted to a group of U-boat commanders at Wilhelmshaven that by sinking armed enemy merchant ships without warning there would be undoubted loss of life. 'Yet,' he said, 'if it is possible for you to save the crews of the merchant ships, do it'.

It was conceded by Berlin that one of the chief reasons for the proclamation was the so-called 'misuse of neutral flags' to deceive U-boat commanders. Since the United States was the largest remaining neutral country, the British tended to use the Stars and Stripes for purposes of deception. On an earlier voyage of the *Lusitania* the veteran Captain Dow, fearing an attack by German submarines as he neared the Irish coast, had hauled up the American flag. On his arrival at Liverpool he explained that he had used the ploy to indicate to any U-boats in the area that Americans were among his passengers. It wasn't his intention to deceive the U-boat prowlers into thinking that the *Lusitania* was an American steamer; they knew perfectly well that the United States had no four-funnel passenger liners the size of the *Lusitania*.

The flag incident aroused anger in Germany. Washington protested to London that the use of neutral flags could only create further risks for neutral ships, while failing to afford protection to British ships. In reply the Admiralty claimed that the flag had been raised on the *Lusitania* at the request of the American passengers on board.

Captain Reginald Hall was able to tell the Cabinet at the start of the German submarine offensive that only two U-boats were ready to sail, the *U-30* and the *U-8*; the *U-20* and the *U-27* did not leave Emden until 25 February. Even then it seemed that only four of the German fleet of 23 submarines were operational. U-boats were temperamental craft; after every voyage they needed a careful overhaul.

The British concentrated their efforts on making the Dover Straits impassable for submarines with a barrage of nets and drifters, assuming that submarines operating off the Irish coast would have to pass through the Dover nets. But U-boats were already entering the western approaches by travelling around the north coast of Scotland and down the west coast of Ireland. The naval authorities then decided that the only way to parry the underwater menace to their combat fleets was to keep the warships in harbour, preferably in safe inlets along the coast of Scotland, protected by screens of minefields and destroyer patrols.

Undeterred, the U-boats turned their attention to merchant shipping. By the middle of March they had sunk four British steamers. At first they acted very much in the restricted fashion that surface raiders had always done. Vessels were warned and passengers and crew given a chance to get away in the lifeboats. But the campaign was soon to be extended beyond the limits of international law.

The U-boat menace in the Irish Sea became a cause for concern to Vice-Admiral Sir Charles Coke. From his base at Queenstown in County Cork Coke had overall command of the entire southern stretch of the Irish coast. He was the first to complain that his defences were entirely inadequate. He wanted more destroyers. But the Admiralty turned the request down flat.

Winston Churchill, the First Lord of the Admiralty, seemed convinced that Germany was paying the price for her militant policies. In the second week of the submarine campaign only three ships had been attacked and all had escaped. By April he was able to report that 'only 23 ships out of more than 6,000 arrivals and departures' had been sunk. 'The failure of the campaign is patent to the world,' he announced. His argument was that not only had the Germans failed to impede the movements of British trade, troops and supplies, but they had suffered losses. Others did not share his optimism. There was criticism of the Admiralty for the sinking of British ships by German mines and torpedoes. It was also suggested that Churchill lacked experience in naval matters and had no real knowledge of naval affairs; his background was Sandhurst, his outlook that of a military man.

By now, however, Churchill had recalled Lord Fisher, a veteran of seventy-five, from retirement to serve as First Sea Lord. It was Fisher who had indicated to Churchill in 1913 that enemy submarines had no alternative but to sink their victims and that 'one flag seen against the light through a periscope seems very much like any other'.

If Churchill had his critics, Captain Hall was not one of them. He had unstinted admiration for the First Lord, especially for his limitless capacity for hard work which he considered 'almost frightening'. When Hall floated his plan to censor the mails it was Churchill who supported him and helped him set up a new department for the work. But Hall was not to know how little thought the Admiralty had given to the defence of the waters around the south coast of Ireland, waters through which ships like the *Lusitania* sailed.

On 29 April, two days before the *Lusitania* was scheduled to leave New York, German-American relations, already strained over the *Falaba* affair, in which the American, Leon C. Thresher, had lost his life when the steamer was torpedoed by the *U-28*, suffered another setback. A German seaplane bombed an American oil tanker, the *Cushing*, in the North Sea off the Dutch coast. The tanker was carrying petroleum from New York to the Netherlands, and, according to the United States Consul at Rotterdam, was flying the American flag under attack. Three bombs were dropped on her, but they caused only slight damage and no lives were lost. The Germans claimed they saw no flag on the vessel nor any recognisable neutral marking. Berlin sent a note of 'deepest regret for the unintentional accident'.

The bombing, like the sinking of the *Falaba*, was not sufficient to inflame public opinion in America.

It was almost 12.30 and heavy smoke was belching from the raked funnels of the *Lusitania*.

Captain Turner was impatient at the delay in sailing. It would have been difficult to convince him that his ship was a target for German secret agents in New York who planned either to place explosives on board or secure conclusive evidence that she was an armed steamer. In the world of espionage Turner was an innocent. Suddenly, as the 'All Ashore' gongs sounded, people kissed and hugged one another while many whispered, 'I wish we were going with you,' before disembarking. The cargo hatches were battened down. Bells rang as officers hurried up the gangways clutching bills of lading and consignment notes for the express cargo.

John Idwal Lewis, the Senior Third Officer, supervising the loading of the mails, was the last man to step off the gangway onto the deck. Chief Officer Piper had already ordered the gangway cleared when suddenly Captain Turner bore down on him. 'Why didn't you tell me you were doing this?' he expostulated.

Piper looked surprised. 'I thought you knew, sir,' he answered quietly.

'Why didn't you *tell* me? I've got a visitor to put ashore. Get that gangway down again!'

Turner's niece Mercedes, who had come on board to bid him goodbye, hurried down the gangway to the pier. Turner returned to the bridge as the hawsers were slackened off. He exchanged his bowler for his Commodore's cap and surveyed the scene below him. On the dockside people were waving hats, handkerchiefs and miniature Stars and Stripes. Passengers waved back as those on the pier flung confetti into the air. Streamers of alphabet flags run from the masts gave the liner the festive atmosphere of a cruise ship. Turner paced the bridge, anxious to be away.

A whistle sounded from a high-funnelled tugboat in the river below; she was ready to nose the giant liner from her moorings and point her knife-like bows downstream. The *Lusitania* replied with three powerful blasts of her deep horn which made some passengers on deck clap their hands to their ears. The bandmaster brought down his baton and the uniformed band on the boat deck struck up 'Tipperary'. At the other end of the deck a Welsh choir began to sing the 'Star-Spangled Banner'.

Oliver Bernard had seen Turner ask for the gangway to be put down. He was surprised to notice that the man who was to guide them on this critical Atlantic voyage was not the stereotyped Commodore he expected, but an old man who wore his gold braid 'as though it were his Sunday best'. He understood that the sailing had been delayed to allow for the transfer of passengers from the *Cameronia*. Already the

*Lusitania* was three and a half hours late. Because of the German warning in the newspapers Bernard felt the voyage had taken on an unusual significance. He wondered if it might even rank as an event in the war itself. But would he come any nearer to the war than this? He had heard a newspaper reporter give Charles Frohman the doubtful assurance, 'Well, if anything happens, we've got your picture'.

Other saloon passengers shrugged off the warning with the nonchalance of habitual transatlantic travellers. Some had already gone to their suites, not much concerned with the late departure. But those second- and third-class passengers who were less travelled and knew of the warning were more anxious. In the early spring Margaret Cox had been advised by her doctor to take her ailing baby away from the heat of Winnipeg for the summer. 'Aren't you from the old country?' he had asked her. 'Then take him home.' She and her husband had disposed of their furniture and sublet their apartment. Cox had joined the Fort Garry Horse, hoping to be despatched to the war; Margaret had booked a private second-class cabin on the *Lusitania* for herself and the baby. When she arrived in New York she went to the Cunard office on State Street to confirm her reservation.

'Aren't you afraid?' a clerk had asked her.

'Of what?' she enquired.

'Why, of being torpedoed!' This was the first she had heard of any warnings, and she was surprised that the clerk should mention it.

Julia Sullivan was almost in tears. She suddenly realised she was leaving the good life of America for the hardships of a remote farm in County Kerry. But she loved Flor and she shook off her fears by telling herself the voyage would be a second honeymoon for them.

Ian Stoughton Holbourn had not left the deck all morning. He was philosophical about life and war and prepared for any eventuality. He watched the preparation for the voyage with interest. If he worried it was for the many children on board; he prayed that they would all reach Liverpool safely. He saw the last of the hawsers thrown off the bollards and winched swiftly on board. The band began to play 'God Be With You Till We Meet Again'.

The throbbing hum of the engines rose to a muffled roar as the massive turbines spun and the four propellers churned the waters of the Hudson into a muddy foam. Almost imperceptibly, the *Lusitania* moved from her pier into the river. Well-wishers dabbed their eyes with their handkerchiefs. The sun suddenly broke through the overcast skies.

One man on board had little interest in farewells. Detective Inspector William Pierpoint strolled anonymously among the crowds on the decks, studying the faces of the passengers intently. If there were German agents on board he was determined to get them.

# PART II

# The Voyage

1-7 May, 1915

*Speed is nothing. Deliver her safe,
bring her back safe—safety is all
that is required.*

—Samuel Cunard to his Captains

# 7

# BEYOND SANDY HOOK
# Day 1: Saturday, 1 May

THE *LUSITANIA* MOVED majestically down the Hudson River, her soaring red and black funnels billowing heavy smoke. The cheers from the crowds on the quayside faded and the waving handkerchiefs merged into a distant white blur as Pier 54 disappeared from the view of the passengers lining the ship's rails.

Standing stiffly beside the Captain, Albert Bestic watched the tugs slipping astern as the waves from the liner's sharp stem tumbled past to be churned into foam by the four mighty propellers. Below him he could see well-dressed passengers strolling the decks, some from the privileged worlds of society and the arts, for seldom did the *Lusitania* sail without celebrities on her passenger list. Albert wasn't envious; he accepted that these people moved in a different social sphere from that of a junior third officer. One of his jobs was to ensure that their baggage labelled *Not Wanted on Voyage* wasn't pilfered.

The vanishing towers of Manhattan and the diminishing figure of Liberty awakened in some passengers a sudden sense of isolation. They were seized with apprehension. As Battery Park and the city skyline receded many passengers remained on deck, reluctant to go below until the New World was lost from view. Among them were Canadians sailing to Europe to fight at the front; Americans, lulled by neutrality, travelling for business or pleasure; and English, returning out of patriotism to their native country. All of them, whatever their doubts, had no choice now but to accept the hazards of the voyage. A few were fatalistic, others attempted to measure the risks. The majority reassured themselves with the prospect of a short voyage, a mere seven days to Liverpool.

Irritated by the long delay in leaving Pier 54, Oliver Bernard paced the promenade deck after lunch. Once the pilot was dropped at Sandy Hook he assumed the Atlantic Blue Riband holder would quickly get into her stride. Yet before they were through the Narrows he had spotted three ships at the distant off-shore limits, guarding the escape route of interned German liners. As the Atlantic opened out he saw that the ships, heaving against the ocean swell, were painted in Royal Navy camouflage, their names obliterated. Bernard asked an officer to identify them and was told they were the *Essex*, the *Bristol* and the *Carmania*, whose grey paint could not conceal the distinctive outlines of the former Cunard aristocrat which William Turner had captained.

Standing at the promenade rail Bernard saw a cutter dropped into the swell from the side of the armed *Carmania*. Twelve seamen rowed the half mile to the overhanging counter for'ard of the *Lusitania*, which heaved to. He watched them slinging mail sacks on board; then the cutter pulled away as the men rowed off again towards the *Carmania*. The bridge telegraph rang out, the *Lusitania*'s engines quivered, and the liner resumed her journey eastward. More time lost, thought Bernard. This was to be his twelfth voyage across the Atlantic, his second on the *Lusitania*, and it looked like being a dull trip. Most of the passengers seemed less sociable than usual. At lunch he had found the saloon steward 'abominably supercilious'.

Staff Captain Anderson, making his rounds that afternoon, anticipated an extremely sociable second class. The dining-room stewards had already organised two sittings at meal-times, with extra tables placed in the passageway outside the dining saloon. Although this section was furnished more luxuriously than second class on any other transatlantic liner, with smoking room, library and lounges, it carried 600 passengers crowded into accommodation designed for a capacity of 460. It was cramped, yet the atmosphere was good-humoured.

In third class, with room for 1,186 passengers, only 373 were booked. Here the accommodation was comfortable, though hardly luxurious. In first class, which offered passengers the amenities of an exclusive club, there was room for 552 in the suites and staterooms, but only 291 were on board. The numbers in saloon and third class may have been smaller than usual, yet the *Lusitania*'s passenger list was the fullest since the outbreak of war. It was a cosmopolitan list with 949 British passengers, among them Canadians, Australians and Irish; 189 Americans, 71 Russians, and 15 Persians. A small number were from Greece, Belgium, Mexico, Cuba, France, Denmark, Holland, Spain, the Argentine, Italy, Switzerland, Finland, Norway and India.

Anxious parents who had heard talk of submarines took down the life-jackets in their cabins that afternoon and as a precaution tried them on their children. The strange, padded garments only made the youngsters laugh with delight. Of the 129 children on board, 39 were infants, 28 of them in second class, eight in third, and three in saloon.

Yet on board a liner that could weather the most violent storms, most passengers felt secure against danger. Since 1907 tens of thousands had travelled on the *Lusitania*. To the young the crossing was an adventure, to many people it was the journey of a lifetime, and even to the handful of experienced voyagers the *Lusitania* offered the comforts of a first-class hotel. Few were ever bored.

*The* U-20 *was a full day ahead of the* Lusitania.

*Spray swept over her narrow decks and conning tower as she ran on the surface through the dark waters of the North Sea towards the Orkneys. Her secret mission would take her along the southern coast of Ireland with the entrance to the Mersey at Liverpool as her final destination, a round trip from*

*Germany of 3,006 miles.*

At exactly seven o'clock the previous morning, Friday, 30 April, her Commander, Kapitänleutnant Walther Schwieger, had taken her out of Emden, west of Wilhelmshaven on the north German coast. The small, grey-bodied submarine had slipped quietly between the cork fenders of the dock, leaving behind the bobbing buoys of the harbour as she glided into the choppy waters of the North Sea. Soon she had cleared the sandy Borkum Reefs and was heading towards the Borkum lightship, 25 miles out, and the crew's last reminder of home.

She carried a wartime complement of 42 men and 7 torpedoes. Every corner of the small craft was stocked with supplies: meat and vegetables next to the torpedoes, boxes of butter under the bunks, salt and spices beneath Schwieger's own bunk. Within a few days the meat and vegetables would be inedible and the men would start eating out of tins. By the end of the patrol the food would be as intolerable as the stinking smell of the overcrowded U-boat itself.

Schwieger was in no doubt about the dangerous nature of his mission. His orders from Berlin were to sink enemy ships, with or without warning, and neutral ships which he suspected might be disguised enemy vessels. The sinking of HMS Pathfinder by the U-21 under Commander von Hersing off the coast of Scotland in the previous September had caused submarine textbooks to be rewritten; it was the first U-boat victory in the war and Hersing returned home a national hero. In January Hersing sank three steamers off the Mersey and that same month the U-20 under Kapitänleutnant Dröscher sank three merchant ships in the English Channel. Berlin was convinced by now that the submarine was the perfect weapon against the British Fleet and the blockade that was strangling Germany. With the submarine they could sever Britain's lines of commerce and destroy the troop transports outward bound in the waters of western and southern England.

The man in charge of the U-boat campaign was Commodore Herman Bauer. At the end of April, acting on instructions from Admiralty Command in Berlin, he ordered the *half-flotilla, comprising the U-20, U-27 and U-30 (which had already left Germany before the other two submarines and was given her orders by radio), to Dartmouth in the English Channel. Bauer's written instructions to his half-flotilla read:*

*Large English troop transports expected starting from Liverpool, Bristol (south of Liverpool), Dartmouth. Get to stations on fastest possible route around Scotland. Hold as long as supplies permit. Submarines to attack transport ships, merchant ships and warships.*

*The fair-haired, blue-eyed Schwieger, who had recently celebrated his thirtieth birthday, came from an old Berlin family. He had entered the naval service at eighteen and was given command of his first submarine, the petrol-driven U-14, at twenty-seven. He had only two interests: submarine warfare and classical music. In December he took over the U-20 from Dröscher. On one of his first missions he fired a torpedo at a British hospital ship off the French coast, mistaking her for a merchant ship. He missed his target, a not uncommon occurrence. Torpedoes often failed to eject because of a faulty trigger mechanism; sometimes a warhead proved a dud; or a defective steering mechanism sent the torpedo on an erratic course. More than sixty per cent of U-boat torpedoes failed to fire.*

*Though basic, Schwieger's U-20 was an effective craft. She was the second of the first four diesel submarines commissioned in 1913 and driven by two eight-cylinder engines. She had four torpedo tubes, and one mounted 8.8 centimetre deck gun. Submerged, she could make only nine knots compared to fifteen on the surface. But Schwieger was not perturbed about such shortcomings. The morale of his crew was high. He was confident about his mission. He had no fears.*

*Before noon he was on the cramped bridge. The early morning fog had cleared. The air smelled good. Below deck he could hear from the squeaking gramophone the strains of* Wir fahren gegen Eng-gell-and . . . *and the crew taking up the chorus. He had inherited the gramophone from Dröscher to while away the lonely hours and had adopted the U-boat's mascots, three dachshunds, from a Portuguese sailing ship he had sunk. Dogs and gramophone broke the tension that could become unbearable when the U-boat was submerged for long spells.*

*Each member of his crew was essential to his mission, from his young wireless operator Rikowsky to his experienced 'war pilot' Lanz. In a crisis he must be able to count on all of them. Seaman Ulbricht, he knew, was temperamental; but so were others, and temperament need not affect courage. Although submarines were cold and dirty craft and a foul prison on long voyages there was no shortage of volunteers. Some officers and men requested a transfer to U-boats from the Fleet. The Navy also sent a number of conscripts from the troublesome province of Alsace into the U-boat service. Schwieger's young quartermaster Voegele was a qualified electrician from Strasbourg. He had been conscripted at the start of the war and assigned to the U-20 not simply because of his electrical skills, but probably because it was a policy of the German war chiefs to keep Alsatians out of the Army where they might cause problems. Voegele was an able crew member, but Schwieger found him less forthcoming than the others, even sullen on occasion.*

*He trusted implicitly his torpedo officer, the youthful, slightly-built Oberleutnant Raimund Weisbach, who came from Breslau and was married with a son. Weisbach had joined the Navy two years after Schwieger. Assigned to the U-20 at the start of the war he had helped to make her one of the most feared U-boats operating off the south coast of Ireland. Living closely with Schwieger he was able to anticipate his Commander's every move.*

*Werner Furbringer, a former officer on the U-20, had developed the same sensitivity towards his Commander; he found Schwieger sensitive, yet not weak, slightly aloof, yet not ruthless. When Furbringer left the U-20 Schwieger gave a small dinner party in his honour at a wine tavern in*

*Wilhelmshaven. At his place at the table Furbringer found a small silver cigar box from Schwieger engraved with the letters DHO-NUF-AKT-APZ, the flag signal, 'Sincere thanks for faithful collaboration'. In his after-dinner speech he summed up his former leader. 'Walther,' he said, 'is an excellent Commander and a splendid man.'*

Charles Frohman sat in the study of his chosen suite wearing a smoking jacket and reading the first of his batch of new playscripts. As he read he munched the sweets with which his valet William Stainton kept him supplied. The impresario had such a sweet tooth that he never travelled without them; some evenings he and a colleague would shut themselves away for what they described as a 'dessert orgy'. Frohman's actress friend Maude Adams had given him an elaborate basket, shaped like a ship and filled with flowers, fruit and sweet-meats, which stood on an occasional table near his desk. His thank-you note to her was among the mails which the ship's pilot brought back to New York: 'The little ship you sent is more wonderful than the big one that takes me away from you.'

He had also written a farewell note to Charles Dillingham, the theatre manager with whom he shared a country house at White Plains in Westchester County; on it he had made a drawing of a liner being chased by a submarine.

His preoccupation with the war had prompted him to stage Justus Miles Forman's play *The Hyphen*. His favourite war poem was about a soldier who had lost his legs. Perhaps it was his illness that made Frohman conscious of suffering. After a fall on the porch of his house at White Plains he had been forced to live like a prisoner in his New York apartment at the Knickerbocker Hotel, tortured with articular rheumatism that racked every joint with pain.

Day and night Dillingham and the actor Paul Potter sat reading and talking at the invalid's bedside, Dillingham in the morning, Potter in the evening. Frohman was so terrified of the dark that he would plead with Potter to tell him stories until he fell asleep. 'More, Paul, more!' he would beg, as the actor talked on, sometimes into the dawn. Frohman fought his illness with such courage that he was able to return to his beloved theatre. But his pain never lessened; still a youngish man, he found such difficulty in walking that whenever he went out he supported himself on a cane he called his 'wife'.

He was friend, confidant, confessor, business manager and artistic adviser to the many artists he managed. Few of his stars could face an opening performance unless they knew that 'C.F.' was seated in a corner back stage. He was satisfied only when several of his productions were before the public in England or America; often he had as many as eight plays in rehearsal at the same time. Driven by fierce ambition, he acquired and dominated actors and authors — and to employ them he bought theatre after theatre.

In twenty-five years only one star had dared to challenge him. At the first morning's rehearsal of a play he made a small point of criticism to the actress Mrs. Patrick Campbell.

'Pardon me, Mr. Frohman,' she interrupted him. 'You forget that I am an artist.'

'All right, Mrs. Campbell,' he said quietly. 'I shall keep your secret.' He limped up the aisle and out of the theatre. He never saw the play or the actress again.

All his correspondence carried the heading *Charles Frohman presents* . . . That afternoon, when he tired of reading scripts, he took a sheet of paper and wrote, as he often did, in his favourite blue pencil, *Charles Frohman has the following stars under his management* . . . Munching another sweet, he began to jot down the names of his own stars and every other name he could think of with a potential for stardom.

George Kessler paced the decks, his mind whirling with business ideas. He was too restless to be part of the leisurely scene. No voyage was short enough for Kessler and he could hardly contain his impatience. At night the Champagne King would lie awake scheming of ways to increase his fortune and ways to spend it. He sought popularity by giving extravagant dinners. He once hired London's best electricians, carpenters and scene painters to transform the courtyard of the Savoy Hotel into a corner of Venice, flooding it to a depth of several feet and serving dinner in a large white gondola. Real swans floated on the water and a magnificent cake was borne to the diners on the back of a circus elephant. Among his guests were Caruso and the great French actress Réjane.

On another occasion he turned the winter garden of the Savoy into a reproduction of the North Pole, with icebergs of silver tissue and fields of plastic snow. His guests sat on white chairs at tables of imitation snow as dwarfs dressed as snowmen held the menu cards for them. At his house on the Thames at Bourne End he once gave a summer banquet, lighting the grounds with 50,000 electric lights.

By contrast, Charles Lauriat was taking a keen interest in the voyage. The Boston bookseller was an amateur sailor, and although this was his twenty-third Atlantic crossing it was his first on board the *Lusitania*. Usually he travelled in smaller and slower ships, but he had chosen the Cunarder on this occasion because he wanted to make his business trip as brief as possible. When the liner docked in Liverpool in a week's time he could reach London by train in a few hours and start work immediately. He estimated that the *Lusitania* was steaming at around twenty knots. She could make a fast crossing, even though her power had been reduced by Cunard and six of the boilers had been shut down in the previous November, an economy which cut the liner's maximum speed from 25 to 21 knots. Lauriat didn't consider the reduction significant: the *Lusitania* was still faster than any other ship on the Atlantic.

However, he could not dismiss certain doubts from his mind. Over lunch he had agreed reluctantly with his Boston neighbour Lothrop Withington that because the *Lusitania* belonged to a country at war, it was a likely target for attack. But would the Germans dare to carry their hostility to such extremes?

Alfred Gwynne Vanderbilt took his customary nap after lunch. That afternoon Ronald Denyer, his valet, ensured that the bulk of his master's luggage was carefully stowed in the baggage room; he retained one large suitcase containing all the clothes the millionaire would need for the voyage.

Donning a silk dressing gown, Vanderbilt stretched out on his comfortable brass bed. The Regal Suite comprised drawing room, dining room and bathroom, with adjoining rooms for his valet. But for all the attention he paid to the opulence around him he might have been relaxing in a suite at the family's Park Avenue hotel. He scarcely noticed the Sheraton dressing table, the brocaded settee, the walls adorned with tapestries, the windows shaped and curtained as in a private house.

Vanderbilt welcomed such travel. He and his wife Margaret occupied a precarious position in Newport society. Even by the standards of Long Island's rich set, their parties were reckless. Newport's inquisitive society had not forgotten the suicide in England of Mrs. Ruiz, and they counted six divorces in the millionaire's establishment, including his own. They were jealous that his trotting horses, valued at $500,000, were the best in the world and that his famous grey team had never been beaten. With his boundless enthusiasm for coaching, Vanderbilt had transformed his Oakland farm into the world's most expensive riding school, surrounding the arena with an enclosed gallery for his friends and adding a white marble swimming pool, a Turkish bath, a squash rackets court, and a trophy room for his cups and prizes.

Despite the war, he was determined to travel to London for the meeting of the International Horse Show Association. Each year he exhibited his horses at Olympia; he once transported twenty-six horses, sixteen coaches and a team of grooms and assistants across the Atlantic. He kept a large apartment in Park Lane and a houseboat at Henley furnished like a floating mansion.

The travels of his sister Gertrude were of a different kind. A tireless philantrophist, she had established a hospital unit in

France to care for wounded soldiers. She even wrote a *Lusitania Journal* about her voyages. She and Alfred were close, and she expected to hear about his trip on the liner. Alfred, though lazy about correspondence, promised himself he would write at least one letter to her before he reached Liverpool. 'Why shouldn't we spend a lot of time abroad?' he once asked her. 'They aren't so bad over there. I think we underrate them.'

In the satinwood music room on the boat deck David Thomas, the Napoleon of the world's coal trade, sat with Margaret listening to the orchestra. He had almost forgotten the German warning that had occupied his thoughts that morning. As with most Welshmen, he needed music. His daughter remarked, 'I cannot understand it. I just feel so low.' He looked at her with surprise. 'How can you say that, Margaret, when you're travelling on the world's greatest liner?'

'Let's not worry, father,' she answered, forcing a smile. 'It's nobody's fault but mine.'

Margaret found the sentimental music boring after the excitement of New York. She had loved every moment of her visit and even forgave the Americans their detachment from the growing anguish of Europeans in the war. Her depression that afternoon puzzled her. Why was she unhappy on the *Lusitania?* Perhaps the truth was that she was returning to a loveless marriage, to a man who no longer enjoyed her company.

Over lunch she and her father had become friendly with their table companions, Dr. Howard Fisher and his sister-in-law Dorothy Conner, who were on their way to start a field hospital in France. Despite their wartime mission they were sociable and amusing and Margaret looked forward to meeting them at dinner. She glanced round at the passengers in the music room, envying their obvious enjoyment, and wondering if anything could disturb their complacent world. She knew her father longed for the day when he would drive up to the front door of his beloved Llanwern, yet evidently he relished the social life on board ship. He had been generous to her, as always, in New York. Her trunks were packed with clothes from the best stores on Fifth Avenue and these she would share with her mother. When she thought of the war raging in Europe, her shopping spree seemed like cheating.

Not far from Thomas and his daughter were the Hubbards. Elbert, sitting upright in his armchair, resembled an Old Testament prophet. Occasionally the Sage of East Aurora pulled a small notebook from his pocket and wrote furiously, to the amusement of those around him. Since his days as an ambitious Chicago cub reporter he had been a compulsive scribbler. That morning before sailing he had dashed off letters to friends and acquaintances. 'Over there,' he wrote to one of them, 'I may meet with a mine or a submarine.'

He and Alice had taken a liking to Ernest Cowper, a young journalist from Toronto, also on his way to Europe to report the war. Cowper was travelling second class, but had crossed over to first to interview some of the notable passengers. Hubbard told him of his plan to recreate the voyage for his magazine *The Philistine*. He would cable his *Lusitania Diary* from London for the delight of millions of readers. He was eager to discuss almost any subject with Cowper — except his Federal Court conviction and his divorce fifteen years earlier to marry schoolteacher Alice.

Like Ernest Cowper, other passengers were prepared to ignore the demarcation line between first and second class.

Hilda Ellis and Sarah Smith conducted Avis Dolphin on a tour of the liner. Strolling through first-class lounges furnished with deep armchairs, expensive paintings, marble fireplaces, grand pianos and rich drapes, Avis risked taking off the tinted glasses she had been ordered to wear after an attack of measles. She wanted to see the splendours clearly, for to an inquisitive small-town girl, the *Lusitania* was a wonderland.

Walking hand-in-hand with her chaperones across acres of deep carpet she was not to know of the segregation imposed during meal times. The saloon dining-room was separated from the second-class saloon on D Deck by a network of galleys and pantries. Avis, however, was too young to be allowed to dine with her companions that evening. By eight o'clock she would be tucked up in bed.

Third-class passengers George Hook and his children Frank and Elsie soon learned that first and second class were officially out of bounds. Hook had planned to travel home second class, but when Mrs. Marsh, the family housekeeper, decided to return to England with her husband and eleven-month old baby boy in third class he declared, 'We won't be separated — let's all travel together' — and he changed to a third-class passage.

They ate together that evening in the third class dining saloon, which was as big as a gymnasium, with banks of tables, separated by a central aisle, stretching the width of the saloon. Here the company was more gregarious. The Hooks made friends with another returning emigrant, Jack Walsh from New York, and Walsh invited Gerda Neilson, the girl he had met on deck that morning, to join them. He had seen her leaning alone over the rail before sailing and had introduced himself. It was the beginning of their romance.

Captain Reginald Hall, Director of Intelligence at the Admiralty, had informed the war staff in Whitehall that German submarines were on their way to the southern Irish coast. On Friday, when the *U-20* had tested her radio with a wireless trial to the Borkum and Ascona stations her messages had been picked up by the British intercept service. Hall knew that the *U-20* and *U-27* would be operating off the Fastnet within a few days. He was concerned at the news. That same Friday a British and a Russian steamer had been torpedoed off the Blaskets on the southern Irish coast.

In the afternoon Hall received further disturbing news. The American tanker *Gulflight* had been attacked by a U-boat off the Scilly Isles. The Captain and two of the crew were reported dead. For the second time Americans had become the victims of a German submarine attack. But Hall was worried by the news for another reason. Within a few days he knew the

*Lusitania* would be sailing through the same waters.

*By four o'clock a heavy fog had come down and, as they were in the steamer lane to the Firth of Forth, Kapitänleutnant Schwieger ordered the U-20 to a depth of 70 feet. In the oil-reeking control room the tall commander crouched anxiously at the patrol periscope. A few months previously when running submerged off the Scottish coast he had sighted two buoys. He had heard a noise as though huge chains were being dragged over the hull of the boat; the men at the diving rudders had shouted that they couldn't control the apparatus. A glance at the gauges had shown that their speed had slowed and the U-20 was sinking fast, staggering helplessly until she hit bottom, one hundred feet down, with a bump. It was then Schwieger realised that the buoys had been supporting a net and his U-boat was caught in the meshes. The men around him were silent. He ordered, 'Reverse engines'. He could only try to back out of the trap. With a straining and a rending the submarine slowly tore her way through the net. The crew exchanged smiles of relief. But Schwieger knew they had been within minutes of death. It was an incident he never wished to speak of again.*

*Now, despite the poor visibility, he stayed with the damp rubber surround of the periscope glass pressed against his forehead. Within an hour the fog lifted and he thought it safe to blow tanks and come to the surface.*

*At 5.15 p.m. the hatches were flung open. Clean air blew down through the fetid hull. The lookouts in their oilskins and sou'westers climbed on deck and Schwieger, his jacket buttoned high, took the bridge. The wind was freshening and the sky was clear. He directed the U-20's course north to Fair Isle.*

As the stewards knocked on stateroom and cabin doors to check that the curtains were drawn to comply with the black-out regulations, the first class passengers were dressing for dinner, the women at pains to ensure that their evening gowns would match the elegance of the Cunard setting. Soon they would gather for the first colourful social event of the voyage.

Down the staircase amidships from the staterooms and by the broad, carpeted stairs from the Grand Entrance, they descended in their finery to the three-tiered dining saloon. Most of them chose the main restaurant on D Deck where a table d'hôte dinner was served, others preferred to dine à la carte in the overhead saloon on the level of C Deck. With cherubs after Boucher smiling down on them from their lofty dome, the diners made their way between marble Corinthian columns to circular tables covered with shining white napery on which the silver sparkled. The centrepiece of this saloon was a magnificent mahogany sideboard gleaming with gilt ornaments. There were few more splendid restaurants in the world than the *Lusitania*'s.

In the galleys, larders, bakehouses and confectionary rooms, an army of cooks, butchers, bakers and scullions prepared the first elaborate meal of the voyage, which would be served by fifty-five waiters, some carrying stacks of plates, others pushing *hors d'oeuvres* trolleys from the kitchens to the dining saloon.

As the strains from the orchestra playing a Strauss waltz drifted down from the balcony the diners took their places in the saloon which had been described as 'a vision of white and gold in Empire style, touched with *vieux rose*'. David Thomas, his daughter and his secretary, Arnold Rhys-Evans, joined Howard Fisher and Dorothy Conner. Margaret looked graceful in a pale blue gown. Charles Frohman, leaning heavily on his cane, was followed at a respectful distance by an entourage that included Charles Klein, Justus Miles Forman, the actresses Josephine Brandell and Rita Jolivet, Rita's brother-in-law George Vernon, and her admirer Wallace Phillips, described as a New York agent for a gun company. They talked loudly as theatre people sometimes do.

George Kessler swaggered through the saloon to join the New York financier Dr. Fred Pearson and his wife. Pearson gave lavish parties at his houses in Mayfair and Dorset, though he would hesitate to claim they were as flamboyant as Kessler's. He spent his fortune travelling the world compulsively buying church organs.

The waiters moved smoothly from table to table as other diners entered the ornate saloon. Shipbuilders Fred Gauntlett, Albert Lloyd Hopkins and Samuel Knox arrived, talking in subdued voices; they were sailing to England at the request of the Navy Secretary to negotiate for the patent of a British submarine design. Charles Frederick Fowles, a New York art dealer, and his wife were joined by the frail Sir Hugh Lane who had changed from his habitual tweeds into evening wear. Charles Lauriat chatted with Lothrop Withington. Marie de Page was in earnest conversation with Dr. James Houghton, who was to assist her husband at his hospital at La Panne; they were joined by Theodate Pope, the middle-aged daughter of a Connecticut car manufacturer. Theodate was on her way to England to meet the spiritualist Sir Oliver Lodge. She was accompanied by her maid Emily Robinson and her soulmate Edwin Friend, fifteen years her junior and, like herself, an enthusiast about psychical research.

The lower tier was soon filled with diners, among them Ogden Hammond, a New York insurance broker; Englishman Charles Bowring, who represented a branch of his family firm in New York; Isaac Lehmann, a New York buyer of US Government supplies; James Brooks, an executive with a New York chain manufacturing company; and Georgina Morell, a wealthy Toronto widow who at seventy-six was the oldest passenger in first class.

Some heads turned discreetly as Lady Allan, tall and dignified in a dark gown, walked to her table with her teenage daughters, Gwen and Anna; she was the wife of Sir Montagu Allan, the last in the male line of a Canadian shipping family. Virginia Loney's entrance did not go unnoticed either. She was startingly mature for her fifteen years and probably the most beautiful young woman on board. With her wealthy Baltimore parents she was on her way to Scotland for a vacation. Almost at the same time a young man of military bearing followed his father to another table in the saloon. William McMillan Adams, the handsome heir of a Boston family, had been home on first leave from the British Army. His father, Arthur Henry Adams, had decided to sail to England with him.

Among the youngest at dinner was William Robert Holt, the fifteen-year-old son of millionaire Canadian banker Sir Robert Holt. His parents, fearing a German invasion of England, had kept him in Canada for the first months of the war. Now, they believed the risk had diminished and William, with two young friends, was on his way to school at Marlborough.

Elbert Hubbard escorted his wife to their table below the orchestra, his floppy silk tie flowing over his shirt front. The pair seemed ill at ease in evening clothes.

When Oliver Bernard strode into the dining saloon he discovered the supercilious steward had given his table to another passenger. Bernard's urchin face darkened. The social discrimination practised by the staff of transatlantic liners infuriated him.

'Perhaps,' he snapped at the man, 'you would tell me why the genius of the engineers who built this ship should be depreciated because you think some passengers are more important than others?'

'I beg your pardon, sir,' the steward replied, stubbornly insisting that Bernard sit at another table.

The designer took his place, still fuming. He looked across to where the Englishman Stewart Mason and Lesley his young bride were seated. But the couple seemed to be ignoring him. When he saw Vanderbilt taking his place at the Captain's table his resentment grew. He disliked millionaires with nothing better to do than travel three thousand miles in wartime to drive a four-in-hand to Brighton. The war would make them richer than ever, he supposed. He turned away contemptuously to read the menu.

The embossed card, with its gilt wreath circling the Cunard

flag, offered oysters on the half shell or *hors d'oeuvres* followed by soup. The choice of fish ranged from *Supreme de Barbue Florentine* to devilled whitebait. The entrées included sautéed chicken, braised gosling and haunches of mutton. Bernard decided not to stint himself.

For those making their first voyage on the *Lusitania* the ceremony of dinner at sea was unforgettable; even for experienced voyagers its appeal seldom waned. As the murmur of voices rose above the music and the clink of china, Captain Turner, who usually delegated Anderson to entertain the guests at his table, proved that he could on occasion be an agreeable host. In his conservative way he ignored the elaborate dishes on the menu and when it came to dessert he chose a rice pudding.

After dinner some passengers went to the music room or the library; others headed for the smoking room to play poker; but most of them, fatigued after the long day, retired to their staterooms.

At midnight Second Officer Hefford with Albert Bestic walked the lengthy corridors of the liner. Few passengers were to be seen. The officers checked that the fire appliances, each housed in a neat glass case, were in order. Then they returned to their quarters abaft the wheelhouse.

Charles Hill, the London director of an Anglo-American tobacco company, lay awake in his stateroom. He was puzzled about a curious incident that day which he had kept from his dinner companions.

During the customary search for stowaways after the liner sailed, the master-at-arms had surprised three men in a steward's pantry near the Grand Entrance on the shelter deck.

Staff Captain Anderson confronted the men, demanding to know who they were, but they refused to give him any information. Suspecting they might be Germans, he sent for the ship's detective William Pierpoint and the interpreter Adolph Pederson.

Anderson knew of the German threats to the *Lusitania*, but

nothing of the espionage ring. When Pierpoint formally arrested the men, Anderson decided to take them to Liverpool for questioning by the authorities. After Pederson confirmed they were Germans the men were locked in the ship's cells. Pierpoint questioned them again later, but was unable to learn if there had been an attempt to plant explosives on the *Lusitania*.

Charles Hill had been chatting with Anderson when one of the masters-at-arms had come hurrying along the deck with the news of the men's discovery. Hill asked the Staff Captain what had happened. 'We have arrested three German suspects,' Anderson admitted, 'and locked them in the cells.'

Why hadn't they been ferried to the *Carmania* or sent back to New York? Hill wanted to know. Anderson dodged the question. 'Our cells,' he assured Hill with good humour, 'are the most comfortable on the Atlantic.'

Captain Turner showed no surprise when Anderson told him what had happened. In forty-five years at sea he had come to regard stowaways as just another shipboard nuisance.

# 8

# THROUGH THE FOG
# Day 2: Sunday, 2 May

SUNDAY MORNING dawned foggy. It was the signal for
the powerful foghorn of the *Lusitania* to bellow its warning
across the hidden expanse of ocean, inviting an echo that
never came.

Captain Turner, tight-lipped and anxious, climbed to the
bridge. He was always summoned when the fog came down.
Shoulders hunched, he huddled in a corner, the peak of his
cap low on his forehead. His eyes searched for the dark blur of
another ship that might suddenly loom out of the im-
penetrable whiteness. He strained to hear the telltale moan of
another foghorn.

The liner had reduced speed. In the bowels of the ship the
engineers, under the veteran Bryce, stood tensely by the
controls, watching the telegraph dials. On the bridge the
telegraph boys waited, ready to crash the levers to 'Full Astern'
should the Captain give the order. Crewmen faded like ghosts
whenever they walked for'ard into the bows. Were it not for
the thrump of the bow wave Turner could easily imagine that
his ship was suspended in air; it was as though the blanket of
fog had stopped the *Lusitania* short in her tracks.

The handful of officers and men remained watchful on the
bridge, knowing that the speed with which an order was given
and obeyed could mean the difference between life and death.
Turner shared these tense moments with them, but he was
confident he could bring his ship safely through the fog.

As he stared ahead the swirling mists lifted and the

*Lusitania* emerged suddenly into the bright early morning sunshine. Tension eased on the bridge. 'The worst is over', declared Turner, certain the fog would not roll in again. Ordering an increase in speed, he turned and went down the companionway to his cabin.

Three decks down in the 'eyes' of the ship Leslie Morton leaned across his bunk to look through the porthole. As the *Lusitania* gathered speed, forging steadily ahead into the Atlantic, it thrilled him to watch the sunlit water cutting away from the liner's bows. His gloomy quarters were like a workhouse dormitory, but at least he had a porthole by his bunk.

Since signing on as a deckhand on Friday he had found the vastness of the *Lusitania* disconcerting. Too many passengers and too much noise. Still, he was prepared to work hard and do as he was told, touching up paintwork and washing down the decks. He had heard the ship was a target for German torpedoes. His crewmates scoffed at such rumours; the *Lusitania* was too fast, they argued, for any submarine. Leslie didn't entirely share their confidence. No ship was unsinkable.

Each crew member lived in a restricted world. George Wynne's world was the hot, noisy first-class kitchens which had a camaraderie of their own. Young Wynne moved among the kitchen staff, whistling as he helped prepare breakfast. The menu was extensive: fruit or fruit juice, followed by grape nuts, oatmeal, hominey or malted milk; kippers, lemon sole, turbot or Yarmouth bloaters; eggs to order or sautéed calf's liver; and Cumberland lamb or Wiltshire bacon with pancakes and maple syrup or baked apples. Passengers could order steak, mutton chops or chicken from the grill. The cold cuts included beef, smoked ox tongue, ham or capon. Scones, oatcakes and toasted muffins were served with tea, coffee or cocoa.

With scant idea of what went on elsewhere on board, George passed the time happily in the kitchens. It pleased him that his father had settled into his job as a scullion, though he complained he was homesick. The boy tried to cheer him up by talking football and reminding him they were only six days from Liverpool.

As George began his kitchen work, John O'Connell was coming off watch. After shovelling coal into the furnaces for four hours the boy's face was blackened and his eyes were burning red. During the last hour when the engineers had ordered more speed, greater effort was expected from the stokers and firemen. In the scorching heat from the furnace John began driving the long steel poker under the burning coals, lifting them to help combustion, forcing the point of the poker upwards by bearing down the handle with his stomach muscles until they ached.

At that moment there was a commotion at the next furnace. A big trimmer who had brought drink on board was grappling with another man on the coal-strewn floor. As they swore and shouted a fireman pushed them roughly apart. Usually a fight could be stopped before an engineer arrived, yet John knew that before the end of the voyage the tension in the boiler rooms would erupt in violence. He wiped his face with the rag he wore around his neck. His lips and nostrils were clogged and sticky with sweat and coal dust. Exhausted, he decided not to take a shower until after the next watch.

In his worn dungarees and thick boots he climbed the 'fiddley', the steel ladder leading to the firemen's messroom. He collected his plate, knife and mug and sat on a bench at the long, fixed table to share breakfast with the men from his watch. He ate in silence, not wanting to join in the coarse talk of the older men among whom he felt out of place. He was scared of many of them and he had to pretend he was as tough as they were. He had been warned to watch for sexual advances, not only from firemen and trimmers, but also from the engineers. He was always wary. He accepted this rough, dirty life because he was lucky to have a job.

Listening to the men talk about the latest news of the war he had to admire their contempt for the German submarines. He never heard anyone suggest the *Lusitania* might be torpedoed, although they must have known that if the liner were sunk they would have little chance of escaping from their steamy underworld. They didn't give a damn. Day and night they worked, ate, played cards, fought and slept. Most of them never went on deck or even saw daylight during the entire voyage. They joked and argued about women, football and the pubs on Scotland Road.

*Oberleutnant Weisbach, the watch officer on the bridge of the U-20, had sighted the approaching enemy flotilla at 4.20 am German time, just before dawn. He shouted a warning to the two lookouts, and the three men leaped down the hatchway in the submarine's conning tower, hands and feet fumbling desperately for a grip on the steel ladder.*

*Weisbach's cry of 'Destroyers!' and the raucous noise of the klaxon woke up everybody. The crew sprang into activity, each man now adept at his job, the result of countless gruelling exercises.*

*Weisbach slammed shut the top hatch, swiftly sealing it with two levers. The last lookout man down, still hanging onto the back of the ladder, slammed and sealed the lower hatch. At the commander's word, 'Dive!' the crew jumped to the valve levers. Diving valves were opened, water rushed into the tanks, and the U-20 swiftly dipped her bow and dived to thirty, then sixty feet.*

*As the submarine levelled out on an even keel, Kapitänleutnant Schwieger ordered, 'Bring her to periscope depth'.*

*As the patrol periscope was run out he peered into the glass. Sweeping the horizon, he saw the ships, at least six of them, steaming southwards about thirty miles off Peterhead in a wide search line; enemy destroyers, he thought, protecting the British Grand Fleet at Scapa Flow. They were directly on course for the U-20 as it headed north towards the stretch of open sea beyond the Orkneys.*

*He had run on the surface all night and the cold air through the open hatches had thoroughly chilled the boat. Even in their leather suits, woollen underwear, thick sweaters and heavy boots, the crew felt miserable. It was damp, too, with*

*condensation running down the insides of the boat. Those who
went back to their hammocks wrapped three or four blankets
around them in search of a little warmth. It was 6.25 am
before the U-20 blew her tanks and resumed cruising on the
surface. Three hours later Schwieger sighted Fair Isle, but
within ten minutes he was forced to dive again to avoid the
bows and guns of the patrolling destroyers.*

*Soon after one o'clock he sighted a further six destroyers
between Ronaldsay and Fair Isle. He attempted to run on the
surface, but against a sea that had suddenly turned rough he
found it impossible. Again he dived to pass the destroyers.*

Captain Turner was tempted to don his bowler hat. Instead,
he picked up his Commodore's cap and made his way along
the boat deck to one of the first-class lounges. Resplendent in
his best gold-braided uniform, he took his place before the
small congregation of worshippers and in a gruff voice began
to read the service. According to custom, he asked God for
blessings on the Royal Family and on those at sea.

Among those gathered in the lounge were Paul Crompton,
his wife and five of their six children, Major and Mrs. Warren
Pearl, Lady Allan and her daughters, Fred Gauntlett and his
shipbuilding colleagues, and Charles Lauriat and Lothrop
Withington.

The service over, Turner spoke briefly to some of the
congregation, but he offered only pleasantries and seemed
impatient to get back to the bridge. Those passengers who
were in his company for the first time found him self-
confident, if slightly old-fashioned. He seemed the epitome of
a transatlantic Commodore, indisputably in command, yet
without arrogance. Most of them realised they had little
chance of dining at his table. For the rest of the voyage the
Captain would remain a distant and enigmatic figure pacing
the bridge.

Turner, however, would have to make another obligatory
appearance at lunch. He seemed displeased when Staff

Captain Anderson reminded him that it was the turn of some members of the aristocracy to join his table, but it would be later in the week before he would need to socialise again. When he returned with relief to the bridge he was told that the *Lusitania* was now five hundred miles out of New York.

Readers of the *New York Tribune*, Turner's favourite newspaper, were informed that Sunday morning that the German torpedo threat had 'failed to reduce to any extent' the *Lusitania*'s passenger list. The account of the sailing, wedged in a single column on Page One between reports of the suffragettes' march along Fifth Avenue and the progress of the war in Europe, claimed that passengers were 'loud in their defiance of the German Embassy's warning to travellers who elected to book transportation on steamships of Great Britain and her allies'. Many, according to the *Tribune*, had laughed at the warning notice. Not only were there no cancellations, but ten additional bookings were made in first class shortly before the liner sailed.

The newspaper referred to rumours on the pier that prominent saloon passengers had received warning telegrams advising them not to sail. These reports had been 'branded as false' by Cunard officials. The *Tribune* readers could not have known about the background to the wireless message sent by Charles Sumner, Cunard's New York manager, to the Captain of the *Lusitania* late on Saturday evening: ASK VANDERBILT FROHMAN KLEIN WHETHER THEY RECEIVED TELEGRAMS WARNING AGAINST SAILING OR THREATENING IF SO SECURE THEM AND RETURN US ANSWER.

Turner had promptly replied: NO ONE RECEIVED TELEGRAMS OF NATURE MENTIONED. Sumner, perhaps to cover up his curious decision to withhold the telegrams from Vanderbilt and other saloon passengers, had sent the wireless message to Turner knowing the Captain's reply would be in the negative. Turner had never seen the telegrams.

When the *Tribune*'s Washington reporter enquired at the

German Embassy about the warning notice, he was informed that its publication was 'entirely an act of friendship and a warning to travellers who may yet be willing to brave the high prices and other more serious restrictions on pleasure visits to Europe'. The Embassy saw nothing irregular in publishing the notice. The State Department, for its part, decided not to take any action.

In Liverpool, five hours ahead of New York time, it was late afternoon. Alfred Booth, the indefatigable chairman of Cunard, was spending an uneasy day. He had read the newspaper reports about the German warning to passengers on British ships and the mysterious telegrams, and was surprised that his office in New York had not thought it worthwhile to cable him with the news.

He wondered whether he should contact Captain Turner to urge him to take special care. On the second day of the *Lusitania*'s homeward voyage, however, when the liner was more than two thousand miles from the danger zone, it seemed premature to worry about submarine attacks. He had implicit faith in his long-serving Commodore and believed the experienced Turner could cope with any emergency. Still, he could not entirely dismiss the nagging fear that the *Lusitania* was sailing into danger.

He decided to contact both his cousin George and the Admiralty next morning. George had travelled frequently to New York where he had worked with Captain Guy Gaunt in the purchase of supplies for the War Office. Alfred, who looked after the shipping affairs of Cunard in Liverpool, valued his cousin's advice. If he agreed that the *Lusitania* was in real danger then Alfred decided he would act at once.

As Oliver Bernard came up the saloon stairway of the liner to take a stroll along the promenade deck after lunch he heard a bugle call summoning crewmen to a lifeboat drill. He stood watching as a dozen crewmen and a bosun lined up opposite No. 14 lifeboat on the portside, just aft of the third funnel. At a command from an officer the men climbed the davits into the boats where they stood for a moment with oars dressed before sitting down, as though waiting for the boat to be launched. Apparently satisfied, the officer ordered the crewmen out of the boat and back to their duties.

How odd, thought Bernard. The lifeboat had not been lowered, even to deck level, and it was this procedure which was the hazardous part of such an emergency. Recalling his own days as a young seaman, he wondered: 'What will happen if all the boats have to be lowered full of passengers?'

The drill proved a diversion for other passengers strolling the decks that afternoon, none of whom had been asked to take part in any emergency exercise. Young Frank and Elsie Hook, neat in their Sunday clothes, were fascinated by the seamen and the bugler. After the drill the spirited Frank wanted to join in the deck games, but Elsie was shy and hung back.

Third-class travel on the *Lusitania* was fairly democratic compared to the early days of transatlantic sailing when it was not uncommon for a ship to transport passengers in steerage on the outward trip and cattle in the same quarters on the way back. It was still mandatory on westward voyages, however, to separate third-class passengers from the rest of the ship by locked gates to prevent emigrants spreading infectious diseases. But on this eastward crossing Frank and Elsie, like other children, wandered unchallenged about the ship. The main disadvantage in third class was the lack of facilities for small children, which meant that mothers had little time to rest. In contrast, children in first class were provided with a nursery on C deck and their own dining saloon. A stewardess supervised an infants' playpen in second class.

Some mothers had transferred from third to second class, when they learned that Cunard had reduced second-class fares from seventy-five to fifty dollars. But even Margaret Cox, nursing her seventeen-month-old Desmond, was finding the voyage in second class exhausting.

In her second-class cabin young Avis Dolphin was violently

seasick, a new and alarming experience for her. She lay in her bunk in misery. Nurse Ellis and Miss Smith brought her lunch on a tray from the dining saloon, but she could not bear to look at food, and refused even the cups of tea they offered her. Not only was she suffering from neuralgia, she was also very homesick.

Charles Frohman, too, had shut himself in his stateroom that afternoon. Although the weather was sunny and fine he had no desire to join his friends on deck. He was feeling unwell and his right knee was intensely painful. Invariably he ate as he worked and visitors always noticed plates of sandwiches on his desk. He used to say, 'A rehearsal accompanied by a sandwich is progress; a rehearsal interrupted by a meal is a delay'. When Charles Klein and Justus Miles Forman called to his suite on their way to dinner, Frohman made an effort to be sociable. His valet was ordered to open a bottle of champagne.

Sensing that Forman was brooding about the failure of *The Hyphen*, which was running to half-empty houses on Broadway, Frohman, who was ready to write off the play as just another miscalculation in the theatrical game, tried to reassure the dramatist. He told him, 'Charley will introduce you to the best theatre people in London' and went on to talk about the future of the theatre, predicting the time when seats would sell for fifty cents, authors' royalties would be cut to a minimum and actors' salaries pared to nothing. Plays about crooks and shop girls would replace drawing-room comedies and nude women would invade the stage as they had done in Paris.

'Of course,' Frohman smiled, 'we won't live to see it.'

Purser James McCubbin kept his promise to second-class passengers Flor and Julia Sullivan. He found them an end cabin overlooking the first-class promenade and sat them at a table next to his own in the second class dining saloon.

'You won't go hungry,' he joked. 'We've got sixty thousand eggs in the store room.'

'Do you say so!' exclaimed Julia. 'Just think of the ten

thousand hens that had to lay them!'

'We have two thousand passengers,' McCubbin explained, 'Each one of them is entitled to four meals a day for the rest of the week.'

By now the first-class passengers had settled in and Mc-Cubbin brought the Sullivans to the great saloon with its vaulted roof and marble fireplaces. He showed them a secluded corner where they could sit, whenever there was a concert or a dance, unnoticed behind a bank of flowers.

Julia was delighted that the *Lusitania* had a swimming pool. Wearing her bathing costume from Florida, she walked proudly to the edge of the pool that afternoon. Head down, arms extended, she dived confidently into the water at the deep end. Surfacing, she swam the length of the pool with easy strokes and then stood waist deep in the shallow end, amused to discover that she was a better swimmer than the wealthy women around her.

Another discovery pleased her, too. As she climbed the ladder from the water and walked back to the deep end, she knew she looked better in her clinging, thigh-length costume than the millionaires' women. After her years with the Branders she had learned to move easily among the rich. For the rest of the week she would enjoy herself at the pool.

*That evening the U-20's batteries were on their last kick and Schwieger knew he could not run submerged much longer. Not only would his craft lose power, but the dangerous currents sweeping round the Orkneys would pull him off course. He ordered the U-20 up to periscope depth.*

*The sea was still choppy. In the tossing water it wasn't easy to hold the submarine at her proper level, but at least the waves and the spray concealed the jumping patrol periscope. He could find no trace of the destroyers until he saw that their smoke was well astern. Relieved, he blew tanks, surfaced, and headed clear of the patrol.*

*For a few more hours the submarine ran on the surface,*

*recharging her batteries. By 10.30 the wind had dropped and the sea was less choppy. Rounding the Orkneys, Schwieger ordered a change of course to 240 degrees to bring them west of the Hebrides on their southward run down the coast of Scotland towards Ireland. Before turning in he noted in his diary, 'Wind NW 5. Sea NW Force 3. Very clear'. He hoped to pass the Hebrides in calm weather. Then he added: 'If the type of blockade of the Fair Isle-Ronaldsay line, such as we met, is not accidental, but intended by the enemy, then it is not advisable to pass in daylight in good visibility'.*

*The U-20 settled down to a steady night's run on the surface. Those who had gone off watch climbed into the bunks and hammocks vacated by the other submariners and fell into an exhausted sleep to the monotonous rhythm of the diesels.*

# 9

# ORDERS TO ZIGZAG
# Day 3: Monday, 3 May

SECOND OFFICER HEFFORD raised his binoculars and focused them briefly on a ship on the distant horizon. The sun was shining from a blue sky as the *Lusitania* passed south of St. John's, Newfoundland. He turned to Albert Bestic beside him on the bridge and remarked: 'Did you know the Admiralty has a new stunt on? They've issued a notice saying that a ship has a better chance of escaping a submarine if she zigzags.'

'What does that mean?' Albert asked. Hefford explained: 'Altering your course every so often. They seem to think this makes it more difficult for a sub to get into position to get a shot in.'

'You mean sort of tack-and-tack like a windjammer?'

'I suppose so. To tell the truth, I'm a bit hazy about it myself. I don't see where the Merchant Service comes into it. All very well for the Navy with nothing to do and plenty of time to do it, but can you guess what Cunard would say if they found their coal bills soaring? And what would the Captain's excuse be? "I was zigzagging, Mr. Booth." They'd soon tell him to go and zigzag with somebody else's ship.'

Hefford was in a talkative mood. Usually the Second Officer was reticent, but sometimes he enjoyed telling Bestic what had been discussed in the Captain's day cabin between Turner and the senior officers. Albert was fascinated by these stories, and he relied on Hefford to keep him informed.

'What about Captain Turner?' he asked. 'Has he got this notice?'

111

'That's where I first heard about it — in the Old Man's inner sanctum.'

From the day they had qualified as officers it had been impressed on them that time was money; successful navigators and engineers were those who made the quickest passage with the minimum of coal, but what Hefford had called a 'stunt' was in fact a confidential Admiralty memorandum to Merchant captains. It specified:

> War experience has shown that fast steamers can considerably reduce the chance of successful surprise submarine attack — that is to say, altering the course at short and irregular intervals, say in ten minutes to half an hour. This course is almost invariably adopted by warships when cruising in an area known to be infested by submarines. The underwater speed of a submarine is very low, and it is exceedingly difficult for her to get into position to deliver an attack unless she can observe and predict the course of the ship attacked. Zigzagging should be carried out whenever the ship is in waters where submarines are believed to be operating, unless the number of ships in the vicinity is great enough to render frequent alterations of course dangerous on account of possible collisions.
>
> Zigzagging is only of service prior to an attack, and when the submarine is submerged. A ship pursued by a submarine on the surface should not zigzag but should proceed at full speed and only alter course as may be necessary to keep the submarine astern.
>
> It is believed that German submarines at present operating are not fitted with beam torpedo tubes; consequently they have to get into a nearly end-on position before they can fire their torpedoes. This information may be of service to Masters in manoeuvring their ships to avoid attack. The underwater speed of even the latest submarines does not exceed nine to ten knots.

As Hefford scanned the horizon again he passed on to Bestic

the gist of the memorandum. 'Perhaps,' Albert suggested, 'the Admiralty was concerned about passenger ships like ours when they issued the notice?'

Hefford said, 'All I know is that some captains have their own ideas about zigzagging.'

Captain Turner looked up in surprise as George Kessler burst into his day cabin. The extrovert wine merchant extended his hand and announced in a loud voice, 'Kessler.'

Turner hesitated, then shook his hand. 'How can I be of assistance, Mr. Kessler?'

After the first lifeboat drill on Sunday Kessler suggested to the Chief Purser, 'It's all very well drilling your crew, but why don't you drill your passengers?' McCubbin had answered, 'Why not speak to Captain Turner about it?' Kessler had taken him at his word.

'You do know, Captain,' he said, 'that there's a torpedo scare?'

'I am aware there's been some talk about submarines,' Turner admitted calmly.

'Then I have a suggestion,' replied the wine merchant. 'I think it would be an excellent idea if each passenger was given a ticket listing the number of the boat he should make for, just in case—you know, in case anything *untoward* happens.'

Turner was impatient with his visitor. 'The company has already considered such a suggestion, Mr. Kessler,' he told him firmly. 'It was made to them after the *Titanic* disaster, but they considered it would not be practicable.'

Kessler was disappointed with the Captain's reaction, and told him so.

'But Mr. Kessler,' Turner said, 'you must understand that I could not possibly act on your advice unless I had received authority.'

Kessler's chief concern was for his own preservation. He was carrying two million dollars in stocks and bonds, an unusual amount to bring on board a liner in wartime, but he was of the opinion that a man should not leave his possessions out of his sight.

Ian Stoughton Holbourn, an authority on classical literature, also had misgivings about the lifeboat drill. But rather than go to the Captain he preferred to speak to individual passengers he met on deck, advising them to try on their lifejackets. Most of them resented the advice of this Scottish academic, conspicuous in his tweed cloak and black hat. None of them wished to be reminded of danger or risk.

Holbourn was returning from his third lecture tour of the United States and these voyages across the Atlantic afforded him an ideal opportunity to work on a book. His bulky manuscript contained the results of twenty years' research into the fundamental theory of beauty. *The Philosophy of Beauty*, the title under which he hoped to publish it before the end of the year, set out to prove that the principle of design is 'the correct relation of the parts to the whole and the whole to the parts'. He particularly disliked the question that modern man applied to anything beautiful: What use is it? The solar system was excellent in itself, Holbourn argued, whether man existed or not. What colossal conceit to think that everything must have reference to themselves. 'We need to cultivate a little humility,' he wrote, 'a little meekness, a little of the artist's spirit of reverent admiration, and then we can grasp the beauty of the world.'

Charles Lauriat, standing at the promenade rail and trying as usual to guess the speed of the ship, wasn't concerned with Holbourn's philosophy or Kessler's schemes. The bookseller was simply anxious to make Liverpool in good time. During the first 24 hours the liner had logged 501 miles, which suggested that she was running to schedule. Since then her speed had dropped, and he mentioned to Lothrop Withington that the run which had been posted at noon was below 500 miles.

'At this rate,' he complained, 'we're not going to make Liverpool on time.'

For the past two evenings Lauriat and Withington had gone

to the first-class smoking room on the upper deck where the betting numbers for the next day's run were auctioned. They planned a further trip to the smoking room that evening. Lauriat enjoyed the informality of the auction, even though he didn't buy a number from the pool.

Ernest Cowper the journalist, evidently relieved to get away from the crowded second-class rooms, crossed again to saloon, this time to talk to his publisher Percy Rogers who was travelling first class. When he encountered Elbert Hubbard afterwards in the lounge, Cowper asked him if he had heard the first-class passengers express any fears of submarines.

Hubbard smiled benignly at him. 'Now, you know they will never torpedo the *Lusitania*.'

'How can you be so sure?' Cowper pressed him.

'I'll tell you how. The Germans have done some darned bad things since the war started, but I don't believe they're all that bad.'

'What about the newspaper warnings?'

Hubbard fondled his flowing velvet tie and continued smiling. 'If I was going to slug you as you came round the corner, would I advertise it in the newspapers?'

Cowper had found no more loquacious passenger than Hubbard; already he had filled pages of his notebook with the Sage's comments.

On the way back to his cabin to transcribe his notes, he could hardly have noticed a small girl with a ribbon in her hair among the children playing in the second class area of the boat deck, but their paths would soon cross. Six-year-old Helen Smith was travelling home to Wales with her parents and six-month-old brother. Her father had emigrated to work with his brothers in Elwood City, Pennsylvania, as an electrician. Helen had been ten months old when she made the westward voyage. Her mother was disillusioned with life in America and the couple had decided to return to Swansea. The family group on the *Lusitania* also included her mother's sister-in-law, travelling with her two teenage boys.

Bellboy William Holton delivered two Marconigrams to the Vanderbilt suite that afternoon. The first from Vanderbilt's wife read: FREDDIE DIED EARLY THIS MORNING LOVE MARGARET. The second, from the millionaire's office, confirmed that his closest friend, Frederick Davies, had died suddenly in New York. Alfred was shocked. During their student days at Yale he and Fred had travelled extensively together. There had been a time when Fred wanted to marry Alfred's sister Gertrude. He had declared his love for her in the fall of 1893 when they were both in their early twenties, but the sceptical Gertrude had written in her diary, 'Love is the source of all earthly happiness, yet it comes and goes in the short space of a day.'

Vanderbilt could not face the company in the dining saloon that evening. He decided to dine in his suite. Another passenger was also absent at dinner. Albert Lloyd Hopkins, the shipbuilder, had received a Marconigram with the sad news that his father, after a day of unconsciousness, had died peacefully.

Julia Sullivan was enjoying the swimming pool. She found the other bathers affable enough, save for one rich middle-aged woman from the midwest. This formidable lady avoided those around her in her concern to chaperone her daughter whom she was bringing to England in search of an eligible peer. Her rolls of fat shook as she waddled to the edge of the pool. She reminded Julia of the porpoises following the ship. If we get torpedoed that fat will keep her afloat, she thought. Later on the shelter deck she noticed the woman plant herself in a deckchair next to her daughter to ward off young men without a title to their name. She wondered what chance such a plain girl had of catching a peer.

While Julia was at the pool her husband Flor had met another Irish passenger, Pat Callan, a big, fair-haired young man from Chicago who was returning to take over his father's business. They introduced him to their friend the Chief Purser to make certain that McCubbin gave him the freedom of the ship. The three of them dined together and then went up in one of the lifts to the first-class smoking room. Pat, who had made his money supplying cattle to the meat packers in Chicago, was keen to join the wealthy men playing poker. It was Flor who spotted the cardsharpers.

'Look at them,' he whispered angrily to his wife. 'They're dressed to perfection and talking like senators while they're fleecing the other lads. Wouldn't I just like to get my hands on them!'

*The light of Sule Skerry led the way for the U-20 into a dawn that promised well. By mid-morning the Butt of Lewis, the most northern point of the Hebrides, was on the port beam. They were soon at Cape Wrath, the northern entry to the passage between the Scottish mainland and the Hebrides known as the Minch, and Schwieger set a course of 205 degrees to skirt the Hebrides on his run down towards the north-west point of Ireland.*

*It was early evening when he launched an attack on an approaching steamer. Pilot Lanz identified her as British, about 2,000 tons, out of Leith, and flying a Danish stern flag. Schwieger decided to take no chances. He would not halt and search her. The British had ordered their merchant captains to fly neutral flags, and when in doubt Schwieger fired.*

*It was to be a clean bow shot at 300 yards. But, as often happened, the trigger didn't recoil, the lock jammed, and the torpedo stayed in the tube. Schwieger cursed his luck. On examination the torpedo crew found the indicator reading 'Open' even though the tube was not fully open.*

*At 8.45 pm Schwieger prepared to attack a second small steamer from eleven metres. But when he fixed her in his sights he decided she was too small to justify wasting a torpedo. Viewed from underwater at dusk a target could be deceptive. At nine o'clock he blew tanks and surfaced. He decided to turn in. The dogs were whining and he heard young Rikowsky climb out of his hammock to feed them. It had been a disappointing day. He closed his diary with the submariner's conventional comment, 'Progress continued.'*

The *Cunard Daily Bulletin*, which the ship's printers, George Mitchel and Fred Davies, distributed among the passengers, carried agency reports from the Dardanelles and the western front. The Germans were experimenting with new chemical devices in France, glass bombs of ether and shells charged with inflammable materials; they were also conscripting men in their sixties for the army.

Under the heading 'German Submarine Torpedoes US Ship' the *Bulletin* also carried an agency report that the American oil tank steamer *Gulflight* had been torpedoed off the Scilly Isles. The Captain had died of shock and two crewmen had jumped overboard and drowned. The damaged tanker had been towed by British patrol ships to a nearby port. These were the only details; the reason for the German attack was a mystery. Reading the report, Ian Stoughton Holbourn noted that the attack had taken place off the southwest tip of Cornwall, close to the southern entrance to St. George's Channel. It was towards these dangerous waters that the *Lusitania* was sailing. Surely his concern for a passenger lifeboat drill was justified?

In the United States that evening there was growing concern among Americans. President Woodrow Wilson, who had intimated unofficially that he would run for re-election the following year, spent most of the evening in the White House with State Secretary Bryan discussing the *Gulflight* incident. They decided to wait for more news before taking any decision on the Government's future course of action. The State Department had sent messages to Ambassadors Gerard in Berlin and Page in London seeking further details. But news editors sifting reports for the next morning's editions had no hesitation in concluding that the torpedoeing of the *Gulflight* had caused utter dismay among State officials. On Wall Street it had also brought about the first setback in prices for months. The *New York Tribune*'s editorial said:

> The *Lusitania*, which sailed from New York last
> Saturday, will be in the war zone, passing within a few
> miles from where the *Gulflight* was torpedoed, within the
> next sixty hours. Among her passengers are large
> numbers of Americans, and what the Administration
> fears now more than all the individual attacks on
> American property, with incidental loss of life, is the
> effect on public sentiment of the loss of American
> passengers in a great sea war disaster. It is frankly ad-
> mitted that the United States would find grave diffi-
> culty in handling such an affair through diplomatic
> interchanges.

The *Tribune* stressed the mounting disquiet in Washington
over the attack on the *Gulflight* for reasons other than the
incident itself. They feared the attack was 'only the beginning
of a more active and daring undersea warfare by Germans
than anything heretofore seen'.

So well-founded did the *Tribune* regard these fears that
they ordered Vance Pitney, their correspondent in London, to
travel to Queenstown, the transatlantic port in southern
Ireland, to await the arrival of the *Lusitania*.

# 10

# PAINTING THE BOATS
# Day 4: Tuesday, 4 May

AS QUARTERMASTER HUGH JOHNSTON held the ship's wheel firmly, he glanced at Captain Turner pacing the portside wing of the bridge. Helmsman Johnston was a wiry youngster from the docks area of Bootle near Liverpool who had grown up with a passion for the sea. He achieved his boyhood ambition when he joined the *Lusitania*; now he looked forward to his two-hour shifts at the wheel. When Turner strode into the wheelhouse, he asked his usual question, 'Everything all right, lad?'

'Yes, sir,' Johnston answered cheerfully. He never had any doubt that the Captain was in full command of the ship. Turner was a strict disciplinarian for whom everything had to be spit and polish. His coolness and unruffled manner made the helmsman envious. But there were times when Johnston sensed that something was on the Captain's mind, especially during the long silences on the bridge. He accepted that the Old Man could be moody, but this was more than temperament.

Turner had said to him one day, 'This war is a terrible thing.' Johnston could only assume that the Captain was thinking about his two sons fighting in France. He never heard him mention his wife and surmised that the Captain's marriage had broken down and he did not want to talk about it. Johnston felt for Captain Turner. He seemed a lonely man.

The sea had a sparkle of innocence that sunny afternoon. The spaciousness and comfort of the *Lusitania* and the monotonous sound of the rushing waters had lulled most passengers and crew into a sense of false security. Three days had passed since the Germans had published their warning notice in the American newspapers and sent their agents to distribute handbills at the gangways, and already their import was fading.

William Holton, delivering messages among the saloon passengers, found the same complacency, and it puzzled him. He thought about the reduction in the liner's speed. He remembered walking along the promenade deck in the previous November and stopping to talk to two junior engineers who had come off duty. 'We don't seem to be moving at our usual speed,' he remarked. 'Economy measures,' one of them had explained. 'We've cut coal consumption on orders from HQ.'

From that day Holton began to keep notes about the voyages. Until November 1914 he calculated that the *Lusitania* had made her round trip in sixteen days, including five and a half days' sea time in each direction. Now the round trip was taking twenty-one days, with a sea time of six and a half days on each run. Some of the crew feared that the reduction in coal consumption and speed was a predisposition for tragedy. Holton shared their concern. He remembered too that on the last eastbound voyage Captain Dow had sailed through the danger zone flying the American flag. Such a deception, Holton was convinced, must surely have come under the hard scrutiny of the Germans.

Since he had been put to work painting the lifeboats Leslie Morton was more cheerful. He had forgotten about his gloomy quarters. Whistling to himself, he lay on his back as he dipped a swab of waste into a pot of grey paint known as 'crab fat' and applied it to the hull of one of the boats. If the boats have to be used in an emergency, at least in this good weather the paintwork will be dry, he thought. Suddenly he heard the sound of running feet. Peeping out from under the hull, he saw two girls in their early teens running along the deck followed by a woman he took to be their nursemaid.

As they came alongside, he thought, 'What lovely children.' They stopped before him, smiling and breathless, and one of them, wearing a white accordion-pleated skirt and a sailor blouse, asked him, 'What are you doing?'

'I'm painting the lifeboat,' he told her. 'And who are you?'

'I'm Anna, and this is Gwen.' They were Lady Allan's daughters, sailing with their mother to join their father in England.

'May we help?' Anna asked him.

'No, thank you,' Morton told her firmly. 'I hardly think this is a job for girls.'

She took no notice of his refusal, but grabbed the paint-covered swab from his hand and daubed it on the boat and then on her spotless white clothes. Morton looked at her aghast. He heard the sound of heavier footsteps and saw bosun John Davies approaching at the double. The girl dropped the waste swab and ran off with her sister. Morton slipped over the side, dropped on to the next deck and hurried forward. He didn't want to argue either with the bosun or a nursemaid.

Albert Bestic found himself with more varied duties on board the *Lusitania* than in any of the smaller ships he had served on. Apart from his watches on the bridge and the midnight tours with Hefford, he completed meteorological forms and wrote up log books, and inevitably there was a daily attendance in the baggage room. Tired, he had settled down for his nap that afternoon when baggage master John Crank knocked on his door.

'Excuse me, sir,' Albert heard him call, 'but we shall have to get another trunk up from the baggage room'.

The Junior Third Officer groaned inwardly. Every afternoon he listened to the same request. The baggage room was a vast, forbidding, dusty area in the bowels of the ship, reached by an electric lift. There was a stairway, but Albert had never seen it used. All the luggage marked 'Not Wanted On Voyage' was stored in this room, yet every day a number of first-class passengers demanded their trunks.

Albert changed into his old uniform and went down in the lift with the baggage master. The *Lusitania* had a strict rule that none of the crew must enter the area unless an officer was present. Albert stayed for more than an hour while a working party searched for one particular trunk among hundreds. It was the only duty that irked him. He wondered why he should have to waste hours every day sitting in this dimly-lit ship's dungeon.

*In the late afternoon Schwieger got his first glimpse of the north-west point of Ireland. On the misty horizon Blackrock lighthouse came in sight on his port bow.*

*He had made two attempts to sink steamers. The first he abandoned because the seas were too rough, the second because the steamer came too close as he manoeuvred for position to fire a bronze torpedo. Before dark the U-20 was running on the surface again. Spray was sweeping over the decks and the conning tower and in spite of their oilskins worn over heavy sweaters and thick woollens the men on lookout were miserably cold. But the sharp evening breeze was preferable to the foul atmosphere below.*

*The long journey around Scotland and the west coast of Ireland was adding some 1,400 miles to the cruise, reducing the time they could spend on patrol. They were to be tossed about for almost two weeks in a steel shell, exposed to enemy ramming and gunfire.*

*It became misty and the darkness was intense when Schwieger went below. He was almost inured to the deadening cold, the smell of hydrogen from the banks of batteries, stale human breath, the cramped bunks, the surreal gloom in the control room dimly lit by red bulbs, the daily ration of a gallon of water for washing, even to the toilets, which worked by a system of valves so complex that if you made a mistake the detritus blew back in your face. There was, too, the inevitable constipation.*

*He instructed Weisbach to call him if any vessel came near. Then he turned in.*

Details of the *Gulflight* incident had reached Washington. Apparently, two British patrol boats had stopped the tanker, on her way from Texas to Rouen, and escorted her into port in the Scilly Isles. Spotting the little convoy, a German submarine assumed the *Gulflight* to be a British ship and fired two torpedoes into her before the Commander noticed the Stars and Stripes flying from her stern. The U-boat had already abandoned her attack when two members of the *Gulflight* crew panicked and jumped overboard, and as the damaged tanker was towed into port the Master died from a heart attack.

One crew member told a reporter: 'At midnight on Saturday Captain Gunter summoned me. I found him in bed and he wanted someone to roll a cigarette for him. He threw up his arms and fainted. From then until the time of his death, which occurred about 3.30 o'clock on Sunday morning, he remained unconscious.'

At the White House it was decided that because the submarine commander had been prevented by fog from seeing the flag the incident could be settled by a German apology, accompanied by a statement that an error had been made. As a consequence, one London newspaper reported an American 'fear of being drawn into the European vortex'. President Wilson and State Secretary Bryan, who had threatened on 10 February to hold Germany to 'strict accountability' for such acts, knew that the Master of the *Gulflight* should not have accepted an armed British escort which exposed him to German attack. Bryan was embarrassed by the assertion of his deputy Robert Lansing that Germany was making 'a determined effort to affront the United States'.

It may have been Lansing who prompted one correspondent to cable London that day, 'In official circles in Washington the conviction prevails that the most serious aspect of the *Gulflight* incident lies in the suspicion that the German Government is making a systematic effort to irritate the United States and show its resentment over the shipment of arms and ammunition.'

Charles Frohman lay on his bed wearing a dressing gown and smoking a cigar. Most of the day he had been in pain, and in the afternoon, when it worsened, he asked Stainton to call Dr McDermott. The young physician had taken over from Dr Poynton, the *Lusitania*'s regular surgeon, who was indisposed. Forcing a smile, Frohman said to the doctor, 'This is not one of my good days.'

However, his mind was fully occupied with theatrical plans which helped him dismiss the pain. He wished for the voyage to be over, believing a change of air would improve his health. He looked forward to London, to the Duke of York's Theatre on Saturday where *Charles Frohman Presents* would be blazing in lights on the facade, above the title *Rosy Rapure by J. M. Barrie*.

When McDermott had gone he limped to his portable phonograph to cheer himself up with 'Alexander's Ragtime Band', his favourite record. Listening to the music, he recalled Maude Adams' advice to him before leaving New York. 'Please rest, C.F.,' she had begged him. He knew this was impossible. For weeks before sailing he had been waging a campaign against cut-price seats on Broadway. Managements were selling theatre seats at prices below those printed on the tickets; if the practice continued he could see the day when playwrights would have to send observers to the box office, as they had done in Paris, to make sure that they were not cheated of their earnings.

Charles Klein was grateful to the impresario for the stand he had taken on behalf of playwrights in New York. Like Frohman, Klein was a nervous, restive man, impatient to sample the London theatre season. A Londoner by birth, he had settled in New York twenty years earlier and found work in the theatre. He doctored scripts for Frohman before turning to playwriting with successful comedies like *A Paltry Million* and *The Lion and the Mouse*. He was working on a new play during the voyage and he brought the first pages to Frohman's suite for his verdict that evening. He tried to persuade the impresario to join his theatrical friends at dinner, but C.F.

shook his head. He was in pain.

Although Sir Hugh Lane felt tired and ill, he nonetheless decided to go down to dinner, and afterwards joined Lady Allan and Dr Fred Pearson and his wife for a game of bridge in the smoking room. He was convinced that the ill-health that had dogged him since childhood would soon kill him, and it had taken great persuasion from his friends before he agreed to travel to New York to give evidence in a lawsuit.

Sir Hugh was haunted by his unfulfilled ambition to build a modern art gallery in Dublin to house his precious collection of paintings by contemporary French, Italian and English artists. The city had rejected his plan for a gallery by Lutyens on a bridge across the Liffey; some complained the damp site would damage the paintings, others that the building would spoil the river view. Angered by Dublin Corporation's refusal, he loaned the collection to the National Gallery in London. His appointment as Director of the National Gallery in Dublin had brought a change of heart. Before leaving for America he took a sheet of National Gallery of Ireland notepaper from his desk and wrote a codicil to his will bequeathing his paintings to Dublin, provided a suitable building was found for them within five years. He had folded and sealed the paper in an envelope, which he placed in the top drawer of his desk. As he played bridge on the homeward voyage of the *Lusitania* it still had not occurred to him that he had forgotten to ask somebody to witness the codicil. For a man who could spot a masterpiece in a dealer's dust heap it was a surprising oversight.

It had been an uneventful evening. The children, tired after their games on the aft promenade deck in the late afternoon, had gone to bed. Young Frank Hook fell asleep still clutching the badge he had won.in a race. As the sun dipped below the horizon in a sky of purple and gold some passengers went dancing, among them the pretty nurse Alice Lines who had been given the evening off by the Warren Pearls. In the first-class smoking-room the Sullivans watched the poker games, and their friend Pat Callan played a few hands. As they returned to their cabin, Julia noticed couples embracing furtively on the boat deck and it amused her to spot the rich woman's daughter trying to hide with a young man in the shade of one of the lifeboats. Julia was certain he was no English peer.

Towards midnight Bestic and Hefford stood on the bridge, waiting to be relieved by First Officer Jones and Third Officer Lewis before setting off on their rounds through the long, carpeted corridors.

To Captain Turner, who had just turned in, everything seemed to be in order. Tomorrow the *Lusitania* would reach the imaginary half-way line. Had he known of the Admiralty's concern about submarine activity in the danger zone, he might not have slept so soundly. But no signals had reached him.

It was a curious Admiralty oversight.

# 11

# THE TURK'S HEAD
# Day 5: Wednesday,
# 5 May

AT NINE O'CLOCK Captain Turner strode onto the bridge and nodded curtly in response to the salute of Albert Bestic.

'Good morning, sir.'

''Morning, Bisset.'

Albert admired his Captain who, blunt-mannered, was yet never too aloof from his officers and men. As usual on a bright morning Turner took an altitude of the sun. Then he paced the bridge wings before retiring to his cabin below.

Albert had noticed an eccentric facet to Turner's character; he discovered that one of the Captain's hobbies was to make varied and complicated fancy knots. On the outward voyage Turner had made an intricate knot using a thin piece of rope. He was proud of his achievement and anxious to show it to someone, yet he hesitated to solicit praise from his officers. Instead, he telephoned his messenger and handed him the piece of knotted rope. 'My compliments to the officers in the wardroom,' he told the boy, 'and tell them I want another Turk's Head just like this one.'

A few of the officers, Albert among them, were enjoying a quick game of bridge during the second dog watch when the bewildered messenger knocked at the door. 'What is it, boy?' Chief Officer Piper snapped at him. He was irritable at the intrusion, having just doubled four spades.

'Compliments of the Captain, sir,' the boy stammered. 'He wants another thingamajig – I – I forget what he calls it. Made like this, sir.' He held up the knotted piece of rope. Piper took the rope from him, glared at it, flung it on the floor and hurled his double hand of four spades on top of it. 'The first damned call I've had this evening,' he swore, 'and what happens? The Old Man wants a bloody fancy knot that hasn't been made since the death of Nelson. What is it anyway?'

Bestic retrieved it from the wardroom floor. 'I think it's a four-stranded Turk's Head, sir,' he suggested. 'It was used in sailing ships for decorative purposes.'

Piper chortled. 'A four-stranded Turk's Head? I haven't heard of such a thing in twenty years. Is the Old Man going daft?'

'Shouldn't we humour him since he sent it along to us, sir?'

'I know why he sent it,' Piper told the officers. 'Because he thinks none of us can do it.' He turned to Albert. 'How about you, Bestic? You're not long out of sail.'

'I could try, sir.'

'Then off you go.'

Bestic went to his cabin and took down a small handbook on knots which he thought he would never need to use again. It was certainly a difficult knot. He studied the instructions and then took a piece of rope and eventually succeeded in making a duplicate. The Captain's knot and the duplicate were returned to the bridge with the wardroom's compliments.

In his day cabin Turner was told that a passenger named Holbourn wished to speak to him. When Holbourn was admitted to the Captain's cabin he complained quietly but forcibly about the lack of passenger drill. On the previous day he had been approached by a deputation of men passengers; they had asked him to stop insisting that passengers should try on their life-jackets. 'You will frighten the women, sir,' they warned him. Holbourn decided he must speak to the Captain.

Turner, who was equally impatient with scholars and millionaires, listened to Holbourn's complaint. 'I understand, Mr. Holbourn,' he said. 'I shall speak to the Chief Officer about it.' Holbourn sensed that Turner resented his interference, and concluded that the Captain was a stubborn man.

E

As for the passengers who had complained to him, he coined a name for them — the Ostrich Club.

He simply could not accept Cunard's perfunctory attitude to crew and passenger boat drills. He noticed that usually only one boat was involved in the daily drill, either No. 13 on the starboard side or No. 14 on the port side, depending on the wind. The remaining twenty-two lifeboats were ignored. Apparently no extra drill or training was demanded, and the Captain seemed unwilling to accede to passengers' requests for drills. Perhaps he thought they were displaying undue concern? Or perhaps he could not come to terms with wartime conditions?

Turner was in a sullen mood after Holbourn's visit. When his friend Chief Engineer Bryce arrived, he cheered up. He and Archie Bryce spoke the same language.

'Everything is in order, Will,' the Chief Engineer assured him.

The liner was averaging 21 knots and Turner could confidently work out his approach to the Liverpool Bar, which he expected to take on Saturday morning at 4.30 am, the estimated time of arrival. There were patches of fog about and if he had to order Bryce to reduce speed as they neared the Irish coast they would be in danger from German submarines. He would be entering the danger zone the next day. The liner's course was set for the Fastnet Rock, off the south-west coast of Ireland.

The submarine activity off the south coast of Ireland could not have fully engaged the volatile mind of Winston Churchill that morning. He had more pressing concerns. Since the attack on the Dardanelles in February the moods of the First Lord of the Admiralty had swung between euphoria and self-doubt. As the instigator of the campaign against the Turks, he was at first convinced that success could be achieved only through a combined naval and military assault. Later, he gambled on a quick naval victory. On 18 March his error was brought home to him when the British and French naval attack foundered in a vicious minefield. His phrase 'By ships alone' to Vice-Marshal Carden had rebounded in a cruel fashion.

He had been committed to the campaign against the Turks on the peninsula of Gallipoli adjoining the Dardanelles, the narrow straits leading from the Aegean Sea into the sea of Marmara. If the Navy once broke through the straits then, he believed, the Turkish capital of Constantinople could be occupied. But the Admirals' cry went up, 'No push without the Army,' and on 25 April Sir Ian Hamilton led the first landing of 30,000 troops.

By 5 May the battle of the peninsula was still undecided, and the Navy's failure was a grievous blow to Churchill's pride. But he was preoccupied with his impending visit to Paris where he hoped to sign a new naval treaty with Italy before visiting Field-Marshal Sir John French, Commander-in-Chief of the British Expeditionary Force in France, at his headquarters at the western front. As for United States opinion in the European war, Churchill believed that one small error in handling the delicate Anglo-American relations could spark off a major crisis. It seemed, however, that the German U-boat campaign, and the attack on the *Gulflight* the previous weekend, had at last lent credibility to the British cause.

Churchill was later to describe the month of April as 'one of painful and harassing suspense'. With his reputation dented, he was stung by the accusation of Lord Fisher, the elderly First Sea Lord, 'You are just simply eaten up with the Dardanelles.'

He had brought 'Jacky' Fisher back to the Admiralty after critics had warned that public confidence in the Navy, especially following the failure to bring the Germans to battle, was ebbing. The First Lord hoped Fisher might help restore this confidence, and he also felt a certain loyalty towards him. Fisher was extremely popular. He was acknowledged as a 'technical innovator of genius' and had encouraged Churchill to improve the conditions and pay of naval ratings. He was seventy-four when Churchill recommended his recall, and had spent five years in retirement. Unfortunately, he was unable to cope with politicians. No sooner was he back at the Admiralty than the two men clashed over the Dardanelles campaign.

Fisher warned Prime Minister Asquith against the 'unsoundness of the Navy in trying to do the job alone' and the 'inevitable weakening of the Grand Fleet'. It was apparent that Churchill's campaign would not succeed. His political career was threatened, and the Tories, who had not forgiven him for going over to the Liberals, had found their scapegoat. Fisher wrote to him on 25 April, 'Really, yesterday, had it not been for the Dardanelles forcing me to stick to you through thick and thin, I would have gone out of the Admiralty never to return.'

Churchill had arrived at the Admiralty with little knowledge of naval affairs. His training at Sandhurst and his experience of war as a young man, 'living gloriously in an atmosphere of battle, murder and sudden death in three continents', as one commentator phrased it, had given him a decidedly military outlook. Now the brunt of criticism for the Navy's failure in the Dardanelles had fallen on him; as the criticism mounted, the short-tempered First Lord considered handing in his resignation.

On the morning of 5 May he went down to the map room at the Admiralty with Fisher and Admiral Sir Henry Oliver, Chief of Naval War Staff. They were joined by Captain Reginald Hall and his colleague Commander Joseph Kenworthy. The five men studied the 30-foot map of the world which covered one wall of the room. It showed the estimated positions of Allied and German shipping; two red squares denoted the positions of the *U-30* and the *U-20*.

Churchill's view of the map can only have been cursory. He pulled his watch from his left-hand waistcoat pocket; he remembered he had promised to meet his wife for lunch. By mid-afternoon he would be on a train for Paris.

As Churchill and his Admiralty colleagues examined the map in Whitehall, Vice-Admiral Sir Charles Henry Coke, who commanded the south coast of Ireland known as Area 21, was

standing on his ornate balcony on the first floor of Admiralty
House at Queenstown. From the imposing vantage point
above the Sloop Garden he could see across the town to the
dockyard, the islands and the distant approaches to the
harbour. He frowned with concern, for he knew that beyond
the harbour entrance German submarines were prowling.

Queenstown was a collection of houses rising like decks of
playing cards from the hilly south side of Great Island,
crowned by the soaring new spire of the neo-Gothic St.
Colman's Cathedral. From his headquarters in this easy-going
town Coke controlled 285 miles of Irish coastline from Dingle
to Carnsore. Although he did not like to admit it, he was only
too aware that his auxiliary patrol, consisting of four torpedo
boats, four armed yachts, sixteen armed trawlers and four
motor boats, the best of them capable of a maximum 11 knots,
could scarcely provide an adequate protection for the area.

As he looked down on the harbour, the 'Senior Officer on
the Coast of Ireland' was troubled by the news of the growing
submarine menace. His little fleet was too sluggish for chasing
submarines, and it was galling to think that a 15-knot U-boat
could dodge impudently beyond the gun range of any of his
craft. Speed was invaluable in such a situation, and though he
had begged the Admiralty to send him a dozen destroyers, the
only ships capable of attacking the U-boats were based across
the channel at Milford Haven in Wales.

Patrolling off the Fastnet Rock that afternoon, under the
command of Vice-Admiral Sir Horace Hood, was the *Juno*,
flagship of the Irish coastal patrol, which was expected to
cover the approach of Allied shipping from the Atlantic. She
carried eleven six-inch guns, and at close quarters could be
deployed in ramming a submarine. But she was an ageing
cruiser, no longer able to reach her former top speed of 19.5
knots. She was not a suitable ship to protect fast passenger
liners like the *Lusitania*.

It had been a proud boast that there was room enough in
Queenstown for the entire British fleet, yet by May 1915 the
great ships were noticeably absent. The Navy's best warships

were suffering defeats in the Dardanelles, guarding the base at Scapa Flow, or patrolling the North Sea in wait for the German High Seas fleet. At Queenstown the ferry boats continued plying between the town quay, known as the Beach, and the dockyard on the island of Haulbowline; but the dockyard was no longer busy and the harbour was almost empty.

With the Grand Fleet stationed north of Scotland, the Admiralty decided that no enemy ships could break through to the Atlantic. Until now it had been only realistic that Churchill, Fisher and the other Admiralty chiefs should have regarded the south coast of Ireland as of no great strategic importance. In spite of the warnings of submarines in the area, they had refused Coke his destroyers. Now there was little they could do.

*It was 2 am German time and pitch dark in the North Atlantic when the lookouts on the U-20 shouted, 'Lights on the port bow!'*

*Oberleutnant Weisbach, the officer on watch, repeated the call and Schwieger hurried to the bridge. Through his binoculars the Commander could make out the navigation and masthead lights of two approaching ships. He ordered the gunners to prepare for an attack. Then, as he began to distinguish sky from water-line, he recognised the ships as patrolling trawlers. He called through the speaking tube, ordering the helmsman to sheer off hard.*

*By dawn a thick belt of fog had come down, and Schwieger decided, now that they had reached the point of approach for large steamers to southwest Ireland, it would be difficult to take evading action. He sang out, 'Make ready for diving!'*

*The U-20 went down 70 feet below the surface. In the early afternoon they blew tanks and rose again. The fog was just as thick. The Fastnet Rock, the navigator reckoned, was on their port beam, even though they could not see it. As the afternoon lengthened and the weather cleared, Schwieger was surprised that, although they were cruising in one of the main Atlantic traffic routes, they had not sighted a single steamer.*

*Just before six in the evening, as the weather became misty again, the lookouts spotted what they took to be a large, full-rigged vessel on the horizon. When Schwieger fixed his glasses on the approaching vessel he saw it was a small, three-masted schooner with the wind filling her square sails. Hardly worth a torpedo, he decided.*

*'No danger,' he called, ordering the engineer to bring the submarine closer.*

*The U-20 increased speed to 12 knots, altering course slightly until the schooner lay right ahead. Bows lifted, white foam streaming past on either quarter, she headed towards her target, as the gunners made ready the deck gun. As they swung behind the schooner's stern, Schwieger grabbed the megapohone. 'What ship are you?' he shouted.*

*'Earl of Lathom! Liverpool!' came an answering voice from the vessel wallowing in the swell.*

*'Abandon ship! Bring your flag and papers alongside.'*

*The Captain and four men clambered over the schooner's side and rowed across to the U-20. Schwieger examined the papers. The broad-beamed* Earl of Lathom *was carrying a cargo of bacon and potatoes from Limerick to Liverpool.*

*As the five men made for the shore, Schwieger ordered his gunners to fire at the abandoned schooner. Twelve grenades bit into her old timber sides before she finally heeled over and sank slowly, dragging her sodden topsails beneath the surface.*

*At dusk that same evening, as they were running on the surface, the fog returned; just after 8.30 they narrowly missed colliding with a steamer which loomed suddenly out of the swirling mists. Schwieger was taken by surprise. He decided to launch a surface attack. For a while, he reckoned, it would be safe enough to remain on the surface.*

*The steamer had slowed down and was probably searching in the murk for the U-boat. Schwieger could not have been more pleased. 'Make the tubes ready,' he ordered.*

*The U-20 was positioned for attack and Schwieger shouted,*

*'First tube, bow shot.' He was aiming for a short, clean shot from about 300 yards.*

*'First tube—Fire!'*

*As the firing button was pressed Schwieger felt the bronze torpedo could not possibly miss. But the steamer captain must have caught a glimpse of the torpedo's wake for the ship suddenly gathered speed and the torpedo passed beneath her stern.*

*Schwieger, peering expectantly through his binoculars, swore. The torpedo had apparently lost momentum as it neared the target.*

*As the steamer came closer the pilot identified her as a Norwegian with neutral markings painted on her tarpaulin. Again Schwieger cursed, and ordered the helmsman to sheer off hard. He did not want to be fired at. And, with growing doubts about the effectiveness of his torpedoes, he decided not to make a second run.*

*'Make ready for diving.' At Schwieger's command they clambered below again to the world of stale air and the smells of men and dogs.*

In New York that afternoon N. L. Mead, representing Wood, Niebhuhr and Co., Customs agents for Cunard, walked down to the Custom House and filed a supplementary manifest for the *Lusitania*. On the previous Friday afternoon, the day before the *Lusitania* sailed, Captain Turner had filed the original ship's manifest at the Custom House, and on this manifest sailing clearance had been granted.

Under the city's health laws it was mandatory to file a supplementary manifest after a ship had sailed if last minute goods or provisions had been loaded. Extra provisions were taken on board the *Lusitania* because of the late transfer of passengers from the *Cameronia*.

Whereas Turner's was a brief two-page manifest, Mead's manifest ran to 24 pages.

Among the items listed on the latter were 1,250 cases of

shrapnel from the Bethlehem Steel Company and 269 bales and 33 cases of raw furs. The furs were shipped by an Alfred Fraser, who had earlier apparently run foul of the War Office by attempting to sell them 100,000 sheepskin coats at an exorbitant profit. Captain Guy Gaunt, the British Embassy's military attaché, retained Fraser on a commission, some said to make use of his name. The 'furs' on the *Lusitania* were addressed to a Liverpool firm which had been engaged in manufacturing gun cotton, but had had no dealings with the fur trade.

Also listed were 240 cases of cartridges from Remington Small Arms addressed to the Royal Arsenal, a consignment from Markt & Hammacher of one case of air rifles and seventeen cases of hardware, and 189 cases of military accoutrements which George Booth had ordered for Kitchener's voluntary army during his last visit to the States.

All the items on the supplementary manifest were checked off at the Custom House that afternoon and the deposition was signed not by Dudley Field Malone, the Collector of Customs, but by a deputy.

Staff Captain Anderson had decided where this supplementary cargo was to be stowed. He loaded the shrapnel cases in the bottom of the liner next to the No. 1 boiler room with a consignment, also listed in the supplementary manifest, of 3,000 boxes of cheese and 700 tubs of butter, in an adjoining hold. Above the boiler rooms he loaded the cartridges, and on the two decks above, which included third-class cabins and the baggage room, he loaded cartridges and furs.

There were bound to be suspicions about this late cargo listed on a manifest which Captain Turner had not seen. Those who accused the British of shipping contraband in their passenger liners would argue that Cunard should have listed most of this cargo before sailing. However, Dudley Field Malone's staff at the Custom House was ready to approve such manifests almost casually.

Avis Dolphin was persuaded by Nurse Ellis to leave her cabin where she had moped for days with neuralgia and seasickness. At the nurse's insistence, she went up to the second-class lounge and lay down on a couch, feeling miserable and staring listlessly as the other passengers talked, read or just dozed. A man who had been sitting nearby, approached her. 'Are you quite comfortable, my girl?' he asked.

'Yes, thank you,' she answered politely, surprised that anybody should be concerned about her well-being on this vast ship.

'I don't think it's possible that you really are,' he said. He walked away, but within minutes returned carrying a pillow wrapped in a shawl.

'There you are,' he said to her, placing it behind her head. 'Now you'll feel more comfortable.' Would she like some fruit? Some tea? Avis thanked him, but she was not ready to think about food. The man sat down beside her, and just then Nurse Ellis came by and she, too, asked Avis if she needed anything.

'I'm not at all hungry,' said the girl.

'Perhaps,' the man suggested to the nurse, 'this young lady would feel a lot better if she sat in the fresh air on deck?'

'Yes, I think she would,' the nurse agreed.

The man led Avis outside and settled her in a deck chair, making her comfortable with the pillow and a rug. Then he sat beside her and introduced himself as Mr. Holbourn, telling her he was returning to Edinburgh to join his wife and three boys. He told her about his island off the north coast of Scotland. 'I'm king,' he said, drawing his cloak about him.

'Are you *really* a king?' Avis asked him.

'Well, perhaps not quite a king,' he smiled. 'In Scotland the term is laird. I am laird of Foula by the rights handed down through Clan Holbourn from centuries immemorial.'

She laughed with him, suddenly roused from her daydreaming. Foula, he explained, was his summer home. 'Of course,' he added, 'my Shetland island is just five square miles. But one hundred and fifty loyal subjects, farmers and fishermen most of them, live there.' He promised Avis, 'I shall make you an honorary subject, my girl. You may come to

Foula and ride on the Shetland ponies and see the brown sheep.'

Avis had never heard of brown sheep, and was fascinated by the promise of pony rides. For the first time since Sunday she forgot about her sickness and loneliness. 'Perhaps, Avis,' the man in the cloak suggested, 'you would like to try some tea and biscuits?'

The girl's mood had brightened with the conversation. Sipping the tea she felt much better. Next day, Holbourn promised, he would read to her and take her for a walk on the *Lusitania*.

# 12

# 'U-BOATS ON THE DOORSTEP'
# Day 6: Thursday, 6 May

THE *LUSITANIA* had surged steadily through the long night. As dawn broke over the dark waters of the Atlantic she was 500 miles from the Irish coast.

In Queenstown Vice-Admiral Sir Charles Coke grew more uneasy hour by hour. The news of the sinking of the *Earl of Lathom* had badly shaken him. Pacing his office at Admiralty House early that morning, he stopped constantly by the casement window and stared anxiously across the great harbour. The U-boats were already on his doorstep.

Their lurking presence preyed on his mind. Why had the Admiralty not given him his destroyers? Since cabling them the previous night about the attack on the *Earl of Lathom* he had received no special orders. The admirals in Whitehall were reluctant to relay messages to Queenstown, apparently believing the Germans would break their code and send a pack of U-boats in pursuit of British ships.

Winston Churchill, the First Lord, had not yet been informed of the sinking of the *Earl of Lathom*. He was then in Paris, breakfasting heartily at the Ritz. After a day's work at the naval convention, which he hoped would be climaxed by Italy's entry into the war on the side of the Allies, he was planning to travel to Sir John French's headquarters at the front.

Lord Fisher, the elderly First Sea Lord, had rested for most of Wednesday. The pressures of office and his differences with Churchill over the Dardanelles had brought him to the verge of a breakdown, and his doctors were concerned about his nervous condition. Until he and Churchill returned to Whitehall it was left to the admirals to counter the U-boat menace off the southern Irish coast. And Churchill was not expected home for three more days.

A number of passengers on board the *Lusitania* were awakened abruptly by a curious thudding sound. The lifeboats, their davits creaking from want of exercise, were being swung out, some of them striking noisily against the ship's sides. The ominous sound made many passengers apprehensive. The more seasoned voyagers soon realised that this was a routine precaution, for there were no alarm bells, no blowing of whistles, no stewards rapping frantically on their cabin doors.

Eleven boats were uncovered; they hung out on each side of the liner, their keels suspended above the rails of the promenade deck. The collapsible wooden boats, which were stowed beneath the lifeboats, were left in place. Each heavy lifeboat could accommodate sixty people, and the *Lusitania* had sufficient life-saving equipment for 2,605 persons; including crew, there were fewer than 2,000 on board.

'What's in the wind?' Albert Bestic asked Hefford.

Hefford, who stood motionless on the bridge staring out to sea, turned slowly to him. 'Submarines,' he replied. 'I hear they've been spotted off the Fastnet. The Admiralty has been keeping Sparks quite busy. He gets reminders for the Old Man about passing harbours at full speed, avoiding headlands and steering a mid-channel course.' The Second Officer was referring to the Admiralty memo to ships' Masters which had been first issued on 10 February.

Albert glanced towards the bridge ladder. He wanted to be sure Turner wasn't about: the Captain discouraged his younger officers from chatting on the bridge. 'It sounds a bit of a mix-up to me,' he remarked to Hefford. 'Don't we always pass harbours at speed—unless we're calling? Avoiding headlands is all very well if you can get sights. I hardly think

the Old Man would barge up the Irish Sea without getting a
fix from some headland. What does he think about it,
anyway?' Hefford lapsed into sudden silence. He stepped aside
to look into the compass and returned his gaze to the sea.

After a while he said, 'Nobody can tell what Turner has on
his mind. He's been yarning with Anderson and Bryce, but I
haven't heard any details. Of course, you may be sure he'll
take all precautions.'

Albert was curious. 'How can we know when there's a
submarine about?'

Hefford answered the younger officer like a knowledgeable
teacher. 'A periscope is the only clue. If there's a feather of
foam at the base it means the sub is manoeuvring to get into
position; if there's no feather it's more dangerous, because the
likelihood is that he's already in position to fire his torpedo. If
you spot anything suspicious, Bestic, you just yell out!'

Albert felt confident that his Captain had taken the
necessary precautions. The lifeboats had been swung out, the
lookouts had been doubled, and as many watertight doors as
was practicable had been closed. What more could be done?
he wondered.

Turner himself was apparently not entirely satisfied. He
called Chief Engineer Bryce and urged him to get more power
from the engines. Bryce went below and instructed his
engineers to adjust the throttles until the revolution counters
climbed higher on the dials. He paced the engine rooms as the
Dirty Gang in the stokehold trundled their barrows along the
heavy planks on top of the coal-strewn floors, 'on the long
run', as they called it, and dumped the contents on the iron
decking for the firemen to fuel the hungry furnaces. The
engineers on duty hurried through the boiler room, checking
the gauges on the bulkheads above the fires, as the pointers on
the dials climbed towards the red danger marks. When Bryce
returned to Turner's day cabin he reported that the steam
pressure on the boilers was almost at its maximum and the
generators were running close to capacity. If the weather held
good the liner might just reach 21 knots, but under present

conditions he couldn't force the speed any higher.

Turner decided to lunch on the bridge. He was annoyed that his speed had been reduced because of the boiler shutdown. If only his *Lusitania* could cruise at her designed maximum speed of 25 knots, she would be in no danger from any submarines.

Shortly after noon Charles Lauriat walked into the first-class smoking lounge and looked to see if the day's run had been posted on the notice board. The last five days had been what he described to friends on board as a 'Lauriat Crossing': good weather, a calm sea and little fog. His only regret was that the liner's speed was not what he had expected. He read the day's run: in the 24 hours until noon the *Lusitania* had logged 484 miles. After the first full run of 24 hours, during which 501 miles were covered, the daily run had never topped 500 miles, although the average speed was 20 knots.

'Another small run,' he remarked, with some disappointment, to Lothrop Withington. They left the lounge together and took the lift down to the dining saloon for lunch. Walking the decks in the forenoon, both men had noticed that all the lifeboats had been uncovered and swung out. At least, Lauriat thought, the Captain is prepared for any emergency.

When Chief Purser McCubbin met the Sullivans that morning, he told them that Captain Turner had received word from the Admiralty to 'follow the northern course and keep a sharp lookout for German submarines'. Because of the large number of Americans on board neither Flor nor Julia believed the U-boats would attack the *Lusitania*. Julia was crestfallen when she heard that the liner would not be calling at Queenstown. But she and Flor decided that, as soon as they reached the Irish coast, they would 'take a hand in spotting submarines'.

*A heavy fog covered the waters off the south-east coast of Ireland.*

*Since midnight the U-20 had run for most of the time submerged. At 8.40 am, German time, Kapitänleutnant Schwieger blew tanks and surfaced. The fog was still heavy, but it had cleared sufficiently for him to remain on the surface with flooded buoyancy tanks. He had gone to the bridge when he saw the shadowy form of a large steamer approaching on his starboard bow. In such poor weather there was little danger of the steamer ramming his U-boat, or even hitting her with gunfire. Without hesitating, he decided on a surface attack. 'Full speed ahead!' he shouted into the speaking tube.*

*Spray splashed over the submarine's lean hull and a streak of foam trailed in her wake as her propellers churned up the dark sea. Immediately the steamer sheered off, but Schwieger was close enough to open fire. He would give his shadowy enemy no warning.*

*For the edgy submarine crew the waiting was over. A buzz of anticipation ran through their enclosed underwater world. Each man guessed what was in the other's mind; each man knew that only the target counted.*

Fred Smyth, the young second cook on the *SS Candidate*, which was bound for the West Indies with a cargo of groceries and hardware, was in the galley clearing up after breakfast when the cabin boy shouted the warning, 'A submarine!'

Smith hurried aft to investigate just as the *U-20*'s first shell struck the *Candidate*'s funnel. He ducked back towards the galley as the shelling turned into a furious bombardment, the shots striking the funnel and the ship's upper parts. The noise panicked the firemen on watch. Smyth heard them throwing down their shovels with a clatter and clambering up the iron stairs to the safety, as they thought, of the deck.

'Get back! Get back to your posts!' Captain Sandiford shouted to them. But the men were already making for the lifeboats. Smyth looked for the chief cook to warn him of what was happening. He found him in the ice-box selecting meat for the crew's dinner. 'Come on!' he yelled. 'We're being shelled by a sub! The stokers are in the boats.'

Uncertain of what to do, he ran to his quarters, and, grabbing his half-filled suitcase, hurried back on deck. The chief officer saw him and yelled, 'Drop it, son! Be satisfied with your life.'

In the swirling fog the submarine had taken up a broadside position some 300 yards distant and the gun crew continued firing at the steamer. Captain Sandiford ordered the helmsman to swing the *Candidate*'s stern to the *U-20* in an effort to avert a torpedo attack. Only when the submarine began directing her shells at the bridge did he halt his steamer, and, reluctantly, order his crew to lower away.

As the boats were swung out the shelling ceased. 'Get a move on!' somebody shouted to Fred Smyth as he stood hesitantly on the deck of the ship he had joined in Liverpool the previous day. Climbing into one of the lifeboats he noticed that the wooden boat deck was pitted with shell-holes.

*From the U-boat's bridge Schwieger watched four boats being lowered from the steamer. One boat was swamped as soon as she hit the sea; the other three boats were launched successfully and, filled with crew members, were rowed away from the stricken steamer. He watched the boats fading into the mist. Then he ordered, 'Stand by for surface fire!'*

*It was a clean bow shot. The bronze torpedo smashed into the area of the ship's engine room with a loud echoing noise, shaking the submarine with the vibration. Schwieger was surprised at how little effect the shot had on the steamer, which remained defiantly afloat. Through the speaking tube he called on the helmsman to steer closer to the target.*

*'Fire at her waterline!' he ordered the gun crews as they swung the gun towards the stern of the target. It was then the U-boat Captain noticed that the steamer's name had not been painted out too successfully. He could read,* Candidate, Liverpool.

Two hundred yards astern of the doomed steamer the crew rested on their oars as the Germans directed their shelling above the propellers in an effort to hasten the death. 'They're finishing her off,' a young crewman exclaimed bitterly.

Suddenly, Fred Smyth saw a naval trawler, armed with one gun, sail through the mist between the lifeboats and the submarine, which had taken up a position astern of the *Candidate*. 'Keep off! Keep off!' the crew in the lifeboat yelled. They did not want to draw the U-boat's gunfire again.

The trawler's small gun was probably inadequate to sink a powerful submarine, but Smyth was convinced that one good shot could hole the U-boat and prevent her from submerging. She would then be a perfect target for ramming. But, to his astonishment, the armed trawler suddenly turned tail and made off. Hell! he swore silently with disappointment. I can't believe she's running away. He watched the retreating trawler, making a mental note of the name on her stern, *Lawrenny Castle SA 52*. The submarine sheered off in another direction. Then the helpless *Candidate* lifted her bow high out of the water and slowly sank.

Captain Sandiford looked around him. The only craft on the surface of the dead calm sea were the three lifeboats, with his crew. It was 10.50 am. He decided to make for the Coningbeg Lightship, the rendezvous for submarine chasers. But first he gave his men permission to eat some hard 'tack', the ship's biscuits, which were the only provisions in the boats. Some of the crewmen smoked cigarettes. Then Sandiford ordered them to start rowing again.

It was three in the afternoon when the *Lord Allendale*, another naval trawler armed with a small gun, reached them and the *Candidate*'s crew climbed aboard. When the trawler was under way again, with the empty lifeboats in tow, Smyth was called to the bridge. Captain Foster was in command, but Smyth was questioned by a naval officer, Lieutenant Stevens, concerning the incident of the *Candidate* and the submarine.

'Did you say that a naval trawler turned tail?'

'Yes, sir.'

'Did you get her name?'

'The *Lawrenny Castle*, sir.'

'That is correct, son,' the Lieutenant remarked. 'She's in my patrol. Please don't forget that name.'

Within an hour the *Lord Allendale* had arrived at the Coningbeg Lightship and soon afterwards the runaway trawler loomed out of the fog and dropped anchor. Lieutenant Stevens went aboard and ordered her captain to proceed to Rosslare, the nearest Irish harbour, under arrest.

*Kapitänleutnant Schwieger, who had changed course to get his craft out of range of the* Lawrenny Castle, *sighted another steamer on the port beam. To manoeuvre into position ahead of the new arrival he needed maximum speed from his engine room. But as the U-20's diesels hammered away, the steamer vanished just as quickly into a fog bank.*

*Schwieger jumped angrily down from the bridge, followed by his lookouts and gun crew, and ordered a crash dive. Running at speed underwater he reached a position ahead of the steamer to allow for a bow shot. But the steamer passed so quickly on the port beam it was impossible to get a sufficient angle of intersection, and he had to abandon his attack.*

*The fog thickened again, so the U-20 continued her journey underwater. By 1.45 pm German time the weather had cleared a little and Schwieger sighted a steamer through his periscope on his port bow. Impatient, he did not wait for pilot Lanz to ascertain her nationality: he ordered a bow shot with a G torpedo.*

*It was a clean shot at 300 yards and it smacked into the steamer close to the foremast. The ship was swamped for'ard and began sinking by the bows. As the crew clambered over the side into small boats Lanz identified the vessel as English and of approximately 6,000 tons. Her name was obliterated and she flew no stern flag.*

*About an hour later, when Schwieger decided to surface, the ship was still partially afloat. For the second time that day* he ordered, 'Stand by for surface fire!' The order was passed along to the bow tubes and acknowledged.

'Fire when ready,' Schwieger snapped into the speaking tube.

'Ready,' Oberleutnant Weisbach answered, holding the liner's forecastle in the crosswires of his periscope.

'Fire!'

The bronze torpedo struck the steamer's forecastle. A loud explosion was followed by a prolonged hissing sound. Schwieger did not wait to see the steamer go down. He and the others on the bridge climbed down the ladder, slammed and secured the hatches, and crowded into the control room as the U-20 submerged to 75 feet. The steamer's sinking, he wrote that afternoon in his diary, was 'as good as certain'.

The fog was now so thick, with visibility reduced to 30 metres, that he decided to remain underwater and head out to sea for the night. His craft was filled with animated conversation and the smell of cooking. Sensing a release of tension among his men, Schwieger put a Wagner record on the gramophone and wound up the handle. He knew his crew would enjoy hearing a jazz tune, or a march, or singing **Denn wir fahren gegen Eng-ell-and**— 'Now we're on our way to England.' He preferred Tannhäuser.

That evening he made a decision that was to change the course of history. He decided to abandon his journey to Liverpool. He noted in his diary the reasons for not continuing with his journey to the operations area, listing five points:

1) he did not expect the foggy weather to improve for days.

2) he could not be expected to evade the destroyers in St. George's Channel and the Irish Sea in time and would need to travel for too long underwater.

3) on a foggy night off Liverpool he could not hope to keep a lookout for outward bound transports without being spotted by the escort destroyers.

4) he was burning so much fuel he would not be able to

*return to Germany around the south coast of Ireland and
he wanted, if at all possible, to avoid returning through
the North Channel in which the U-20 had met patrols on
her last long-distance trip.*

*5) he had only three torpedoes left, and his orders were
to save two torpedoes for his return passage. Already he
had fired four torpedoes, and one of them had missed its
target. That left him with a single torpedo with which to
sink another ship.*

*Schwieger decided instead to cruise in the Irish Channel, south
of the entrance to the Bristol Channel, until his fuel gauges
showed that he had three-fifths of his oil left. In this area he
would have more opportunities for attack, and certainly there
would be less enemy counter-action.*

Charles Frohman beamed as he entertained passengers and
Cunard staff in his suite. Evidently he was in less pain, and
with the end of the voyage in sight, he looked forward to
Barrie's play at the Duke of York's on Saturday evening. Playing
the genial host, he wore a dark suit with a dark silk tie under a
stiff white collar, the Napoleonic ring on his little finger his
only concession to theatrical flamboyance. He was anxious to
make up for the days spent alone on the voyage.

Trays of canapés were laid on the occasional tables and on
his desk, from which Stainton had tidied the playscripts.
Champagne glasses were filled and the drawing room was
vibrant with talk and laughter. Like other passengers that
evening Frohman was relaxing among friends.

Vanderbilt was among the guests, somewhat subdued after
the death of his friend. Charles Klein, Justus Miles Forman
and the actresses Rita Jolivet and Josephine Brandell had
grouped themselves, as usual, around the impresario. Captain
Turner joined the party for a few moments, as did Anderson.
So democratic was Frohman that he ordered Stainton to pour
champagne for the ship's barbers, Lott Gadd and Reg Nice.

He had not forgotten the days he spent counting newspapers for ten dollars a week.

Rita Jolivet remarked that he probably read more playscripts than any theatre manager in the world. Her brother-in-law George Vernon reminded him of his plans to present plays on board the *Mauretania*, the *Lusitania*'s sister ship.

'Yes, I did dream of a mid-Atlantic theatre,' sighed the impresario. 'But my leading lady succumbed to *mal de mer*.' He was cheerful again. Saturday was less than two days away, and then he would be dining at the Savoy Hotel with Barrie.

In another suite George Kessler dispensed cocktails to a group that included Georgina Morell, the oldest passenger in saloon, Fred Gauntlett and his ship-building colleagues, Charles Lauriat, Theodate Pope and her companion Edwin Friend, Isaac Lehmann, and Kessler's close friends on the voyage, the Fred Pearsons. Staff Captain Anderson looked in and was almost as convivial as Kessler, who was still surprised that he had been unable to persuade Captain Turner to introduce boat drill for the passengers.

'Can you explain it?' he asked the Staff Captain.

'That is the Captain's decision,' Anderson told him.

Kessler, impatient to reach England, did not want his arrival delayed by submarines. On Wednesday he had received a Marconigram from a business associate in the City:

HAVE URGENT INSTRUCTIONS FROM NEW YORK TO SEE YOU IMMEDIATELY KINDLY WIRE BY MARCONI NAME YOUR HOTEL LONDON SO THAT I CAN CALL ON YOU ON ARRIVAL

The one-page *Cunard Daily Bulletin* had been filled that morning with reports of the war that were so optimistic they might have been deliberately chosen. The party guests discussed what they had read of the Allied advances on the western front and in the Dardanelles and the prospect of Italy entering the war on the side of the Allies. The news cheered Mrs. Morell, who worried about her son and grandson, both with the British forces, and her daughter who was a Red Cross nurse at the front.

In another stateroom Charles and Mary Plamondon opened a bottle of champagne to celebrate their thirty-sixth wedding anniversary. Plamondon, who was president of his own manufacturing company in Chicago, had noted in his diary that afternoon, 'Going to evening concert for sailors and seamen's home.'

Margaret Mackworth was one of the few first-class passengers to be bored by the voyage. As she dressed for dinner, preparing to join Howard Fisher and Dorothy Conner, she thought how uneventful the crossing had been. She remarked on this to her father, but the coal magnate did not appear to be listening; he had enjoyed his trip on the *Lusitania* and was looking forward to the concert in the first class lounge after dinner.

Alice Lines planned to go to the concert and to the dancing that would follow. While the Pearls were at cocktails she fed baby Audrey. A steward knocked on her cabin door and asked if he might draw the porthole curtains. 'We're getting close to Ireland,' he explained. 'We must black out the ports.' Throughout the voyage Alice had experienced no hint of danger. The lifeboat drill that morning had not bothered her, and apart from her duties in looking after the children, she felt almost spoilt. The food was 'tip top', as she put it, and every morning her own steward brought her tea. During the day she ate with the children in their dining room; at night she joined the Pearls in the first-class dining room while Greta or one of the stewardesses looked after the baby. Greta preferred to take the older children to the four o'clock nursery tea while Alice enjoyed afternoon tea on deck and listened to the ship's orchestra. At six o'clock she and Greta had supervised the children's evening meal in the nursery. Now, with the children safely in bed, the girls began to dress for dinner and the concert.

Traditionally, the concert would have been held on the last evening of the voyage, but the *Lusitania* was scheduled to arrive in Liverpool so early on Saturday that Anderson decided to allow plenty of time on Friday for packing and disembarkation, and organised the concert for Thursday evening.

He invited the Sullivans, among other passengers, to sing or recite, but they declined. Julia was told he had 'scoured the ship for performers to amuse the rich passengers' and had been luckiest in third class. So late did the cocktail parties run that the orchestra on the balcony of the first-class dining saloon played to a meagre group of diners until long after eight o'clock.

When Charles Lauriat hurried to his cabin before going down to dinner he noticed that the shades had been drawn and that his bedroom steward had written a note for the night watchman, listing which portholes were open when he went off duty.

A few moments before Alfred Gwynne Vanderbilt left his suite to go to dinner his valet was handed a Marconigram by one of the bellboys. 'Cable for Mr. Vanderbilt,' the boy sang out. It read:

HOPE YOU HAVE SAFE CROSSING LOOKING FOR-
WARD VERY MUCH TO SEEING YOU SOON MAY
BARWELL

Since the news of the death of his college friend Fred Davies had reached him he had been moody and depressed. The Frohman party had lifted his spirits and now he was reassured that Miss Barwell was waiting for him in England. He went down to dinner with a jaunty step.

None of the passengers preparing for dinner or the concert could have known that while editors of newspapers on both sides of the Atlantic may have had misgivings about the voyage of the *Lusitania*, the liner had been absent from the news columns for some days, save for a six-paragraph item cabled on Wednesday to the London *Evening News* by their New York correspondent.

In an interview Captain Max Müller, superintendent of the North German Lloyd Line, claimed that Germany was preparing for a naval offensive of 'unparalleled severity' to oust the British from the seas. While other nations were building battleships, Germany was working day and night perfecting her submarines. Britain may have temporarily succeeded in crippling German overseas trade, Müller declared, but Germany was now ready to retaliate, and Americans with no business in the war zone were travelling at their own risk.

'As for the *Lusitania*,' Müller warned, 'we will get her surely.'

Captain Turner returned from the Frohman party to a cabin desk littered with paperwork. He was about to attend to it when bellboy William Holton handed him a message from the wireless room:

SUBMARINES ACTIVE OFF SOUTH COAST OF IRELAND

To Turner the message seemed incomplete. Surely there were more details? 'Wait a moment, boy,' he called to Holton, scribbling a query on his scratch pad which he tore off and gave to the boy who hurried up to the Marconi room. Turner climbed the companionway to the bridge. He was puzzled about the seven-word warning, the first direct message to the *Lusitania*. Within minutes Holton had located him on the bridge and handed him another wireless message. The wording was identical. Turner decided against going down to dinner. Anderson could take his place at the Captain's table. He was the soul of geniality and a fund of apparently inexhaustible anecdotes. No better officer to join in the chatter with the 'monkeys'.

Soon it would be dark. In the bows he could see the figures of two crewmen instead of the usual one. Two more men were in the crow's nest. The boats were uncovered and swung out. All non-essential watertight doors were closed. The stewards were even now making sure the passenger portholes were blacked out. He had taken all necessary precautions.

Although he did not know it, the message had been repeated through the wireless station at Valentia on the Irish coast and had come directly from Vice-Admiral Coke at Queenstown. It had been Coke's decision to send the warning directly to the *Lusitania*. Turner was still on the bridge soon after 8.30 when a bellboy arrived with a repeat of the message the Admiralty had first issued just after midnight:

AVOID HEADLANDS PASS HARBOURS AT FULL SPEED STEER MID-CHANNEL COURSE SUBMARINES OFF FASTNET

The *Lusitania* would probably round the Fastnet Rock before morning, and Turner intended giving it a wide berth.

After dinner the first-class lounge filled rapidly for the concert. The passengers, who had reached the boat-deck lounge from the dining saloon two or three decks down, by the grand staircase or the electric lifts, made themselves comfortable in the Sheraton armchairs and settees, the men in evening dress, the women in décolleté gowns. Charles Frohman, attracted by any theatrical event, came in with his entourage; Lady Allan brought her daughters, while the Cromptons left their young family in bed. The Hubbards looked more like performers in a costume drama than members of an audience. D. A. Thomas had persuaded his daughter to accompany him to hear the Welsh choir. Rita Jolivet and Josephine Brandell, unwilling to share the stage with artistes who were not professional, sat with men friends they had met on board. A group of young women passengers enlisted to sell programmes to raise money for the seamen's fund moved among the audience. 'I'm sorry, but I've already bought a programme,' Alfred Gwynne Vanderbilt remarked to a Canadian girl who approached him. She was about to apologise when he took from his pigskin wallet a five-dollar bill.

'There,' he told her, 'that's for your lovely smile.' Blushing, she said, 'I shall have to look for change. Our programmes cost only ten cents.'

'Certainly not,' replied Vanderbilt firmly.

When everybody had settled down and the members of the Gwent choir were singing their opening chorus the Sullivans slipped quietly into the lounge and sat behind a bank of flowers under the palm trees which reminded Julia of Florida. Listening to the choir, her gaze wandered to the delicately-painted ceilings. So deep was the carpet beneath her feet she felt it might easily creep over her shoes. 'Flor,' she whispered to her husband, 'isn't this place twice as beautiful as a convent chapel?'

He nodded assent. 'And twice as big,' he said.

A pianist played the Irving Berlin number 'I Love a Piano' and a Scots comedian told jokes that made no sense to the Americans.

Regular transatlantic passengers noticed Captain Turner making his way during the interval through the crowded lounge to the concert area. They anticipated the customary speech of farewell. In gruff tones Turner thanked his audience for travelling on the *Lusitania* and hoped their voyage had been pleasant. He said there had been warnings of submarines in the war zone. 'But of course,' he reassured them, 'there is no cause for alarm. We shall be arriving at Liverpool early on Saturday morning.'

The Commodore exuded confidence, yet few of the passengers had failed to notice the boats swung out, deck lights extinguished and heavy curtains covering the portholes.

'Are we in any danger, Captain?' a man's voice called out.

'In wartime,' Turner replied, 'there is always danger. But I must repeat that there is no cause for alarm.' He wished them a pleasant evening's entertainment and then added, 'I will make one request to those gentlemen who are fond of cigars. Please do not light them on deck.'

Most of his listeners were ready to accept the Captain's word. They waited for the rest of the programme. A young tenor in the choir, Gwyn Parry Jones, sang Welsh songs and operatic arias. Julia Sullivan whispered to her husband, 'This is as good as the Metropolitan any day.' Towards the end of the concert a woman sang a popular song of the season, 'When I Leave This World Behind'. Julia applauded enthusiastically.

Oliver Bernard arrived late, and saw Stewart Mason and his bride sitting together. They had cut him from the moment they had come on board. Vanderbilt was there, too. He looked around disapprovingly at the other passengers in the smoke-filled saloon, most of them rich people who thought heaven was in Newport and then turned it into a Coney Island for millionaires with their tawdry mansions. Even the best architects were willing to design homes for them like royal brothels. If only I were given another innings in life, he thought bitterly, I would show these fools something better than a pile of expensive luggage on the *Lusitania*. If only I had been given a decent start, instead of having to climb from the bottom of the ladder which the rich enjoyed kicking away, I would find something better to do with a fortune than prance around Paris or the Pyramids. He noticed the audience was split into groups of twos and threes, as though determined to keep to themselves. A submarine, he could not help thinking cynically, would soon make this lot sociable.

Still sullen, he made no attempt to join the performers and the less inhibited among the audience in the chorus of 'For He's a Jolly Good Fellow'. It was sung for Staff Captain Anderson, who was singing as heartily as those around him. The Sullivans joined in too. 'We hadn't a note in us, but could screech with the best of them,' Julia later recalled.

The concert over, Charles Lauriat decided to buy a number in the ship's pool. He had not bought one during the voyage, but he was confident the *Lusitania* would put on extra speed for her dash up the Channel to Liverpool. He bought number 499, the highest in the pool, for fifteen dollars.

The Sullivans and Pat Callan went to the first-class smoking room to watch the card games. At one table Lady Allan and Sir Hugh Lane played bridge with the Pearsons. To Julia, the Irish peer with the haunted eyes looked terribly frail, 'more like a girl than a man'.

One of the wealthy men playing poker suddenly gave an angry shout and Julia turned to see him snatch the cards which a well-dressed sharper had played. She had never heard such a commotion. She turned to Flor. 'Gentleman or rowdy,' she commented, 'they're all the same when you rouse them.'

Other players jumped up from their seats and within minutes Anderson came hurrying into the room. The players argued hotly with one another and with the Staff Captain. He silenced them. 'Gentlemen,' he said, 'I must ask you to leave the lounge. If you call to my cabin tomorrow afternoon I shall do my best to judge your dispute.'

Few of the men were prepared to resume their games. Some of the bridge players were shocked by the scene. As the Sullivans made their way out of the lounge they overheard Sir Hugh Lane excuse himself to his companions.

On deck it was a cool May night. Julia noticed young couples strolling the decks and embracing in dark corners and at the top of companionways, as though wishing to delay the ending of the voyage. She saw the rich woman's daughter again, talking softly to her young man in the lee of one of the lifeboats.

Jack Walsh and Gerda Nielson had their own favourite corner in the third-class lounge, but it was a large and impersonal place, so after dark they walked on deck, their arms around each other. The young engineer told Gerda about his adventures as a soldier in the South Africa war; he had been in the battle of Spion Kop and at the siege of Ladysmith. After leaving the army he had gone to 'make good' as an engineer in California and then sailed to Honolulu to work as a mechanic at the Marconi wireless station. Over ten years he had saved two thousand dollars which he was bringing home to Manchester. He felt happy; he had not known anybody when he boarded the liner in New York, yet now he was close friends with George Hook and his family, and had fallen in love with Gerda. He came to a decision: he would propose to Gerda Neilson.

At midnight First Officer Jones and Third Officer Lewis

relieved Hefford and Bestic on the bridge. At the foot of the bridge ladder the two masters-at-arms were waiting to accompany them on their respective rounds. Bestic followed his guide along carpeted corridors, past staterooms where passengers were sleeping. In 36 hours they would step ashore at Liverpool. 'Made it?' they would echo the greetings of relatives or friends. 'Of course we made it. You didn't believe the Germans could catch a ship like the *Lusitania?*' And they would glance back at the majestic liner alongside the Landing Stage where for seven years she had arrived with the punctuality of an express train.

# 13

# DANGER ZONE
# Day 7: Friday, 7 May

CAPTAIN TURNER strode onto the bridge at dawn. He had slept fitfully. The realisation that the *Lusitania* would reach the official danger zone before morning had kept him awake. He would have been more perturbed had he known that since Saturday 23 merchant vessels had been torpedoed in these waters. But the Admiralty had not informed him of the attacks.

He had been called to the bridge when the fog swept down, and had ordered the speed to be reduced to 18 knots. Steaming at 21 knots his 30,000-ton liner would arrive at the Liverpool Bar before full tide, and she would lie off the Mersey, exposed to the enemy, waiting for the tide and the pilot; at a slower speed she could probably reach the Bar at full tide and be carried across at four in the morning. Above him the masthead kept appearing and disappearing, moisture clinging in myriad white beads to the signal halyards. Every two minutes the deep foghorn, activated by an automatic switch, bellowed its warning into the swirling mists. In the chill air he shivered.

First Officer Jones and Junior Third Officer Lewis were with him on the bridge. They had heard about the latest submarine warnings; to these were added the hazards of fog and the liner's arrival in the danger zone. None of them yet knew that yesterday the *Candidate* and the *Centurion* were sunk off the Irish coast.

Lewis and Jones remained on watch when Turner left the

bridge and went below to his cabin for his favourite breakfast
of kippers and boiled eggs. Even in a crisis he never lost his
hearty appetite. He had placed eight look-outs on two-hour
watches; two in the bows, two in the crow's nest, two in the
stern and a quartermaster on each bridge wing. But though
his officers on the bridge craned to see what lay ahead they
could discern nothing through the fog beyond the two
shadowy figures in oilskins in the bows.

Word had gone round among the passengers on Thursday
night that the *Lusitania* was nearing her landfall. So excited
was Julia Sullivan that she persuaded her husband and Pat
Callan to venture on deck at dawn for the first glimpse of the
mountains of Kerry. Pat promised to recite a poem, 'A Dream
of Ireland':

*I feel the touch of a Munster breeze.*
*Thank God my exile has ended.*

But it was so cold, dark and foggy that they left the deck
hurriedly, deciding to return after breakfast.

Albert Bestic listened to the muffled sound of the foghorn as
he sat at breakfast before going on watch. How different it
sounded in the saloon compared to the bellow just above his
head when he stood on the bridge. Yet invariably passengers
complained.

Over breakfast, David Thomas grumbled to his daughter
and Dorothy Conner, 'That wretched foghorn gives our
whereabouts away.'

Dorothy teased him. 'Really?' she said. 'I was just hoping
we'd get some sort of thrill going up the Channel!'

To Josephine Brandell the foghorn made 'a noisy hooting'
and did nothing to dispel her fears which had been aroused by
Captain Turner's talk of submarines. She had asked another
passenger to allow her to sleep in her cabin, and the woman
had spent most of the night trying to calm her. On her way
down to breakfast the actress noticed that some people, afraid
to remain in the staterooms, had taken blankets from their
beds and were sleeping in the lounges.

Impresario Charles Frohman on board the *Lusitania* on the morning the liner sailed from New York's Pier 54

Millionaire Alfred Gwynne Vanderbilt photographed before the *Lusitania* sailed from New York on 1st May 1915

# CUNARD

## EUROPE VIA LIVERPOOL
# LUSITANIA

Fastest and Largest Steamer now in Atlantic Service Sails
SATURDAY, MAY 1, 10 A.M.
Transylvania, Fri., May 7, 5 P.M.
Orduna, - - Tues., May 18, 10 A.M.
Tuscania, - - Fri., May 21, 5 P.M.
LUSITANIA, Sat., May 29, 10 A.M.
Transylvania, Fri., June 4, 5 P.M.

Gibraltar–Genoa–Naples–Piraeus
S.S. Carpathia, Thur., May 13, Noon

ROUND THE WORLD TOURS
Through bookings to all principal Ports
of the World.
Company's Office, 21-24 State St., N. Y.

## NOTICE!

TRAVELLERS intending to embark on the Atlantic voyage are reminded that a state of war exists between Germany and her allies and Great Britain and her allies; that the zone of war includes the waters adjacent to the British Isles; that, in accordance with formal notice given by the Imperial German Government, vessels flying the flag of Great Britain, or of any of her allies, are liable to destruction in those waters and that travellers sailing in the war zone on ships of Great Britain or her allies do so at their own risk.

### IMPERIAL GERMAN EMBASSY
WASHINGTON, D. C., APRIL 22, 1915.

The *Lusitania*, Cunard's 'Ocean Queen' in 1915

*Right:* The warning announcement from the Imperial German Embassy to travellers appeared in New York newspapers on the morning the *Lusitania* sailed on her last voyage

The domed dining- room of
the *Lusitania*

Breakfast menu
from the *Lusitania*

· CUNARD · LINE ·

R.M.S. "Lusitania"          Sunday, April 18, 1915

## BREAKFAST

Compote of French Plums

Rolled Oats

Yarmouth Bloaters

Boiled & Fried Eggs—to order

Wiltshire Bacon          Cambridge Sausages
American Dry Hash Cakes
French Fried Potatoes·

· · · COLD · · ·
Ox Tongue                    Roast Beef

Fresh Rolls

Marmalade            Jam

Tea          Coffee          Cocoa

SECOND CABIN

Kapitänleutnant Walther Schwieger, who commanded the *U-20*

Oberleutnant Raimund Weisbach, the officer on board the *U-20* who fired the torpedo that sank the *Lusitania*

*U-20* docked with other German submarines — a German wartime photograph

# THE SPHERE

AN ILLUSTRATED NEWSPAPER FOR THE HOME

With which is incorporated
"BLACK & WHITE"

Volume LXI. No. 799. | {REGISTERED AT THE GENERAL / POST OFFICE AS A NEWSPAPER} | London, May 15, 1915 | [WITH SUPPLEMENT] | Price Sixpence.

The sinking of the *Lusitania* pictured by an artist 'with the assistance of eye witnesses'

# THE NEW YORK HERALD.

PART II.  NEW YORK, SATURDAY, MAY 8, 1915.  TWENTY-TWO PAGES  PRICE THREE CENTS.

# THE LUSITANIA IS SUNK;
# 1,000 PROBABLY ARE LOST

LAST PICTURE OF THE LUSITANIA TAKEN AS SHE LEFT NEW YORK HARBOR.

## GERMANS TORPEDO THE GIANT STEAMSHIP AND SHE FOUNDERS EIGHT MILES FROM IRISH COAST

Ten Boats Are Lowered and Officers Work Heroically, but Inrush of Water Through Great Holes in Vessel's Bottom Sends Her Down, Bow First, in Twenty Minutes.

**TWO FEARFUL MISSILES TEAR THROUGH SIDE NEAR BOW AND AT THE ENGINE ROOM**

Great Ship Is Nearing St. George's Channel as the Unseen Enemy Launches Torpedoes That Bend Her Hull.

[Special Cable to the Herald.]

Herald Bureau,
No. 130 Fleet Street,
London, Saturday.

The steamship Lusitania, of the Cunard line, one of the largest and finest vessels in the world, was nearing the entrance to St. George's Channel, between the Irish and English coasts, yesterday afternoon with 1,254 passengers from New York and a crew of 816, when an unseen German submarine discharged two torpedoes which

## RESCUE VESSELS SPEED TO THE SCENE TO PICK UP SURVIVORS; ONLY 500 ARE ACCOUNTED FO

Wireless Call for Help Is Caught by Many Passing Craft and Land Stations, but Naval Observer Ashore Sees Ship Disappear Before Aid Can Reach Her.

**TUG ARRIVES AT QUEENSTOWN WITH 150 SURVIVORS FOUND IN BOA**

Numerous Distinguished Passengers Aboard, but No List Saved Can Be Obtained—Rescued Are Hurried to Hospitals and Many Are Reported Dead from Injuries.

### 1,000 LIVES LOST, LAST ESTIMATE.

London, Saturday, 4:30 A. M.

A DUBLIN despatch to the Exchange Telegraph Company says the latest reports indicate a loss of life on the Lusitania of above one thousand.

Channel, leading to the Irish Sea, in which German submarines have been reported recently, and was proceeding to her destination when the submarine crept upon her, and, according to the officers of the Cunard line, without warning fired the torpedo at her hull.

From the fact that latest advices say the giantess of the seas sank within twenty minutes or twenty-one minutes some idea can be gained of the size of the great holes opened in her hull.

The Titanic, of the White Star line, remained afloat two hours after the hull had been pierced by an iceberg, and as the Lusitania went to the bottom so quickly it is believed her hull was damaged much more extensively than was that of the Titanic.

Not a word has come from Ireland concerning the submarine that wrought the awful havoc. Apparently the death dealing craft revealed herself beneath the surface of the water and escaped unseen.

**WIRELESS CATCHES APPEAL FOR HELP.**

The first information that the Lusitania had been torpedoed came from the wireless station at Old Head, Kinsale, on the coast. The marine observer there had seen the steamship steaming but badly. The wireless operator then picked up this message from the Lusitania

Send help quickly. Am listing badly.

Half a dozen vessels were hurried out from Kinsale to where the Lusitania was lying helpless. She was then eight miles out from Kinsale. The first message was received about ten minutes after two o'clock in the afternoon. All reports agree that the Lusitania suddenly plunged to the bottom at thirty-three minutes after she had been torpedoed. In that receptance, twenty minutes after she had been torpedoed. In that period given to the lifeboats on board had to be launched, and it is reported from Kinsale that they way put into the sea crowded with people.

So brief was the period given to the 2,075 persons on board

### George A. Kessler One of Those Saved, Cable Message to Cunard Office Says

At ten minutes after eleven o'clock last night officers of the Cunard line in this city announced that cable messages were being received in London and Liverpool giving names and addresses of the survivors. The work of obtaining the names is so slow that as it was announced such persons now being taken to the authorities may serve.

The first message received was from Liverpool and ran as follows:—

**"GENERAL LASSETTER'S WIFE AND SON ARE SAFE."**

**"MRS. J. T. SMITH, OF BRACEVILLE, OHIO, AND MR. GEORGE A. KESSLER, OF NEW YORK CITY, BOTH ARE SAFE."**

Just before the Cunard offices closed for the night the message announced:—

**"MISS IRENE PAYNTER IS SAVED"**

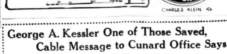

---

Albert Bestic, Junior Third Officer on the *Lusitania*, pictured in later years.

The loss of the *Lusitania* as reported by the *New York Herald* on 8 May 1915

Helen Smith, a survivor from the *Lusitania*, with dolls given to her in Queenstown

Coffins of *Lusitania* victims are buried in one of the mass graves at Old Church cemetery near Queenstown

The Stars and Stripes flies at half mast from the US Consulate at Queenstown. In the background is the Town Hall which was used as a temporary morgue

Captain Turner, wearing a shrunken uniform, walks through Queenstown on the morning after the sinking

Recruiting poster used in Ireland after the sinking of the *Lusitania*

Winston Churchill in Whitehall
in 1915

Lord Mersey walking in London

*Below:* The inquiry at Central Hall, Westminster, June 1915. Lord
Mersey presides as Captain Turner (on the right at witness table)
gives evidence before examining counsel, Sir Edward Carson
(standing, back to camera). Seated at the extreme right of the
platform is Nurse Alice Lines

Harold Boulton also saw passengers sleeping in the lounges. As he went to breakfast they were gathering up pillows and blankets and going off to get dressed. Boulton, who had been on a visit to the United States after a medical discharge from the British Army, asked a crew member if they were travelling slowly because of the fog. 'It's not only the fog, sir,' he was informed. 'We're saving coal and keeping reserve steam up so that if we spot a submarine we can muster enough speed to get us out of danger.'

Drinking his coffee in the first-class dining saloon James Brooks of Bridgeport, Connecticut, thought the liner's speed had been reduced 'very appreciably', and it worried him. He had seen the lifeboats swung out with their rudders attached, and had noticed that, with the exception of two lifeboats amidships on each side of the vessel, the four-foot-long chain appeared to be still attached to each davit and boat in addition to the rope, tackle and fall used for lowering the lifeboat into the water. To leave these chains attached would surely prove dangerous in an emergency?

Charlotte Pye, travelling second class with her eighteen-month old baby Marjorie, thought the passengers at breakfast looked upset. She was on her way from Edmonton to England and her husband had suggested that she travel on the *Lusitania* because it was the fastest ship. When she went on deck after breakfast she met H. L. Gwyer, a young clergyman, also from Edmonton, who was travelling with his bride.

'Did you know we are in the danger zone?' he asked her.

She was suddenly concerned. 'Will it be safe for us?'

'Well,' he told her, 'I suppose something *may* happen, so I've decided to stay on deck tonight.'

Margaret Cox took her baby son Desmond to a late breakfast. An attentive steward made a disparaging comment, 'Some of these people don't know how to eat. Just look – the tablecloths and linen get so dirty.' Other passengers had eaten at her table that morning and she had to agree with him.

'I suggest you come to the first luncheon sitting,' the steward advised her. 'Everything will be so much fresher. There's such a crush at second sitting and the food isn't warm enough.' He was persuasive, but in the end she declined. The steward seemed disappointed, but he promised to keep a 'nice pork chop' for her.

Oliver Bernard was irritable at breakfast; the foghorn spoiled his appetite. If the passengers were apprehensive now that they were in the danger zone, they would hardly be reassured by this continuous bellowing; he could not understand why Captain Turner should want to announce his liner's whereabouts to the enemy, especially when German submarines were prowling in the area. Mistakenly, he calculated that the liner's speed was down to ten knots. Obviously the matter was 'in the hands of God and the Admiralty'. He had found no evidence of anxiety on the part of the *Lusitania*'s officers, and around him at breakfast there seemed to be an air of expectation, as though everybody was waiting for the fog to lift so that the liner could show her paces.

A muffled bellow woke Charles Lauriat. As soon as he identified the foghorn he turned over and went to sleep again. While the weather was disagreeable he had no intention of getting up.

*The fog hung like a pall around Walter Schwieger. Since dawn his U-boat had been running on the surface. He stood on the bridge while the batteries were recharged, his gloved hands gripping the rail, his leather jacket buttoned high. The submarine moved slowly, one diesel propelling the boat on the surface while the other charged the batteries with the tail clutch out. Schwieger was still mulling over his plan to return to Germany instead of carrying on to his patrol station off Liverpool. After seven days at sea he sensed that tension was building up among his men. Even with the cold morning air blowing through the hatches the atmosphere below was fetid and crew members lay inert in their hammocks or in bunks squeezed between hull and torpedo tubes. The gramophone was silent. Hearing the dogs yelping radio operator Otto*

*Rikowsky fed them; he longed for fresh food.*

*He had mentioned his plan to Weisbach. If he had wavered for a time the fog that morning decided him. The longer he remained on the surface in this weather the greater the risk of his U-boat being rammed thus reducing his chance of scoring a lethal shot against an enemy ship. At exactly ten o'clock German time he noted in his diary: 'Since the fog is still dense, I have decided to start the return journey now.' The U-20 was now less than 100 miles from the* Lusitania *in the Irish channel. But at such a range the submarine's hydrophones could not hope to pick up the sound of the liner's propellers beating underwater.*

Soon after 9 am Vice-Admiral Coke learned about Thursday's sinking of the *Centurion*. He had already passed reports of local sightings of submarines to the Admiralty and was deeply worried about the danger they posed outside the harbour. Looking from the first floor windows in Admiralty House at Queenstown he could not discern in the fog even the forts of Camden and Carlisle flanking the harbour mouth. Why had it taken the Admiralty a full day to inform him about the *Centurion*? He could only assume that the lack of response to his messages stemmed from the divisions at Whitehall caused by personal animosities among the 'charity Admirals'.

Churchill was in France that morning on his way to Sir John French's headquarters at the war front, planning to see for himself the attack which French was planning for daybreak on Sunday and worried that the task facing the Allied troops might be impossible.

Lord Fisher was aghast at Churchill's impulsive changes of plan. 'Winston has so monopolised all initiative at the Admiralty and fires off such a multitude of departmental memos,' he wrote, 'that all my colleagues are no longer superintending Lords, but only a First Lord's registry.'

The two men had totally different habits. Churchill liked to work into the small hours and sleep late; Fisher worked early in the morning, tired quickly in the afternoon, and went to bed at nine. Churchill mistrusted senior naval officers he could not dominate, and he made no secret of his ambition that Asquith should put him 'unreservedly at the disposal of the military authorities'. He would much rather run the Army than preside at the Admiralty. He irritated the First Sea Lord with his habit of consulting him only after he had already sent signals to the Fleet. On the morning of 7 May Fisher was apparently unable to make a decision, or else he did not comprehend the crisis off the south Irish coast. The situation demanded Churchill's presence, for with every passing hour the *Lusitania*'s position was becoming more perilous.

Vice-Admiral Coke, a nervous administrator, was frustrated by the inadequacy of his patrol. Judging by the reports from lookout stations along the coast from Waterford to Cape Clear, Area 2I was, for all he knew, infested with submarines. Only 15 of his 40 small ships, known derisively to other commands as the 'Gilbert and Sullivan Navy', were patrolling the 180 miles of coastline; the remainder were in for repair or coaling. That morning the cruiser *Juno* was steaming back to Queenstown, having been delayed by the fog. Even this flagship of the Irish Coast Patrol was showing her age. Her tired engines couldn't produce more than 18 knots, and, in spite of her brave display of eleven six-inch guns, she was vulnerable with submarines about. An alert U-boat commander would have no trouble in diving out of harm's way if the *Juno* attempted to ram.

Pacing between his desk and the windows Coke was as much concerned for the safety of his patrol as he was for the approaching *Lusitania*. His vessels had been instructed to direct their attention to the points at which the shipping lanes converged, such as Brow Head and the Coningbeg Lightship, with orders to warn merchant ships to avoid headlands, keep a mid-channel course and pass harbours at full speed. From the reports that reached him once a week he knew that merchant vessels were ignoring these instructions. His patrol had frequently to hoist the signal MTC, 'Keep Further Out', to force steamers and sailing ships away from the coast.

Coke heard about the sinking of the *Candidate* just before eleven am. He was now more alarmed. The largest and fastest ship in Area 2I was due off Queenstown within hours. He decided to send another direct message to her. It began with a query in code, QUESTOR, requesting the liner to signal the code she held. The *Lusitania* replied with WESTRONA, indicating that she held the first edition of the Merchant Vessel Code. Coke then sent two warnings to the liner about the submarine presence. He even wondered if it might be wiser, considering the danger was increasing with every hour, to divert the *Lusitania* into Queenstown. A few months previously the *Transylvania*, then under Captain Turner, and the *Ausonia* had both been called into Queenstown because they were transporting large guns from the States.

In Liverpool Alfred Booth was as shocked as Coke at the news of the sinkings of the *Candidate* and *Centurion*. Instead of sending a message to Captain Turner, he went directly to Admiral Stileman, the Senior Naval Officer at Liverpool, and asked him to inform the liner that two merchant ships had been sunk. Alfred and George Booth agreed that the *Lusitania* was in a perilous situation. Because of the danger both of them assumed she would be diverted into Queenstown.

Since midnight the *Lord Allendale* of Grimsby had lain at anchor in one of the bays off Milford Haven with 44 of the *Candidate*'s crew on board. At ten am a powerful naval motor-launch manned by bluejackets drew alongside and Captain Sandiford stepped into it.

Then Lieutenant Stevens, smart in his gold-braided uniform, ordered Fred Smyth, 'You, too, son.' The *Candidate*'s second cook followed him over the side into the launch. They were driven quickly away from the *Lord Allendale* to the embarkation steps, close to the Admiralty offices.

When Smyth was shown into Admiral Dale's room the Admiral was engaged and passed him over to a junior officer who asked him a number of questions in a businesslike manner. Smyth was then told to wait outside, and after a short while the officer returned with three typed copies of his statement concerning the events of 6 May which he asked him to sign. The young cook was curious to know what would happen to his statement. Lieutenant Stevens told him, 'A copy will go to Mr. Churchill, the First Lord.'

Fred Smyth left the offices, convinced that the Admiralty would act on his statement. He was now a seaman without a ship, and he could not forgive the Captain of the armed trawler for his unexpected turnabout.

As though from a gigantic cocoon of cotton wool the *Lusitania* emerged from the fogbelt into the bright morning sunshine. It was the cue for Captain Turner to step from his corner on the bridge and issue his orders. At once the foghorn's defiant trumpeting ceased. The engines resumed their familiar throb. It was just after eleven am.

Now that the weather had improved Turner should have felt more secure, but the submarine warnings through the Valentia station to the *Lusitania*'s wireless room were persistent. At 11.52 am a warning from the Admiralty to the Queenstown Command reached him:

SUBMARINES ACTIVE IN SOUTHERN PART IRISH CHANNEL LAST HEARD OF TWENTY MILES SOUTH OF CONINGBEG LIGHT

Turner was convinced that more than one submarine was operating in the area. As the liner steamed steadily on at 18 knots he ordered helmsman Tom Evans to steer a serpentine course; this was Turner's interpretation of the Admiralty instructions to zigzag.

Hefford and Bestic noticed the passengers emerging from saloons and smoke-rooms to walk the promenade deck or settle in deckchairs. Around noon they heard the sound of raised voices and saw passengers gesturing excitedly on the portside. On the horizon an irregular pencilled line had suddenly appeared. The long-awaited coast of Ireland.

Julia Sullivan could hardly believe her eyes. She grabbed her husband's arm. 'Flor,' she cried, 'in next to no time we'll be passing Piper's Hill!' After years of exile she longed to glimpse her birthplace again. She talked like an excited child, convinced she could already see the whitewashed houses on Cape Clear. Flor suggested they ask Purser McCubbin if they could borrow his binoculars. McCubbin was on the boatdeck tossing a medicine ball to Charles Bowring and Elbert Hubbard. Since early morning, the Hubbards had been on deck, and now that land was sighted Elbert believed he was nearer to his meeting with the Kaiser.

Once the fog had cleared Charles Lauriat decided to get up. He shaved, dressed and went to the smoking-room to study the notice of Thursday's run. During the past 24 hours they had travelled only 462 miles. He was surprised. He stepped on deck to take a walk before lunch and view the distant Irish coast. Even now, it seemed the *Lusitania* was not steaming at top speed; she was just 'lounging along'.

Oliver Bernard, leaning over the promenade rail, could not raise the enthusiasm of the other passengers about the coast of Ireland. As the liner cleared the fog and sailed into what promised to be a perfect early summer's day he decided her progress was 'disappointingly slow'. 'Is the Commodore waiting for something to happen?' he wondered. 'Is he really calling Count Bernstorff's bluff?'

*Off Galley Head the* U-20, *cruising at an underwater depth of 75 feet for fear of being rammed, was less than 40 miles from the* Lusitania. *Soon after ten o'clock Schwieger had taken his submarine up to eleven metres to find that the fog had cleared and the weather was sunny. At one o'clock German time, they heard the sound of powerful propellers passing overhead.*

*Rikowsky held tightly to his radio operator's chair as the submarine began rolling heavily. Schwieger ordered 'zero metres' and, as the U-boat rose, he peered through the periscope to see an old cruiser with two masts and two funnels. 'Quickly!' he called to the pilot. 'Take a look.'*

*Lanz peered into the glass and decided, 'British warship. Pelorus Class."*

*'Donnerwetter!' Rikowsky heard his Commander swear. 'A prize—and we've missed her.'*

*Even at the U-20's best underwater speed the Juno was drawing further away from them, zigzagging out of sight towards Queenstown. No point in getting the torpedo tubes ready, Schwieger told Weisbach. They could never catch her. He blew tanks at one o'clock and when they surfaced there was no other shipping in sight. He went below and noted in his diary, 'Waiting off Queenstown does not seem worthwhile.' It was time for him to start the long journey around the Fastnet and home to Germany.*

For a veteran who had crossed the Atlantic many times William Turner was strangely confused. The landfall was probably Brow Head, not far from the Fastnet Rock, but he could not understand why they had not passed the Fastnet during the night. By now they should be close to Queenstown. If the landfall was Brow Head then the next headland would be Galley Head. He was still guessing at his true position when, just after noon, he was handed another Admiralty message:

SUBMARINES FIVE MILES SOUTH OF CAPE CLEAR PROCEEDING WEST WHEN SIGHTED AT 10 AM.

If these submarines were astern then the *Lusitania* had been saved from danger by the fog.

Straining for landmarks, Hefford and Bestic caught a blurred patch of white through their binoculars. It could have been the lighthouse on the Old Head of Kinsale, the next prominent headland after Galley Head and Seven Heads, yet neither of them was certain. Having run for almost 500 miles without a 'fix', or a four-point bearing, they needed confirmation of their position. The *Lusitania* was on a course S 67 degrees E when Captain Turner suddenly ordered Evans to alter course 30 degrees towards the land. Third Officer Lewis had inspected the lower decks to make sure the ports were closed. Chief Engineer Bryce had prepared the boilers for an emergency run. Once the white-washed lighthouse tower with its contrasting black bands had been positively identified Turner was confident he could steer safely up the Irish Sea to Liverpool.

One passenger had spent most of the voyage in his cabin.

Since leaving New York Theodore Naish from Kansas City had been seasick. His wife Belle kept assuring him as they crossed the Atlantic that the occasional whitecaps were no higher than six inches. The liner may have pitched a little at times, she told him, but the breeze was light and the weather delightfully warm. 'Theodore,' she declared, 'it's just like the Detroit river on a summer's afternoon.' But her words did not cure her husband's seasickness. Belle had been upset by Thursday's boat drill. The boats seemed so small and the passengers so numerous she was convinced that their only hope in an emergency lay in their life-jackets. Her husband did all he could to calm her. She went to the second-class dining saloon and brought some lunch to Theodore. 'Why don't you go on deck and take a look at the Irish islands?' he suggested. 'They're very pretty.'

'Your word is good enough for me, Theodore,' Belle replied, encouraging him to eat. 'We'll see them on our return trip.'

'Why not go up, dear,' he persisted, 'just to see what's doing.'

She promised him that as soon as he ate his lunch she would go on deck, just to please him.

The children in first class were the first to lunch. Alice Lines and Greta Lorenson took the three older Pearl children to the nursery lunch, leaving the baby sleeping in Alice's cabin. Other passengers at this moment were packing suitcases in readiness for next morning's disembarkation. In their second-class cabin Jane McFarquhar and her daughter Grace laid out new clothes, deciding to change after lunch and discard those they had worn on the voyage. Then they went on deck to see the coast. As they lingered at the rail, looking across the smooth, sunlit waters towards Ireland, Mrs. McFarquhar thought, 'We are now at the end of the voyage, and there has been no sign of danger.'

James Leary of New York missed the first luncheon sitting because he had slept late. He became confused about the time after his steward covered the skylight of his cabin on B deck with sheets of blotting paper as a blackout precaution. When Leary dressed and came on deck it was after 12.30.

As the liner made her sudden 30 degree turn Ian Stoughton Holbourn was on the promenade deck explaining the workings of the ship to Avis Dolphin. He had gradually brought the girl out of herself by talking about his Shetland island and the ponies and seabirds. Avis had listened enraptured as he recited stirring poems about the sea, and when she remarked that girls' books were always so dull he promised to write a story for her that would be as thrilling as a boy's adventure book. He went out of his way to introduce her to other children on board, and Avis made friends with Ailsa Booth-Jones, an eight-year-old who was travelling with her parents and four-year-old brother. On Thursday Ailsa had proudly shown Holbourn the four prizes she had won in the deck games. To him these children were the life and charm of the voyage.

Fireman John O'Connell had spent his morning in a different world. He was so dirty when he came off duty that he stripped, washed, shaved and changed his shirt and dungarees before sitting down to lunch. As he ate he listened to the other firemen reading from the morning's *Cunard Daily Bulletin*. The main headline, set in heavy type, read, 'Reports of German Victory a Hoax'. The story claimed that Berlin's enthusiasm had turned to gloom as French troops scored a series of gains for the Allies in spite of the enemy's use of poison gas. No mention was made of submarines. On the last stage of the voyage Staff Captain Anderson did not want to upset his passengers. Even the British and American papers that morning carried no reports of the sinkings of the *Candidate* and *Centurion*, yet with the loss of the two merchant vessels the total of ships sunk by the Germans since the declaration of the war zone on 18 February had reached 90. Column after column in the London papers reported fierce fighting and brilliant advances in the Dardanelles. The *New York Tribune* mentioned German submarine activity in the North Sea, but made no reference to the south coast of Ireland. The newspapers had forgotten the *Lusitania*.

As the liner steamed towards the Old Head of Kinsale George Wynne was preparing Jerusalem artichokes for dinner. In singlet and check trousers he joked with another assistant cook and talked about the good times they would have next night in Liverpool. His father had not been impressed by the luxury of the *Lusitania*; he still hoped for a job ashore to be near his wife and the rest of the family.

Leslie Morton had come on duty at noon. He would take over as extra lookout at four bells, or two o'clock, but he was spending the first two hours, along with most of the deckhands on the starboard watch, in the baggage room, sending up luggage and mail by lift to the upper decks in readiness for the liner's arrival in Liverpool.

*Schwieger's* U-20 *was running on the surface at two o'clock German time, when the chief engine room artificer Friedrich Sellmer, who was on deck, shouted, 'Ship!'*

*Turning his binoculars Schwieger picked out an astonishing and totally unexpected sight. From his vantage point on the bridge he could make out the four stacks and two masts of a steamer approaching from south south-west, making towards Galley Head at a course at right angles to the submarine.*

*She was about 13 miles away, he calculated. He summoned pilot Lanz, who climbed quickly to the bridge and confirmed Schwieger's first impression. She was a large passenger steamer.*

*Schwieger ordered, 'Diving stations!' Those on the deck and on the bridge scrambled below, slamming and securing the hatches behind them. Within minutes the U-20 was running at 30 feet below the surface, at her best speed of 9 knots, on a course converging with that of the steamer.*

*Otto Rikowsky heard Lanz remark that the steamer was zigzagging slightly. He thought, 'Well, then we can't get near her.' But Schwieger was hoping against the odds that she might change course to starboard so that he could attack.*

*At 1.35 pm– 2.35 German time– he saw the steamer turn suddenly to starboard, exactly as he had hoped. He wrote in his log, 'Proceeded at high speed to obtain ahead position.'*

# 14

# LAND SIGHTED

MARGARET MACKWORTH looked across the luncheon table. 'Home tomorrow! Aren't you pleased, father?'

Thomas returned his daughter's smile. 'I would be more pleased, my dear, if I believed that wretched siren hasn't given our whereabouts away.' For his sake Margaret avoided further mention of her boredom on the voyage. She knew her father would be happy to see Llanwern with its flowers in bloom again.

In the first-class dining saloon the passengers sat down to first luncheon. They chatted to one another across the spotless napery. The mood was lighthearted, and already many of them were looking forward to the ceremony that evening of the last dinner at sea. Few were prepared to resume the talk of submarine threats; most were eager to discuss what lay ahead in England. Danger seemed very remote in that sumptuous setting.

Oliver Bernard noticed that, true to tradition on the last day of a voyage, passengers were more friendly towards one another. The murmur of conversation rose above the orchestra. The atmosphere in the dining saloon seemed more animated than at any time since the liner had left New York. Even his fellow-countrymen appeared to have shed their aloofness.

Charles Frohman, seated at a centre table, forgot for a while the pain in his right knee as, drawing on a fat cigar, he regaled his friends with theatrical anecdotes.

The erect young officer William McMillan Adams led his

father to their favourite table. Theodate Pope sat with James Houghton and Edwin Friend, talking incessantly about psychic matters. Lady Allan lunched with her lively young daughters, Gwen and Anna. Vanderbilt was enjoying lunch at the Captain's table with Staff Captain Anderson; later the jovial Anderson would give his decision on the previous night's card game dispute. As he had done so often during the voyage, William Pierpoint sat alone.

As though reluctant to turn away from the sight of land, the Hubbards paced the decks. Julia and Flor Sullivan were still at the promenade rail, scanning the coast with Purser Mc-Cubbin's binoculars. Julia's hands trembled when the glasses found Glandore, nestling close to the harbour that runs into Rosscarbery Bay. 'Sweet Glandore,' she whispered happily to herself, regretting they could not land at Queenstown. Rosscarbery was her birthplace, and when she saw Piper's Hill with its fields spread out like the skirt of a check apron she recited to her husband a rhyme she remembered from childhood:

> *Parkmore and Parkeen,*
> *Laggawn and Lisheen,*
> *The Reask, the Ray and the Carrig;*
> *The Meadow, the Mock,*
> *The Field of the Rock,*
> *The Garden, the Close and the Haggard.*

'Have you an air for it?' he asked.

Julia handed him the glasses. 'You know well, Flor, that none of us could sing. But we were great dancers.' They lingered at the rail as the Seven Heads hid the welcome view of Glandore and the liner steamed close to the Old Head of Kinsale.

Sir Hugh Lane leaned over the promenade rail. Wistfully, he gazed at the shores of his native county Cork. He must have recalled his childhood days when, unable to join in the sports of his older brothers, he preferred to look at the paintings and ornaments in the houses he visited. Even then, the aesthetic boy dreamed of creating a gallery of pictures, a dream that was to become the abiding passion of his life. He turned away and went down to the dining saloon where Josephine Brandell had interrupted her lunch to make a collection among the diners for the members of the orchestra.

Oliver Bernard gave Josephine a coin and rose from his table. He was impatient with an American woman who prattled on about her choice of lifeboat should the *Lusitania* be torpedoed. He silenced her with the remark, 'My choice would be a raft.' He paid his wine bill and bade 'Good afternoon' to Theodate Pope and her friends as he passed their table and went up the saloon stairway. On reaching the port promenade deck he had the impression the liner had come to a standstill. Then he realised she was 'crawling along'. Irritated by such desultory progress, he crossed in front of the bridge to the starboard side and walked aft along the deck to the verandah café known as the Palm Lounge. 'I have had sufficient exercise on this deck,' he reflected, 'to last me for a lifetime.'

Before entering the café he leaned against a screen, looking pensively across the smooth expanse of ocean. The sea was perfectly still, like an opaque sheet of polished indigo; the horizon, as far as the eye could see, was undisturbed by the sails or smokestacks of any other vessel.

Harold Boulton had also arrived at the Palm Lounge. He sat at a table, lit a cigarette and ordered a steward to bring him coffee. Commander Foster Stackhouse joined him and the two men began chatting. Stackhouse told him he was planning an expedition to the Antarctic, but Boulton was convinced the explorer was on a secret mission for the British Government. It was a delicate matter, and he did not raise it that afternoon; instead, he discussed with Stackhouse the possibility of their being torpedoed.

George Kessler went directly to the smoking room on the boat deck to play bridge. convinced that for twenty pounds he had bought the lucky number in the pool, 480. Fred Pearson and Charles Klein were talking volubly about church organs.

'Didn't you know,' Klein asked Kessler, 'that Fred and I are the Aeolian Company's best customers?'

The Irishman Michael Byrne stepped from the Grand Entrance and, having lit a cigar, began to stroll around the deck. About the same time the businessman Charles Bowring took the lift down to lunch, leaving the Hubbards tossing a tennis ball back and forth. It was just 1.30 pm when Charles Lauriat returned to his stateroom and pulled on a sweater, before replacing the jacket of his knickerbocker suit. He then went on deck determined to take 'a real walk'.

At 1.30 pm First Officer Hefford and Albert Bestic finished lunch and went to the bridge to relieve Jones and Lewis. The distinguishing marks on the lighthouse were now plainly visible, and they identified the outline of the Old Head of Kinsale.

At last Captain Turner knew where he was. He ordered helmsman Evans to swing the wheel to bring the liner back to its original course 67 degrees east. As the *Lusitania* turned towards starboard, he instructed Albert, 'Bisset, take a fix'. When the four-point bearing was completed the *Lusitania*'s true position would be established beyond doubt.

It may have been because he felt himself alone off the Irish coast without an armed trawler in sight that Turner made this decision. Conscious of the submarine menace, he was nevertheless unaware that 23 ships had been sunk in the area since Saturday. At a speed of three knots below her maximum he held his ship on a steady course 12 miles off the coast, in close proximity to headlands, abandoning his earlier serpentine tactics. Either he had decided to ignore the Admiralty's advice to 'zigzag, avoid headlands, steer a mid-channel course and pass harbours at full speed' or these instructions, of which he had received copies in February or April, lay forgotten on his desk.

He left the bridge, and went below to his day cabin. That morning he had begun another complicated knot. When it was finished he would present it to the officers during afternoon tea.

At 1.50 Bestic began to take a four-point bearing of the lighthouse tower from which he could calculate its distance as soon as it came abeam. At two o'clock Third Officer Lewis relieved him, and Albert started down the bridge ladder to his cabin. On the way he met telegraphist Robert Leith. 'Well, Sparks,' he asked cheerfully, 'what's your latest crime story?'

'If you mean submarines,' Leith told him, 'we heard that one was spotted off Cape Clear at ten o'clock.'

'That's way astern of us now.'

'Another was spotted a few miles south of the Coningbeg. That's ahead of us.'

'Yes, but eight miles away.' Bestic reckoned the lightship was four hours' steaming time from the Old Head. By then the submarine would probably have moved into the Bristol Channel. These U-boats didn't stay long in one place, although he did not see any warships on the horizon to trouble them. He went to his cabin, planning the afternoon in his mind. He would sleep until eight bells, then join the officers in the wardroom for afternoon tea before going on watch. But first he must bring the log up to date. He had written the words *RMS Lusitania, 7 May 1915* when he heard an abrupt knock on his door. He guessed it was the unwelcome baggage master. 'You again?' he called. 'Same old story, I suppose?'

'I'm sorry, sir,' Crank apologised on entering. 'But on account of the weather being so fine, like, we've got orders to get some of the baggage on deck ready to go ashore in the morning. The men are waiting for you, sir.' Albert sighed. He would have to spend at least another hour in the bowels of the liner. 'All right,' he answered, 'I'll come with you.' Reaching for his cap, he remembered he was wearing his new uniform. 'Just a moment,' he called. 'I've got the glad rags on. I'll have to change. You go on down and I'll follow you in a few minutes.'

'Very good, sir.' Crank closed the cabin door and went below.

Belle Naish went on deck at her husband's prompting, and was surprised to find the land so close. It seemed to her as if she could reach out and touch the trees, the green fields, the black-banded white lighthouse. Looking down at the water, she thought, 'I could run faster than we are moving.'

Six-year-old Helen Smith followed her parents from the second-class dining saloon to their cabin where her mother insisted she change into travelling clothes. 'Tomorrow morning,' she told her, 'we shall be landing in Liverpool.' While her parents packed after the seven-day voyage, leaving out only what they would need for going ashore, Helen wandered, as she often did, alone on deck.

Norah Bretherton and her children had finished first luncheon. Norah carried Elizabeth to the second-class playpen on B deck, entrusting her to the care of a stewardess, and then took young Paul down to their C deck cabin to put him to bed for his afternoon nap. Charlotte Pye sat with her baby Marjorie. Close by, Margaret Cox ate her lunch, holding baby Desmond on her knee. Avis Dolphin arrived for second luncheon with Nurse Ellis and Miss Smith.

Mary Maycock, who had been working in America as a companion to the Astor family, had packed her cabin luggage. Wearing a silk blouse, dark skirt and high laced boots, she sat at a desk in the second-class library writing a letter to her brothers Tom and Arthur in New York, telling them she had sighted land. In her trunk, along with her certificate of graduation as a hairdresser and beautician, was the trousseau she had bought for her wedding in her native Yorkshire.

One second-class passenger had crossed into first class that afternoon. Newspaperman Ernest Cowper, his notebook almost filled, went in search of Elbert Hubbard for a final interview.

In third class Elsie Hook stood at the entrance to first and second class. Before lunch she had been talking to some girls about flowers when a smartly-dressed young man remarked, 'Do you like flowers? I've got some in my cabin. I shall bring you a rose after lunch.' She was waiting for him with her father and Frank, when an insistent woman passenger asked her to post a letter. For a moment Elsie hesitated; then she set off to post it in the box on D deck.

The Hooks' friend Jack Walsh had finished lunch and was sitting in a corner of the third-class lounge on C deck with Gerda. The couple held hands and Jack kissed Gerda softly on the cheek. They were very much in love. She had accepted his proposal the night before and they agreed to marry as soon as they reached England.

*The liner's white superstructure, gleaming in the afternoon sun, filled Schwieger's periscope glass. He could hardly believe what he saw.*

*He ordered the helmsman to bring the U-20 up a little, then down a little, manoeuvring into position for attack. Having made her turn to starboard the liner was about 700 metres from the submarine, presenting a perfect target. From the forward torpedo room Oberleutnant Weisbach reported to his Commander, 'Tubes clear.'*

*Schwieger fixed his attention on the liner in his periscope. The watertight doors dividing each section of the narrow hull had been closed for diving, and the submarine was charged with tension: by now every man knew they were stalking a big passenger liner.*

*'Stand by first tube!' Schwieger rapped out.*

*It was now that Quartermaster Charles Voegele suddenly paled. He stood motionless in the cramped control area as though unable to telephone the command to the torpedo station. The young Alsatian was never a favourite with Schwieger. 'Stand by first tube!' the Commander repeated sharply.*

*Voegele ignored him. Tense and shaking, he muttered, 'I will not attack a ship with women and children on board.' The other men stared at him in disbelief. It was unheard of to disobey an order. Voegele would surely face a court martial on his return to Germany.*

*Schwieger did not take his eyes from the periscope. If he had heard Voegele's words he did not betray the fact. Another man took the telephone from the quartermaster and quickly passed the command to the torpedo room. Seconds had passed, yet Schwieger believed the prize was still within his grasp. Peering into the glass as he gripped the periscope handles he kept the liner in his sights. It was no time to worry about a mutinous quartermaster.*

*As the bow cap was opened and the torpedo tube filled with sea water, the call came back from Weisbach, 'Torpedo ready.'*

Charles Lauriat, warm in the sweater he wore beneath his jacket, came up the main companionway and stepped onto the portside deck. He noticed the Hubbards standing by the rail just forward of the entrance. It wouldn't be long, he remarked to Elbert, before he had his interview with the Kaiser. Hubbard had loaned him a copy of *The Philistine* which contained the vitriolic attack on Wilhelm II.

'You've read my piece, Mr. Lauriat,' Elbert Hubbard replied. 'Do you really think I'll be a welcome visitor in Germany?'

In the dining saloon Charles Hill suddenly remembered he had made an appointment for two pm with Miss Hale, the ship's typist, to dictate some business letters. 'You must excuse me, gentlemen,' he apologised to his companions as he stood up, 'I really must hustle.'

He hurried to the lift, intending to go to the A deck library where the typist was waiting for him, but the lift boy assumed he was going to his cabin and stopped the lift at the promenade deck. Hill stepped out to find himself on B deck. About to re-enter, he noticed Chief Steward Fred Jones outside the Grand Entrance on the starboard side. Remembering he wanted to tell Jones he needed the typist again Hill stepped onto the deck.

Alice Lines had left Greta Lorenson in charge of Amy and Susan in the nursery and had gone down to her first-class cabin to prepare the baby's food. Stuart was with her and Alice said to the boy, 'Come on, let me take your shoes off. Then you can lie on the bed and have a nap.'

As soon as the boy was comfortable she began to feed the baby.

*Kapitänleutnant Schwieger ordered, 'Fire one!'*

*In the torpedo room Weisbach pulled the firing lever. A fierce hissing swept through the submarine as the high-pressure air was blasted into the tube, releasing the torpedo. The boat shivered. The men felt an intense pressure in their ears. Schwieger continued staring into the glass.*

*Seconds passed and nothing happened. Had they missed? The U-20 had only two more torpedoes, and these were needed for the voyage home; a fan of torpedoes in the direction of the target was out of the question. Silent and tense, the crew waited.*

*Schwieger had shot his torpedo at a distance of 700 yards and a depth of 3 metres; it was travelling at 22 knots towards a ship that was steaming, by his estimation, at 18 knots. He reckoned it would take about 60 seconds for the single torpedo to reach its target.*

# 15

# A WHITE STREAK

OLIVER BERNARD leaned idly against the outside screen of the Palm Lounge as the *Lusitania* steamed parallel to the Irish coast. It was soon after two o'clock. He was staring vacantly at the bright blue sea when he caught sight of a flickering swirl of sunlight in the sparkling water. Something had disturbed the indigo surface a few hundred yards away on the starboard bow. A porpoise, perhaps? Bernard was shaken out of his reverie. 'What is that streak in the water?' he asked himself. 'It's spreading. It's coming closer.'

The attention of other passengers on the starboard side of the decks was caught by the disturbance. Michael Byrne also thought he saw a porpoise, although he missed the customary leap of the fish. When he looked more closely he was certain that what he was seeing below the surface was a submarine.

Ernest Cowper, delayed in his search for Elbert Hubbard by the ship's doctor who held him in conversation, saw a conning tower about 1,000 yards distant. Joseph Myers, who had been relaxing in the Palm Lounge, had walked into the sunshine towards the starboard side of the deck with Frank Kellett when he noticed a periscope projecting above the surface some 700 yards away. From his vantage point on the boat deck he could see clearly the submerged hull and conning tower of a submarine. He caught Kellett's arm. 'Look, there's a submarine!' he exclaimed.

'My God,' a startled Myers muttered to Kellett, 'we're lost!'

James Brooks walked up the broad staircase from the dining saloon. As he stepped from the Grand Entrance onto the starboard side of the boat deck he heard friends calling him from the Marconi deck. He climbed the companionway to join them. Passing along the starboard rail close to the Marconi office he noticed the white wake of a torpedo approaching on a diagonal course. It was between ten and fifteen feet in length, two feet in diameter and appeared to be travelling about 35 miles an hour. He said flatly, 'That's a torpedo.'

As Charles Hill crossed from the Grand Entrance to speak to the Chief Steward at the rail, Jones turned to him and said in amazement, 'Good God, Mr. Hill, here comes a torpedo!'

Glancing in the direction of the man's finger, Hill observed the periscope of a submarine, but not the torpedo itself. Then he noticed a line of disturbance in the water forming a pronounced curve. He said calmly to Jones, 'It looks as though it might cross our bows.' It did not seem to him that the periscope, which was ahead of the *Lusitania* and to starboard, was more than 200 yards away.

Joseph Myers was mesmerised by the sight of the torpedo cutting through the water like a razor. He watched it describe a distinct arc as it rose from the submarine, then ran along the surface before taking a final downward plunge close to the ship's side somewhere between, as he thought, the second and third funnels. Myers, Kellett, Brooks, Cowper, all of them saw the telltale streak of white foam. It had an hypnotic effect on them.

Oliver Bernard glanced instinctively for'ard. Have they noticed anything on the bridge? he wondered. Since leaving New York the passengers had chattered endlessly about submarines; now that it was happening did they believe it? He heard the voice of an American woman asking nonchalantly, 'That isn't a torpedo, is it?' He wanted to convince himself that the deadly, frothy track snaking towards them like an express train was anything but a torpedo. Too sick to answer, he turned his head away.

Leslie Morton was the first crew member to realise something was wrong. Just before 2.10 pm he was looking out on the starboard bow when he noticed a slight turmoil in the sea. An enormous bubble had broken the surface about a thousand yards from the liner. A few seconds later he saw a white streak running along the top of the water as though an invisible hand was drawing a line on a blackboard with a piece of chalk, a line that was heading to intercept the course of the *Lusitania*. Snatching up the megaphone, he yelled to the bridge, 'Torpedo on the starboard side, sir!'

As Albert Bestic, buttoning the jacket of his old uniform, stepped from his cabin onto the deck outside the officers' quarters abaft the bridge he heard Morton's warning shout. A few seconds later seaman Tom Quinn saw the telltale froth from the crow's nest and shouted into the speaking tube, 'Torpedo! Starboard side, sir!' Stopping to glance seawards, Albert saw a lengthening streak of white foam heading swiftly towards the liner. Instinctively he gripped the rails of the ladder, his knuckles whitening. He thought, 'This is the approach of death.'

Captain Turner dropped the knot he was fashioning on his desk when he heard Hefford repeat the lookout's warning call. He dashed from his cabin up the stairs to the bridge. But it was too late for the helmsman to take evading action.

As the blue-white foam disappeared beneath the starboard counter, Oliver Bernard stood hypnotized. Holding onto the verandah rail, he shut his eyes, and trembled as a severe shock ran through the deck as though a tug had rammed the liner's enormous hull.

D. A. Thomas and Margaret had left the dining saloon and were walking towards the lift. The coal magnate said, 'You know, Margaret, I think we might stay up on deck tonight.' Not wanting her to think he was frightened of submarine threats, he added with a forced smile, 'Just to see if you get your thrill.' Before she could answer they heard 'a dull thud-like sound', from just below them, in the middle of the liner.

Other passengers were later to describe the sound more vividly. Michael Byrne, standing on the starboard side of the boat deck directly beneath the Captain's bridge, heard a detonation 'like a million-ton hammer hitting a steel boiler a hundred feet high and a hundred feet long'. To Joseph Myers it was 'like a peal of thunder accompanied immediately by a flash of lightning'. James Brooks who, like Myers and Bernard, had seen the torpedo disappear beneath the counter of the ship, heard 'a dull explosion'. Standing beside the Hubbards Charles Lauriat heard 'a heavy, rather muffled sound' as the ship trembled under the force of the blow. Leaning together over the rail the startled Charles Hill and Chief Steward Jones saw the torpedo penetrate the side of the ship with a sound 'like the slamming of a door'. Belle Naish had turned from the rail and was halfway to the second-class entrance when she heard 'a crash'.

At lunch in the first-class dining saloon Charles Bowring felt 'a violent shock' as crockery and cutlery jumped off the table. William Holt, who had gone to the lounge to read a novel, heard 'a dull crash'. In second class, Dr Carl Foss of New York, travelling with a group of physicians to join the Red Cross in the field, was finishing lunch when 'a loud, voluminous boom', made him spill his coffee. Jane McFarquhar glanced in alarm at her daughter Grace as 'a rumbling noise' seemed to come from beneath the dining saloon. To Isaac Lehmann, who had been joined by Maurice Medbury, another New Yorker, in the first-class smoking room, the sound was 'like the boom of a cannon'. He exclaimed to Medbury, 'They've got us at last! Let's get outside!'

Julia Sullivan had retrieved the Chief Purser's binoculars from her husband and was focussing on her beloved shoreline, hoping that Piper's Hill might peep out again between the Seven Heads. She was so overwhelmed by the sight of Ireland after her years of exile that Flor had to give her jacket a gentle tug to calm her, a tug that for Julia set off 'the most dreadful explosion the world has ever heard'. It shook the liner, 'lifting her up and then throwing her down and rolling her from side to side'. Terrified, she grabbed her husband to save herself from falling.

Reaching the navigation bridge Captain Turner was just in time to see the sheer of the torpedo in the water before it struck the starboard side of his ship. To his ears the report was 'like the banging of a door on a windy day'. Then he heard a 'second report of the same kind'. In fact, a number of passengers, particularly those on deck, were adamant about this second explosion.

To Charles Lauriat it 'followed quickly on the first'. He did not think it could have been caused by a second torpedo, for the sound was certainly different; it was more like a boiler exploding in the engine room. Ralph McCredy, a young doctor returning to Dublin from Canada, would recall 'a terrific explosion, followed by another'. Harold Boulton, sitting over coffee in the Palm Lounge, was listening patiently as Commander Foster Stackhouse explained why it was 'quite impossible' for the *Lusitania* to be torpedoed. The explorer assured him, 'She has reserve speed ready to put on. She is probably unsinkable. And in any event, if you know the sea you can spot a periscope two miles away . . .' His words were cut short by 'two almost simultaneous explosions'.

William McMillan Adams dropped his novel in the first class lounge and dashed into the companionway as the first explosion shook the liner 'from stem to stern'. He was scanning the sea for a submarine when he heard a second, and greater, explosion. It sounded to him 'as though the mast had fallen down'. Michael Byrne was to describe this explosion as 'awful'. He saw the bow of the great liner lift out of the water. Everything amidships seemed to part and give way right up to the superstructure of the boat deck on which he was standing.

Oliver Bernard opened his eyes to see a monstrous column of debris and water rising high in the air.

Albert Bestic stood aghast as deck planks, boats, coal dust and water were hurled skywards. Had it not been for the lookout's warning cry he would have been walking past the exact spot on his way to the baggage room. As the debris descended in an avalanche, landing noisily on the deck or splashing into the sea to float astern, he turned and ran towards the bridge,

utterly incredulous that anything could disturb the well-oiled
routine of the liner. There was work to be done this afternoon,
baggage to be sent on deck, the Captain's log to be written up.
He simply could not accept the possibility that the majestic
*Lusitania* would come limping up the Mersey, or perhaps even
into Queenstown.

In the bow Leslie Morton had heard 'a tremendous explosion followed instantly by a second one'. As water and
debris went shooting into the air he dived down the scuttle to
the fo'c's'le to see if his brother was safe. He met him coming
up from his bunk, dazed with sleep and wearing only a shirt.
John asked him sleepily, 'What the hell are you doing with the
ship?'

Alarmed and fearful, first-class passengers rose hurriedly
from their tables as splintered glass fell from windows and
portholes into the dining saloon. The string orchestra, perhaps
hoping to prevent panic, continued playing 'The Blue
Danube'.

Josephine Brandell, having completed her silver collection
for the musicians, had sat down to finish her lunch when her
companion cried, 'They've done it!' The fears which had
obsessed the actress during the entire voyage were being
realised.

Samuel Knox and Albert Hopkins made for the dining
saloon exit, but Fred Gauntlet delayed, calling to the stewards
to close the open ports. Although he repeated his request,
none of them seemed to hear him.

In the second-class dining saloon crockery fell from the
tables as Charlotte Pye and her baby were thrown to the floor
by the force of the explosion. Margaret Cox felt as though the
room was about to collapse on top of them. Her attentive
steward had just served her with a pork chop cooked in bread
crumbs which had taken twenty minutes to prepare, and she
observed that the person next to her was eating a dessert of
pears and blancmange. Avis Dolphin had also been looking
forward to dessert when the lights flickered and went out and
diners scrambled to their feet. She thought, 'What a shame

I'm going to miss dessert.' Ian Stoughton Holbourn shouted to her and her two companions across the tables, 'Stay where you are!'

Women began screaming as they struggled through the crowded room to the entrance doors leading to the stairways. Clasping her baby close to her, Margaret Cox pushed through the frantic diners towards her steward, now closing the ports. 'Tell me what to do,' she begged him. 'Whatever you say I'll do it.'

'Get up the stairs,' he advised her. 'Get up as quickly as you can.'

Flames, smoke and splintered glass blew into the portside stateroom of Major Warren Pearl on E deck. He was not a man to panic. He knew Amy had gone on deck; his children were probably in their cabins with their nursemaids. Aware of the risks of the voyage, he had drilled his wife and the nurses on how to act in an emergency. Alice Lines was in her cabin; she at once wrapped Audrey in a shawl which she tied in a knot around her neck. Then she took hold of Stuart's hand. 'Come along,' she said firmly to the boy. 'We won't wait for anything.'

In third class Elsie Hook was standing on the stairway leading down to the third-class dining room when she felt the liner suddenly lurch. She could see people eating lunch in the saloon. Not waiting for their reaction she turned and ran back on deck. Her father and brother Frank came hurrying towards her.

On the first-class promenade deck Charles Lauriat turned to look in the direction of the explosion. He saw coal and debris hurled into the air and heard the crash of falling gratings and deck planks. He was standing well forward on the portside, looking back to the point of the explosion on the starboard side. Instinctively he glanced at his watch. It showed eight minutes past two, Greenwich time. Turning to the Hubbards, he said, 'Why don't you go to your stateroom and fetch your life-jackets?' Their room was on D deck and it would not take them long to get there and back. But they did not seem to be listening to him. They stood motionless by the rail, Elbert holding his wife close. They seemed powerless to act.

Those on deck nearest the point of explosion felt the impact more severely. James Brooks was struck so violently by the force of water cascading near the for'ard funnel that he fell sprawling on the deck behind the Marconi office. The first explosion lifted the ship hard to port, the second enveloped the deck in steam so dense he struggled for breath. 'Let's get away from here,' a frightened Isaac Lehmann urged Maurice Medbury as they hurried from the smoking room. The two men rushed towards the deck as debris crashed onto the roof of the Palm Lounge. After that Lehmann did not see Medbury again.

Oliver Bernard ducked into the Palm Lounge to avoid the wreckage descending in all directions. He thought the torpedo had struck close to the bridge and that hundreds must already be dead, trimmers and stokers in the boiler rooms, passengers in the forward cabins. Then the water tanks burst, releasing their contents in an enormous cascade. He looked up to see the canvas awning, which was stretched across the entrance to the café, sagging as though about to split apart beneath the weight of water and debris. He scrambled outside again, convinced the great luxury liner was tilting right over, just as if she were in dry dock and the underpinning on the starboard side had been knocked away.

*The crew of the* U-20 *had waited in suspense after Weisbach fired the torpedo. The only sound to break the silence was the steady humming of the electric motors. One of the dogs in the bunks yelped plaintively.*

*Through his periscope glass Schwieger followed the streak of white foam as the torpedo darted through the water towards the unidentified great liner. He saw it strike home between the first and second funnels. The detonation that followed sounded 'like a small click'. But the second explosion was so powerful that the light bulbs in the control room fell out and the submarine began to rock heavily. An enormous cloud plumed skywards over the for'ard funnel. Above the point of impact the superstructure was torn asunder and fire and smoke enveloped the liner.*

*Schwieger gripped the periscope handles. Usually a U-boat had to dive deep immediately after an attack. Today, with no destroyers in sight, he could stay close to his wounded victim, fascinated by what he saw. The liner seemed to have lost way and was listing to starboard.*

*He was sure the second explosion could not have been caused by his G torpedo; he could only assume that a violent internal explosion had rent the liner. The Germans knew that passenger ships were being used to carry arms and contraband to Allied ports. Was the liner carrying munitions?*

*He did not of course know of the shells, rifle bullets, shrapnel and gun cotton that had gone aboard the* Lusitania *at New York, almost all of it listed in the supplementary manifest. This cargo might well have caused the powerful second explosion; but then, so might the pressure of steam. Captain Dow had expressed a fear in February that if struck in her boilers by a torpedo the* Lusitania *would be destroyed.*

*'Run up the patrol periscope,' Schwieger ordered, a hint of emotion in his voice. 'The ship is sinking. Anybody who wants can take a look.'*

# 16

# DISTRESS CALL

SOOT AND COAL DUST went shooting upwards with debris and steaming water after the second explosion ripped through the bottom bows of the liner. The dust now rained down on the tilting bridge and upper deck, momentarily blinding the Captain and his officers and men.

Turner shouted, 'Hard a-port!'

Young Hugh Johnston, who had taken over the wheel from Evans at two o'clock, had heard Second Officer Hefford echo the lookout's cry, 'Here comes a torpedo!' Believing his Captain's first impulse was to beach the liner at Kinsale, the harbour which was on the beam, he swung the wheel, his eyes intent on the indicator, singing back, 'Hard a-port, sir!'

But the pull of the bow to port was unalterable. The compass needle was jumping wildly as the *Lusitania*, listing to starboard, began tracing a helpless arc. Turner called to Johnston, 'Hard a-starboard!' Johnston swung the wheel in the opposite direction, singing out, 'Hard a-starboard, sir!' Still the massive liner would not respond.

'All right, boy,' Turner snapped. 'Mr. Hefford,' he called urgently to his Second Officer, 'take a look. See what list she's got.'

Hefford glanced at the compass. 'Fifteen degrees to starboard, sir.'

'Watch if she goes any further.'

Hefford repeated to Johnston, 'Watch the indicator. Sing out if she goes any further.'

Turner had sent Chief Officer Piper for'ard to secure an open hatch in the bows. He had ordered all watertight doors to

191

be closed, and Hefford had given this order from the bridge; but because of the power failure it was by no means certain that all doors were still controlled from there.

Bestic came up the stairway to the bridge convinced that the crew members who had gone to wait for him in the baggage room, men who could launch and handle lifeboats, were dead or dying because of the power failure, which must have trapped the steel cage between decks. He told himself, She won't sink. Didn't the *Titanic* float for four hours? So he was astonished to hear the Captain order, 'Boat stations!'

As Albert turned back he thought he heard in the eerie silence that enveloped the great ship the solitary cry of a seagull. Then, suddenly, the murmur of voices rose like the wind in a forest.

Telegraphist Robert Leith ran from the second-class dining saloon where he had been lunching and elbowed his way through the frightened crowds in the passageway. Taking two steps at a time, he climbed four flights, finally reaching the Marconi office by a narrow ladder. His junior, David McCormick, was already at the keyboard. Leith took over from him, tapping out the desperate message: COME AT ONCE BIG LIST TEN MILES SOUTH OLD HEAD KINSALE.

Ian Stoughton Holbourn made his way through the crush of passengers in the dining saloon to reach Avis Dolphin and her nurses. 'Don't panic,' he told them calmly. 'Come to my cabin. I'll find you some life-jackets.' Shepherding them towards the entrance doors he heard the crash of crockery sliding from the tables. Stewards were calling, 'Keep your places! There's no danger!' But the diners, who seemed alarmed, though not panic-stricken, went on pushing their way up the stairs.

On reaching his cabin just off the main stairs Holbourn took down a life-jacket and tied it on Avis. He tied a second life-jacket on Nurse Ellis, but when he turned to give the third to Sarah Smith, she brushed it aside. 'I won't take it,' she said.

Holbourn was taken aback. 'But why not?'

'Because you have a wife and children. You're going to need

it desperately.'

He didn't wait to argue. 'Come quickly,' he ordered. 'We will get you to a lifeboat.'

Margaret Cox was among the diners jostling to get to the top of the stairs. She thought, 'If I had taken the waiter's advice about first lunch I would be sleeping two flights down at this moment.' Mabel Docherty, carrying her eight-month-old baby boy, the youngest infant in second class, was also struggling to escape from the dining saloon. She knew she must get to the boat deck, yet she kept thinking, 'I haven't taken the money from my trunk or even a wrap to cover us.'

Nora Bretherton, who had been at the first sitting, was on her way down with her little boy Paul to put him to bed in their C deck cabin when the explosion rocked the ship. For a few seconds she hesitated on the stairs midway between B and C decks, unable to decide which way to go. Then she ran back up to B deck to snatch her baby from the playpen.

Jane McFarquhar and her daughter Grace were among the last passengers to reach the boat deck from the second-class dining saloon. As they slowly forced their way up the stairs other passengers pushed them from side to side, and they emerged on the boat deck to find crowds gathering on the high side of the liner, determined to get into the lifeboats. The McFarquhars saw fear in their faces. They realised the liner could be in mortal danger. Self preservation was now their sole priority.

'There's no chance here,' Mrs. McFarquhar, trying to keep calm, said to Grace. 'We must get to the other side.'

Belle Naish, her clothes soaked by the water that showered on the deck, was confronted by a tide of passengers pouring out of the companionway. She wanted desperately to join her husband on D deck, but these people were cursing and shrieking. Terrified that the crowd would carry her over the rail of the tilting deck into the sea, she doggedly fought her way through them. By the time she reached D deck the last passengers in the thinning group were trying to help one another.

G

She found Theodore, who had forgotten the discomfort of his seasickness, freeing the tapes of their life-jackets. She helped him on with his jacket, then he with hers, and to save time they each tied the other's tapes at the neck, chest and waist.

When they heard the stewards telling passengers to collect any valuables from their cabins before going to the lifeboats the Sullivans were seized with apprehension. They struggled through the crowded passageways off the promenade deck; some passengers had fallen when the explosion rocked the liner and seemed unable to get to their feet.

The cabin door was jammed. Flor kicked it roughly with his heel until it gave way. Pulling their trunk from beneath his bunk, he swiftly cut the leather straps with a pocket knife and flung the contents on the floor to find the oilskin envelope which held their shares and most of their savings. 'At least we'll have our money,' Julia reassured him. He stuffed the Treasury notes into his pocket and Julia pinned the envelope containing the shares to the inside of her life-jacket.

Ernest Cowper could find no trace of the Hubbards. He turned to the ship's doctor. 'What do you think?' he asked him. 'Will she sink?'

The doctor shrugged. 'All I know is we should get ready to leave — now!'

Cowper realised how heavily the liner was listing when he saw a man in a life-jacket sliding helplessly down the deck on all fours. A small child came running towards him. 'Please, mister,' she pleaded, 'will you take me with you?' He lifted her in his arms and carried her to a corner of the second-class promenade deck. 'What's your name?' he asked her.

'Helen,' she said shyly. Helen Smith had wandered alone on deck and become separated from her parents. Her aunt, whose two boys were playing somewhere on the ship, saw Helen's mother running frantically along the deck in search of her child, her long hair falling loose around her shoulders.

'Wait here, Helen,' Cowper told the small girl. 'I'll be right back. Then you can come with me.' He ran down two flights of stairs to fetch a life-jacket, but his cabin was in darkness. Empty-handed, he turned and made his way up to the promenade deck again.

In third class Harold Taylor rushed into his cabin wearing only a shirt and trousers and announced philosophically to his young bride, 'Well, that's it. We've been hit.'

'Hit?' she cried.

'Yeah. We've been torpedoed!' Lucy Taylor flung a coat around her shoulders and they hurried out. As they climbed the stairs she realised she wasn't wearing any shoes.

In the fo'c's'le Leslie Morton was yelling to his brother, 'We've been torpedoed!'

John stared at him in such astonishment that Leslie had to shake him by the shoulders. 'Don't you know what this means? Come on, we've got to get to our boat stations!'

George Wynne was in the saloon vegetable locker when he heard someone shout, 'We've been hit!' A young assistant cook yelled, 'We've had it!' George ran from the locker towards C deck. His only concern was to find his father. He saw him almost immediately, coming up the stairs from the sleeping quarters. His face was deadly pale. When he saw George he turned, shouting, 'Stay where you are, son — I'll get you a life-jacket!'

In the bowels of the liner many of the 'dirty gang' who had been fuelling the furnaces were deafened by concussion. The risk of being scalded alive by escaping steam sent them running towards the escape ladders, throwing down their shovels and slices as they went.

In No. 1 boiler room, below the first funnel, leading fireman Albert Martin had seen the torpedo slam past him before it exploded between a group of boilers. The shell between the forward and centre coal bunker doors on the starboard side burst like paper as the sea water flooded in. Choked with dust and steam, fireman Tom Madden attempted to escape through the bulkhead door amidships, but it was shut tight. Unable to force it and not knowing where to find the release levers, he tried to turn back, but the swiftly rising waters swept him off his feet and carried him like flotsam across the boiler room to the starboard side. Grabbing a floating coal barrow he began to work his way slowly and painfully to the escape ladder in the portside ventilator. He fumbled frantically in the darkness until he found the bottom rungs and slowly began his climb to freedom.

In No. 2 boiler room, beneath the second funnel, the water rushing from the forward bunkers burst through the hatches and knocked fireman Leslie Plummer off his feet with such tremendous force that he was carried past one boiler to the next until he was slammed against the bulkhead. He fought to get clear of the dirty, salty water and regain his feet, determined to reach the empty No. 4 boiler room and the ladder to the firemen's quarters.

The same dark, relentless tide carried trimmer Eugene McDermott and fireman William Mallin ten feet above the floor, sweeping them helplessly towards a grating, the lower end of a ventilating shaft, at the top of which they could glimpse daylight. It was high above the water and it was some time before McDermott was able to catch hold of the grating. With all his strength he hauled himself onto it and began to climb the shaft ladder which led to the deck around the funnel. When he emerged into daylight he could not find fireman Mallin. In fact, many of the 'dirty gang' had perished, and McDermott was the only man to escape from No. 2 boiler room.

Albert Martin made for the forward starboard ventilator leading to the bridge deck, singing out in the darkness, 'Everyone follow me!' He wondered if any men in the first boiler room were alive. As the water rose higher he recognised the answering voice of Third Engineer Cole, 'Alright, Martin! Go ahead!' Reaching the escape ladder he dragged himself out of the water and began the slow climb to the top.

Trimmer Tom Lawson, who had been on the starboard side of No. 1 boiler-room had run through the smoke-filled central passageway into the forward stokehold when he heard Albert

Martin's voice some distance ahead. Suddenly he was engulfed in a rush of water, but he found his feet and waded on in the darkness, guided by the fireman's voice. He had been so deafened by the explosion that he had no idea how far away Martin was. He had reached the end of the passageway when one of the centre starboard boilers was lifted off its chocks and rolled against the port boiler, sealing the passageway behind him. There was no way back. Half-drowned, he managed to reach the ladder ahead where a small group of men were climbing towards the light.

Only six of them, including Lawson and Martin, reached the bridge deck. As they dropped down onto the boat deck Lawson heard Anderson calling to the passengers, 'Please keep calm! She won't go any further.'

Directly across the expanse of sunlit water in the fishing town of Kinsale, less than twelve miles from where some two thousand people on the *Lusitania* were fighting for their lives, Police Constable Jim Speight left the barracks near the water's edge. He had just come on duty and was walking along the winding road when he heard an explosion offshore. Training his field glasses on the spot, he saw smoke rising from a big liner. He turned and hurried back to the barracks to raise the alarm.

Jane Deasy, a girl in her early twenties whose father kept a bar and shop in the last house on the edge of Kinsale harbour, was at lunch in the family dining-room. She was looking from the window at the fishing boats in the harbour when she saw three or four policemen running towards the pier. She watched them talking excitedly to the fishermen in the boats. The fishermen began casting off and raising their sails.

Her young brother burst into the room shouting, 'The *Lusitania*'s going down off the Head!' All week long the fishermen had been 'watching and waiting' for the *Lusitania*. Jane had heard them talking about the liner as though they expected some disaster. 'I'm away on my bike,' her brother declared. As he cycled to the lighthouse she went down to the pier to see the last of the boats heading out of the harbour towards the stricken liner.

Ten miles west of Kinsale Tim Keohane, the coxswain of the Courtmacsherry lifeboat, was on coast watch at Barry's Point on the other side of the Old Head. Hearing the distant explosion, he looked through his glasses across Courtmacsherry Bay to see a large liner listing, with smoke pouring from her upper decks. He recognised the *Lusitania* and started to run the three miles back to the village of Courtmacsherry and the rectory where the Reverend Forde, the lifeboat secretary, lived. As he passed the cottage of John Murphy and his son Jerry, two of the lifeboat crew, he did not stop to talk to them, but shouted, 'Come on! The *Lusitania*'s going down out there!'

As mounting panic swept through second and third class, the smaller number of first-class passengers maintained an outward composure, as though determined not to be caught in a vulgar stampede.

Margaret Mackworth and her father had been in the lift near the dining saloon when they heard that 'dull, thud-like sound'. They stepped out and Thomas crossed to a porthole, but Lady Mackworth would not wait. The stairs seemed safer and she could not bear the thought of remaining below decks a moment longer than necessary in a ship that might be sinking; she had made up her mind that if anything happened to the *Lusitania* she would make straight for the boat deck. Now she fought to control that impulse, knowing she must first go to the stateroom for her life-jacket. As she started up the stairs the liner was already listing. 'Why am I not more frightened?' she wondered. She found herself breaking into a run: 'Now I'm beginning to get frightened, but I must not let myself.' On her way down the corridor leading to her stateroom on D deck she collided with a stewardess running towards her. Lady Mackworth wasted precious seconds apologising to the woman. Then, hurrying back with her life-jacket, she dashed into her father's parlour suite and collected his too. She climbed to the boat deck, making for the portside, certain it would be safer on a deck that was high out of the water. But where was her father?

'Stay here if you wish,' Charles Lauriat told the Hubbards impatiently. 'I'll fetch some life-jackets for you.' He hurried to his stateroom, the most forward on D deck, and tied on a life-jacket. From his suitcase he took a small leather case containing his business papers and money, which he stuffed in a pocket of his jacket, and removed two other life-jackets from their shelf. When he returned to the portside deck the Hubbards had gone.

Charles Frohman had come from luncheon with his usual lively group and was on the upper promenade deck chatting with George Vernon. Captain Alick Scott, an English officer on his way home from India, had joined them just as the torpedo struck. Frohman was quite calm. Smoking a fresh cigar, he simply said, 'This is going to be a close call.'

Scott started to move away. 'Stay there! I'll fetch some life-jackets.'

'Why not stay where you are, Captain Scott?' the impresario suggested. 'We shall have more chance by staying here than rushing off to the boats.'

But Scott ignored him and dashed off.

Rita Jolivet, who had come from her cabin wearing a life-jacket, found Frohman unperturbed. Above the rising sound of frantic voices he began to talk calmly about the Germans and the war. He asked the actress and her brother-in-law if they had heard the rumour that German agents had been arrested on board during the voyage. When Scott returned with two life-jackets, one for Vernon, the other for Frohman, the latter protested that Scott had none for himself. Reluctantly he allowed the officer to fasten a jacket on him. 'Now, Captain, you must get yourself a life-jacket,' he insisted.

Scott shrugged. 'If I'm going to die, it's only for once.'

Frohman, looking even more tubby in the patent Body Belt, smiled at him and continued puffing his cigar. Turning away from the growing commotion on the decks, he leaned with one arm on the rail, gazing out to sea. Almost in a whisper, he said, 'I didn't think they would do it.'

Dr James Houghton left his cabin in search of Marie de Page and found her standing on B deck without a life-jacket. He removed his own and fastened it around her. Lady Allan was nearby with her frightened daughters and maid. The force of the explosion had thrown her against the rail and she was wincing in pain, certain her arm was broken.

Charles Hill had left the Chief Steward to make his way to cabin B52 in the hope of finding a friend of his, Mrs. Witherbee, and her four-year-old son. Their cabin was empty. Sea water was already pouring through the open porthole. He continued on to his own cabin to collect his despatch case and overcoat. His steward Percy Penny helped him into a life-jacket, although he was wearing none himself. 'I think you should go straight to the boat deck, sir,' Percy advised him.

On the starboard side of the boat deck William McMillan Adams was standing, appalled but fascinated by the scenes of confusion, when his father came up and took him by the arm. William noticed he had put on his overcoat and cap. Together they crossed to the portside, which was highest out of the water. 'We must give some assistance,' his father said.

Holding young Stuart Pearl's hand tightly, and reassuring herself that the baby tied in her shawl was safe, Alice Lines made for the stairs leading from her cabin to the boat deck. 'No matter what happens,' she warned Stuart, 'hang on to me. If I fall down, hang on to me. Don't let go.' She continued talking to him as they climbed the stairs. The boy began to sob. 'Now, Stuart, don't cry,' she said to him soothingly. 'Do as you're told and Nurse will look after you.'

They met Greta coming down with baby Susan. Alice suddenly panicked. Where was her beloved little Amy? 'What have you done with my baby?' she cried.

Greta was sobbing with fright. 'A stewardess took her to a lifeboat. Oh, what are we to do?'

'Don't bother with anybody else,' Alice said emphatically. 'Just watch the children.'

Georgina Morrell had been sleeping soundly, as she usually did after lunch, when the torpedo struck. Her maid awoke her abruptly. 'We're sinking. There's no time to dress.'

The elderly woman sat up in bed, staring in disbelief at the maid who began to help her fasten a life-jacket over her nightgown.

'What *are* you doing?' she asked.

'Quickly, dear,' the maid told her. 'We must get to the lifeboats.'

Unable to reach his suite, David Thomas turned back and made for the boat deck. Michael Byrne, who had gone to the Palm Lounge, watched the first-class passengers emerging on deck. Most of them seemed 'transfixed where they stood'. As he leaned against the café screen, he saw Anderson on the port bridge wing shouting, 'Keep the boat deck clear!' 'Impossible,' Byrne thought. 'Most of the crew and passengers are already on deck by now.'

Harold Boulton went down to his stateroom to fetch his life-jacket. His friend Mrs. Lassetter and her son, Lieutenant Frederick Lassetter of the King's Own Light Infantry, had a nearby suite and he knocked on their door. There was no reply, so he crossed to his own stateroom and pressed the light switch. The power had failed. In the darkness he groped for his life-jacket which had been on its shelf during the voyage, but it had gone. As he continued along the corridor leading to the entrance stairs the liner was listing so heavily to starboard that he found himself walking with one foot on the floor and the other on the wall. At the end of the corridor a steward was handing out life-jackets. Boulton took one and strapped it on. He had started up the staircase leading to the Grand Entrance when the liner lurched further to starboard and he found himself tumbling down the stairs. He landed awkwardly at the feet of an attractive woman and her daughter. Embarrassed, he picked himself up and managed to ask politely, 'Is there anything I can do to help?'

They regarded him with some disdain. 'No, thank you,' the woman said. 'There is nothing you can do. The Captain says the ship cannot sink. We have no intention of becoming alarmed.'

Boulton climbed the tilting staircase with difficulty. On reaching the Grand Entrance he noticed the lift had jammed halfway between floors and was filled with people who had been coming up from lunch. They were screaming and struggling frantically to release the gates. Boulton thought, 'They are trapped like rats.'

Near the Marconi office James Brooks, his face and clothes covered in soot, scrambled to his feet. He ran down to the portside of the boat deck and into the smoking room. It was almost empty. Making for the entrance doors at the other side of the room he collided with the six half-naked stokehold crew, filthier than himself with grease and dirt, who had escaped through a forward ventilating shaft. He pushed past them, suddenly panic-stricken, not knowing where he was running.

High on the bridge, Hugh Johnston, desperation in his young face, could coax no reaction from the rudder.

Frustrated, Turner ordered, 'Full astern!' There was no response from the engine room. The men below were either scrambling to safety or were dead. Her engines powerless, the ship was still making headway, lurching blindly like a wounded animal. A bluff-bowed cargo steamer would have lost way in a couple of minutes, but Turner had no means of stopping the relentless curving progress of his ship. The mighty *Lusitania* ploughed on. Her beautiful knife-like bows, so much admired from the day of her launching, were proving her undoing. Like his Captain, helmsman Johnston, spinning the wheel helplessly, knew that the fastest liner on the Atlantic was out of control.

Chief electrician George Hutchinson, who had earlier checked the watertight compartments and found them in working order, feared the worst had happened. He ran to the dynamo. He must keep the current flowing to the wireless station in the Marconi office. But there Robert Leith was watching the needle dropping inexorably down the dial until it struck zero. Immediately he switched to the emergency dynamo, continuing to tap out the desperate message: COME AT ONCE BIG LIST TEN MILES OLD HEAD KINSALE.

It was 2.14 pm. Leith did not think there was much time left.

# 17

# BOAT STATIONS

CAPTAIN TURNER BEGAN to fear the unthinkable. Was his magnificent ship really doomed?

He had ordered the swung-out lifeboats to be lowered to the rails, but told Anderson not to allow any boats into the water until headway was sufficiently off the ship. The safety of his passengers and crew was uppermost in his mind, and he was confident that the *Lusitania*'s forty-eight lifeboats were adequate; twenty-twenty-two were wooden, clinker-built boats suspended from davits on either side of the liner, twenty-six were collapsibles of wood and canvas, lighter than conventional lifeboats and designed to be easily released from their housings. Most of the collapsibles were stowed beneath the conventional boats. Anderson was responsible for the portside lifeboats which were numbered evenly; the odd-numbered boats on the starboard side were the responsibility of First Officer Jones.

Because of the liner's headway it seemed impossible that the boats could be lowered. They swung so far inwards on the portside and so far out on starboard that even if the *Lusitania* slowed to a stop they would be difficult to launch. Many of the crew were inexperienced in handling the boats; Turner had already admitted to 'green hands' among his men. Albert Bestic hurried down the bridge ladder to his allotted portside boats, numbered 2 to 10; the fifth boat, No. 10, was his own. He ordered the frightened passengers who were pouring out of saloons and cabins to stand back against the bulkhead so as to be clear of the davits. They stood waiting, as though dazed.

None of them had been given lifeboat drill; few of them had read the written instructions in their cabins. They expected guidance from the officers and crew. But Albert had received no orders to lower the boats.

A man frantic with fear suddenly broke from the crowd. Leaping onto a collapsible, he climbed from it into the first lifeboat. Albert turned to a burly seaman, and jerking his thumb towards the passenger said quietly, 'Get him out!' The seaman vaulted into the lifeboat. Seizing an axe, he advanced until the weapon was within an inch of the passenger's face. 'Hop it,' he growled. The passenger obeyed and climbed back onto the deck.

On the starboard side bellboy William Holton reached his station to find that his boat, No. 5, the third from for'ard, had been blasted off the side by the explosion. It was floating astern, apparently undamaged. He heard Anderson's voice from the bridge, 'The boats must not be lowered. The ship is not going to sink.' He agreed with the Staff Captain. He did not think that lifeboats filled with passengers could be safely lowered into the water while the liner was moving because of the risk of one boat landing on top of the other.

When fireman Eugene McDermott heard Anderson's order, he left his boat station, No. 18 on the portside, and slipped down the ladder to the fireman's quarters to find a life-jacket. Below decks it was so dark that he could not even grope his way to his bunk. He climbed back up to the third-class promenade where passengers were shouting and screaming. A third-class passenger grabbed him. The young fireman thought at first that he was about to strike him, but the man pleaded, 'Will you look after my mother and sister?' The two women were nearby, pale-faced and crying.

'Take them to a saloon,' the passenger begged him.

McDermott thought it would be safer to direct them to a lifeboat, but he agreed to do as the man asked. He led the women into the empty third-class saloon and persuaded them to wait there. As he stepped on deck again he wondered how many of his mates in the stokehold were alive. He had no life-jacket, but at least he could swim.

In a passageway leading onto C deck a young crew member, his eyes wide with terror, ran past George Wynne shouting, 'Get out! We're lost!' In his mind's eye Wynne saw again the anguished expression on his father's face as he had turned to look back at him before going in search of a life-jacket. Joseph Wynne had not returned. George decided he could wait no longer. He dashed up to the boat deck where people were milling around the lifeboats. He searched desperately for his father, but could not see him in the crowd.

Wearing her life-jacket and holding a jacket for her father, Lady Mackworth stepped into the sunlight on the port side of the boat deck. 'Do you mind,' she asked Dr. Howard Fisher and the nurse, Dorothy Conner, 'if I stay beside you until Father returns?'

Before they could answer a stream of hysterical third-class passengers swarmed up from below decks. White-faced and panic-stricken, they pushed their way to the nearest lifeboat, knocking aside an officer who tried to stop them climbing into the boat. The self-possessed Lady Mackworth turned to the nurse. 'I always thought,' she remarked, 'that a shipwreck was a well-organised affair.'

Dorothy agreed. 'So did I. But I've learned a devil of a lot in the last few moments.'

David Thomas, who had come on deck to look for his daughter, stood aside when he saw the passengers storming the boats. At a fellow-passenger's suggestion he accepted an inflatable lifebelt and blew it up. When he put it on it did not seem very secure; he thought that at any moment it would collapse. By now the stairways were clear and he decided to go down to his cabin. His life-jacket was gone; he did not know his daughter had taken it. He recalled there were jackets in the wardrobe and found three there. By the time he reached the boat deck again the liner was listing so heavily it was difficult to walk up the port side. Looking around him he observed only 'absolute confusion' and 'an entire absence of discipline' among the crew.

Charles Lauriat was unperturbed as he walked as far as the bridge. He heard Turner and Anderson shouting, 'Don't lower the boats.' In a calm, clear voice, a woman called up to Turner, 'Captain, what on earth do you want us to do?'

'Stay where you are, madam,' Turner told her. 'This ship is all right.'

'Where do you get your information, Captain?'

'From the engine room,' he answered abruptly.

Lauriat turned and walked back through the crowds. Many passengers were wearing their life-jackets incorrectly. One man had put an arm through one armhole and his head through the other; another wore his life-jacket upside down around his waist. But when he approached them to explain how they should adjust them, they hurried away, convinced he wanted to take the jackets from them.

Noting the ever-deepening list of the liner, Lauriat was convinced she would not stay afloat for long. He went down to his stateroom on B deck. It was plunged in darkness. He placed his hand unerringly on a box of matches he kept on the table by his bed. Striking a light, he opened his travelling bag and pocketed his passport and some personal papers. Then he made his way back along the main passageway, walking in the angle formed by the floor and the side walls of the staterooms.

Glancing down the cross passages on the starboard side he saw that the portholes were open, the sunlit water alarmingly close to them. The ports in the dining saloon on D deck, he remembered, had been open during lunch. If the *Lusitania* was sinking fast it was surely because water was pouring through these and other ports on the lower decks at a rate of many tons a minute. It amazed him that all the ports had not been sealed when the *Lusitania* entered the danger zone.

Soon after the command not to lower the boats had been given Harold Boulton heard Anderson appealing: 'Will the gentlemen kindly assist me in getting the women and children out of the boats and on to the upper decks?' By then Boulton had found Frederick Lasseter and his mother, and Mrs.

Lasseter had been placed in one of the lifeboats. At Anderson's request the two men now helped her and the other women out of the boat again. Boulton turned to look for'ard and saw the liner's bows slowly dipping beneath the water. He said to Lasseter gravely, 'This ship is going to sink.'

On the port side of the Palm Lounge, Oliver Bernard met Lesley Mason. When she recognised him she screamed, 'Where is my husband?' She was no longer the self-assured young bride who had snubbed him throughout the voyage. 'Your husband will soon be here,' he tried to reassure her. 'We shall be going ashore directly.'

Above the din of trampling feet and excited voices, the girl screamed at him again, 'Where is my husband? Where is Stewart?' She was hysterical. Grabbing her by the shoulders, he shook her violently, shouting, 'Listen to me! If you stay right here your husband will find you. They'll be lowering the boats from this side!'

She made a pathetic effort to smile. He was uncertain whether she had understood him, so he added, 'If you go running around this town of a ship, you'll never meet up with him. Understand? Now stay here and I'll find some life-jackets.' She nodded tearfully. As he pushed through the crowds on the port promenade he heard an officer shout, 'Nobody in the boats yet. Keep back, everybody.'

Reaching the Grand Entrance he almost bumped into Vanderbilt who was standing calmly in the foyer, wearing a grey pin-stripe suit and a polka-dot tie, and holding a lady's purple jewel case. He looked as casual as though waiting for the next race at Ascot. He grinned at Bernard, evidently amused by the excitement. The designer ignored him and made for the stairs, forgetting how heavily the liner was listing. He lost his balance and fell sideways, tumbling down the broad staircase and crashing painfully at the bottom on B deck.

As he got to his feet he heard the passengers trapped in the cage of the electric lift shrieking and beating on the grille gates. He could only ignore those death screams as he

stumbled on down the dark, deserted passageway, falling
several times, until he reached the Masons' cabin. 'Stewart!
Stewart!' he called out. Hearing no reply, he continued to his
own cabin at the end of the passageway.

In the darkness he felt for his life-jacket on top of the
wardrobe, pulled it down, and made for the stairs again. He
did not want to be drowned like a rat in the dark.

When he got back to the Palm Lounge, Lesley Mason had
gone. Having taken such trouble to find the silly girl a life-
jacket he felt angry. A demented woman passenger rushed at
him, screaming, 'Where did you get that? Where did you get
it?' Without a word of protest he allowed her to snatch the
jacket from him.

The order for passengers to clear the decks had been heard by
William McMillan Adams and his father. Looking at the
lifeboats swinging dangerously inwards on the port side, young
McMillan Adams knew they would have to be pushed over the
rail of the ship before they could be launched. But passengers
were ignoring the orders from the officers. They were climbing
into the boats and refusing to leave them.

Only one seaman was waiting to help when Albert Bestic
reached No. 2 lifeboat, the first boat on the port side. It was
crowded with passengers, most of them women in full-length
skirts. He took his place at the stern davit, the seaman at the
for'ard davit, and then called to McMillan Adams, his father
and another man in the crowd to help push the lifeboat over
the side. As the boat swung out Albert heard a sharp crack.
Either somebody had loosened one of the guys or it had
snapped under the strain. 'Stand back!' he yelled. But so fast
did the bow of the lifeboat spin inwards that it swept
passengers off the collapsible and slid forward to smash
against the superstructure of the bridge, crushing people in its
path.

Horrified, Albert turned to see the second boat, No. 4, also
out of control, come hurtling down the deck to smash against
the first boat. Pushing his way to the next boat, No. 6, he

found Anderson pleading with women and children to get out. Albert helped him clear the boat of passengers so they could push it over the side. Anderson then got the idea that if the tanks on the port side of the liner were flooded the list might be checked. 'Go to the bridge, Bestic,' he called. 'Tell them to trim the port tanks.'

Albert made his way for'ard again. Climbing the ladder, he hung onto the bridge rail and shouted Anderson's request to the Captain. But it was too late. The remaining crew members who could have trimmed the tanks were already on the boat deck. Although Turner had decided against launching the boats because of the headway of the liner and the tilt of the deck some crew members and passengers on the starboard refused to accept his decision. They now took matters into their own hands.

Convinced the liner could never recover her buoyancy, Leslie Morton ran to the starboard side. There's no hope for her now, he thought. From the feel of the planking beneath his feet he sensed the *Lusitania* was lost. Many of the seamen needed to launch the boats were lying dead, drowned in the baggage room he had left that afternoon to go on lookout. Although the starboard boats were in charge of First Officer Jones, Morton heard one of the other officers give the order to lower away.

The boats that had swung clear of the stricken liner were prevented from swinging further only by the snubbing chains that held them to the edge of the deck. Bolder passengers had jumped seven feet down into Morton's boat, No. 11. He helped women passengers across the gap until the order was given, 'Lower away!'

The heeling liner was sweeping in a giant semi-circle, still travelling through the water at about five knots. Morton at the stern davit and another seaman at the for'ard end let the falls run. The lifeboat dropped cleanly into the water. It fell back a boat's length, then came up alongside the listing liner, directly under the next lifeboat, No. 13, which was still in the davits.

Morton was about to swing himself over the side and go

down the ropes to push his lifeboat away from the liner's side when the falls on No. 13 gave way with a rush. The boat fell past him, its occupants screaming, onto No. 11. Hearing the terrible screams of the crushed, maimed and dying below him, all he could feel was a cold shock at the suddenness of death. He pushed through the desperate throng in search of his brother John at the for'ard boats. He saw people losing their hold on the deck, sliding down and over the side into the sea. He saw wives separated from their husbands and lifted into boats and children torn from their parents and handed over the heads of the crowd from seaman to seaman. The crescendo of pleading voices, as hundreds realised the liner was sinking too fast for them to get away, became a bizarre chorus to the death drama in the boats.

From his vantage point on the bridge ladder Bestic saw passengers climbing into the remaining portside boats and trying frantically to release the falls. Three more boats crashed onto the deck, careering towards the bodies and wreckage already piled against the superstructure. Sickened, he turned away from the carnage and went to rejoin the Staff Captain at No. 12 boat, the sixth boat from for'ard, which hung amidships. Anderson was in his shirt sleeves, grim-faced, almost unrecognisable as the sociable, good-humoured man who had presided at the Captain's table.

They manhandled No. 12 lifeboat over the side. It scraped and bumped its way down the protruding rivets of the hull until it seemed the sides would be ripped out before it reached the water. When it came level with the promenade deck the keel swung so far inboard it looked as if the boat would crash on the deck as the other five had done. It rocked dangerously as men on the promenade deck tried to climb aboard and those in the boat beat them off with oars. The struggle panicked the seaman at the stern davits into letting go the falls. The stern dropped swiftly and the passengers were toppled into the sea. For a few seconds No. 12 lifeboat hung precariously by the bow fall. Then the rope snapped and the boat bucketed down the rivets, crashing onto the passengers struggling for their lives in the water.

The sight of No. 12 lifeboat falling into the sea was too much for Isaac Lehmann. He rushed down to D deck, only to find that someone had already been to his stateroom and taken his life-jacket. For a moment he hesitated. Then he flung open his dress suitcase and took out his revolver. He thought, quite clearly, 'This will be useful if someone is doing the wrong thing.' On his way up to the boat deck he met his steward William Barnes. 'Get me a life-jacket, Barnes,' he ordered. Impatiently, he stood waiting until the steward returned and fastened on the jacket. Stepping onto the boat deck Lehmann encountered Purser McCubbin and the ship's surgeon. The two men looked at him quizzically. 'Please stay calm, Mr. Lehmann. There's no chance of her going down.'

Boat No. 14, with the businessman Charles Hill aboard, was pushed by Anderson and Bestic over the side. Hill sat in the bow wondering what had happened to the three Germans who had been arrested on the first day out of New York. There had been no further talk of them among the officers or crew. If they were locked in the ship's cells they were lost.

As the lifeboat passed the promenade deck five or six stokers helped push it away from the liner's side. Then the men at the davits lost control. The bow falls became fouled and the boat dropped almost vertically, tossing the passengers sitting near the stern into the sea. Hill was held in by his seat and, to his amazement, the boat finally hit the surface right side up. Water began pouring through the planking and, as people in the sea attempted to climb aboard, it capsized.

Three times it capsized, three times it righted itself, and each time Hill hauled himself back into the waterlogged boat. He began to laugh crazily at the absurdity of the situation, and seeing the ship's barber Lott Gadd taking charge of the boat, he laughed some more, thinking, 'I haven't paid him for my week's shaving.'

At 2.15 pm in Admiralty House at Queenstown Vice-Admiral

Sir Charles Coke received a message from the wireless station at Valentia: LUSITANIA IN DISTRESS OFF KINSALE BELIEVED SINKING. One minute later it was followed by a message from Corkbeg: INTERCEPT SOS FROM LUSITANIA WE THINK WE ARE OFF KINSALE.

Shaken, he ordered his driver to take him in the Admiralty car down the hilly streets to the Naval Pier. As he came downstairs his duty officer handed him a message from Galley Head: LUSITANIA TEN MILES SOUTH EAST APPARENTLY SINKING. Although he had worried about the *Lusitania*'s safety since the submarine sightings earlier in the week, he was not prepared for such a crisis.

The ageing *Juno*, which had been delayed by fog, had arrived in Queenstown harbour. Vice-Admiral Hood came ashore in a launch and he and Coke conferred rapidly about what should be done. Both agreed that the submarine risk to the *Juno* must be kept to a minimum; she was not an escort vessel, but if the *Lusitania* was in real distress Coke said the *Juno* must go to her at once. As the launch took Hood back to the cruiser Coke ordered every available craft to the rescue. His resources were meagre. The only vessels ready to sail were the tugs *Stormcock* and *Warrior* and the small examination steamer *Julia*. The trawlers *Ebro* and *Congo* and the armed yacht *Greta* were under repair in the dockyard; other craft were on patrol far from the *Lusitania*. Craft coaling in the harbour, including the trawlers *Brock*, *Bradford* and *Flying Fox* and three old torpedo boats, *050*, *052* and *055*, began to raise steam. Coke ordered torpedo boat commander R. W. Myburgh to warn the outer patrol to join in the rescue if signals failed to reach them from the coast stations. Then he ordered a message to be sent to the *Indian Empire*, the only vessel equipped with wireless, now about 50 miles from the *Lusitania*.

Deeply worried, but convinced he could do no more, Coke was driven back to Admiralty House. Another message had arrived from Corkbeg: FROM LUSITANIA COME AT ONCE BIG LIST PLEASE INFORM ADMIRAL. From his first floor balcony he could see the tugs *Stormcock* and *Warrior* leaving the harbour. The *Juno* was still getting up a full head of steam. He knew it would be hours before the first of his inadequate fleet of steam trawlers could hope to reach the great liner.

When Isaac Lehmann regained the portside boat deck he saw that lifeboat No. 16 was gone. It had ripped its planking along the ship's side and disintegrated as soon as it hit the water.

About forty people were standing on the canvas covers of the collapsible beneath No. 18 lifeboat, which was filled with people. A seaman was standing, axe in hand, as though waiting for orders. 'Why aren't you putting this boat into the water?' Lehmann shouted angrily at him. He could see the *Lusitania*'s bows was now almost submerged. 'Who has charge of this lifeboat?' he demanded.

The seaman with the axe muttered, 'The Captain has given orders not to launch any boats.'

'To hell with the Captain!' Lehmann yelled. 'Can't you see the ship is sinking?' The women in the lifeboat stared in terror as he pointed his revolver straight at the seaman. 'I will shoot to kill the first man who disobeys my order to launch this boat!'

At once the seaman swung the axe to release the pin. The lifeboat swung inboard, crushing the passengers on the collapsibles, smashing those standing on deck against the smoking room windows, then careering through the crowd aft to slide out of control towards the bridge superstructure.

Lehmann was flung to the deck. He lay there, hardly believing what had happened, unable to find his revolver. The runaway boat had killed most of the people on the collapsible; others were so maimed they could not move. He felt a sudden stabbing pain in his leg, and looked down to see blood pouring from it. He was badly injured. Slowly and painfully, as steaming water from the boilers cascaded over him, he began to crawl towards the rail.

Albert Martin was one of the few crew members who had

escaped from below decks. He stood handing out life-jackets and helping passengers put them on. He remained calm in the terrified crowd.

Desperation showed in the faces of many of the women as Norah Bretherton reached the portside boat deck carrying her baby. She climbed onto one of the collapsibles on the starboard side, pleading with the men around her to take her baby in the boat. She heard a man shout, 'Lower her. She's full.' A voice directed her, 'Get into the next boat.' Her friend Mrs. Secchi from New York, already in the boat, called to the men, 'Take this lady and her baby.'

Mrs. Bretherton caught sight of a passenger in the same boat who had been friendly to her boy during the voyage. 'You know my Paul,' she called to him. 'Will you get him from the cabin?' He looked at her without a hint of recognition in his eyes. In sudden panic she thrust her baby into a seaman's arms and ran down the stairs to D deck, falling from side to side on the swaying liner. Smoke was pouring up through the floor in the passageway, but she ran headlong into her cabin, snatched up her three-year-old son, and carried him back to the boat deck.

A number of pregnant women passengers were on board the *Lusitania*. The chaos on the decks was more terrifying for them; some had fallen and were unable to regain their feet. Margaret Cox had noticed them and been told they were on their way to join their husbands serving with the Canadian Army. She saw one pregnant mother among the crowds on deck trying to keep her three small children close to her. Her own baby Desmond was flung from her arms when she lost her footing on the tilting deck. She saw him tumbling towards the rails and fell to her hands and knees in her struggle to catch him.

Tossed about on the crowded tilting deck as she carried her baby, Charlotte Pye was in tears. 'Don't cry, lady,' a man called to her. 'It's all right.'

'No, it's not all right,' she sobbed. 'I haven't got a life-jacket.'

'I'll get you one,' he promised. But he returned without one. 'Here,' he urged her, 'take mine.'

He helped her into his jacket, tied the baby securely to her, and then led her to a lifeboat on the starboard side. Only by walking across two oars laid together could Mrs. Pye reach the boat from the rails of the liner. A crewman told her she would have to unstrap her baby to reach the lifeboat. She did so, and when she was in the boat her baby was handed to her.

Mabel Docherty was carrying her baby William on her left arm as she hauled herself up a slippery, swinging rope to the boat deck. The urgency of the moment banished her fear. As she made for the starboard boats an officer told her, 'There is no need to hurry, madam. Stay where you are. The ship is quite safe.' But she ignored him and climbed into a boat already filled with passengers.

A compulsion to run had seized businessman James Brooks. He raced around the decks, not knowing where he wanted to go. Past the crowded lifeboats on the starboard side, through the concert room to the Grand Entrance he ran on, keeping his balance by holding onto chairs and tables. But back on deck again he found he was calmer. Slowing his pace as he reached the bridge, he looked up to see Captain Turner, wearing a life-jacket, raise his hand. 'Don't lower any more boats,' Turner shouted. 'It's all right.' Brooks turned and walked aft again. As he passed a lifeboat he heard a crew member say, 'To hell with him. We'll damn well get this one away!'

An officer assured Belle Naish, 'She's all right. She'll float for an hour.' Gauging the widening angle between the deck rail and the horizon Mrs. Naish knew this simply wasn't true. 'We're sinking fast,' she told Theodore. 'It can't be long now.'

The couple continued helping passengers don their life-jackets correctly. One woman was persuaded to remove her fur coat before putting on her life-jacket. They tied another woman's life-jacket tapes securely, but could not persuade her to remove an enormous hat with a long floating veil. A woman in a heavy woollen coat with a large fur collar had strapped a child of about two years inside her life-jacket. 'If you want to save your child,' Theodore advised, 'you'd better take him out of that life-jacket, or else you'll both go down.'

'And you'd better take your coat off,' added Belle.

By now the wet deck on the port side was almost perpendicular. Jane McFarquhar thought there would be more chance of escape on the starboard side. 'We must get there or die,' she told herself. When they reached the other side her daughter lost her balance and slid helplessly down to the edge of the deck where only the iron rail prevented her from falling over. A steward called to Mrs. McFarquhar to go on. 'I'll look after her,' he said, helping Grace to her feet.

He led them from chair to chair through a first-class saloon until they reached the companionway leading to one of the lifeboats. 'Come right on,' an officer called to them. In front of them a lifeboat, filled with passengers, was suspended from the davits, but it hung about three feet from the side of the liner. Jane McFarquhar climbed onto the cover of the collapsible and, summoning her courage, made a spring, landing awkwardly in the open boat. A few seconds later her daughter was helped across the gap.

When they reached the boat deck the Sullivans heard Pat Callan calling their names. As soon as he caught sight of them he worked his arms like flails to make a place for them by a lifeboat, now almost level with the rails. He and Flor jumped in, expecting Julia to follow. But she wouldn't jump. Moving back into the crowd she cried that her husband must join her. Infuriated, Flor fought his way out of the boat, pushing past the passengers who were struggling to get in.

'I'm mad at you,' he yelled at her, trying to pull her back to the boat. But she stood her ground stubbornly. As the seamen lowered the boat, now packed with people, the long deck suddenly tilted further and Julia saw the lifeboat dropping by the bow. One of the falls had slipped and she saw the boat's occupants spilling like apples into the water.

Flor led her away from the crowds. He pulled the bundle of

Treasury notes from his hip pocket. Pushing the money into the bodice of her dress, he kissed her. 'Here, Julia,' he said softly. 'You can swim. You'll need this by and by.'

She was astonished. His farewell shook her out of her nightmare. 'Nonsense, Flor,' she said fiercely. 'Come on. We'll get away from this crowd. We'll find a place we can jump from.'

As lifeboat No. 17 on the starboard side emptied its occupants into the sea Lady Mackworth turned away. She did not want to look at such 'horrible things'. It had not occurred to her, nor to Howard Fisher or his sister-in-law, to attempt to get into a lifeboat themselves. The whitefaced stream of passengers rushing from one boat to another reminded her of a swarm of bees who had lost their queen. She could see no children. Could they survive in this crowd? Then she thought, though she regretted it immediately, 'Death would be better than to be part of this terror-infected mob.'

Howard Fisher decided to go below to fetch life-jackets for Dorothy and himself. While he was away a rumour swept the crowd that the danger was over and the liner was righting herself. The two women looked at each other and began to laugh with relief. 'You've had your thrill,' Margaret Mackworth said to the younger woman.

'And I never want another,' Dorothy answered.

But when Fisher returned carrying two life-jackets he looked shaken. He told them he had waded through deep water below to get them. The situation was worsening. Calmly, Margaret unhooked her skirt. She would drop it off where she stood so that it would not impede her in the water.

Running towards her father and brother on the third-class promenade, Elsie Hook spotted a wad of dollar bills which somebody had dropped on the deck. 'Look, Dad!' she cried, picking them up and thrusting them at her father.

'Throw them away,' he warned her. 'They may cost you your life.'

It was the girl's first intimation of real danger. She stood with her father and Frank by the starboard rail, her hands grasping the ledge, praying, 'Please God, save us.' Nearby two elderly women were clasping each other and crying. 'Don't worry,' Elsie told them. 'God will save you.'

*Kapitänleutnant Schwieger, his eyes still focussed on the incredible drama in the glass of his periscope, called again, 'Anybody who wants can take a look.'*

*He stood aside as Pilot Lanz gripped the handles and swivelled the periscope. The veteran merchant mariner knew of five passenger liners with four smokestacks sailing in these waters:* Britannic, Olympic, *(the sister ship of the* Titanic*),* Aquitania, Mauretania *and* Lusitania. *The* Mauretania *was transporting troops to the Dardanelles, and he quickly identified the sinking liner. 'Mein Gott,' he exclaimed, 'das ist die Lusitania!'*

*Excited cheering broke from the crew. Schwieger had received reports that the* Lusitania *was expected off the Irish coast at this time. The Cunard company publicised sailing departures in advance and Germany kept submarine commanders informed of the movements of Allied ships. He expressed no surprise at his pilot's identification; what astonished him was that his unreliable G torpedo had caused such devastation.*

*Oberleutnant Weisbach, who had been called from the torpedo room, stepped forward to the patrol periscope to view the stricken liner. She's going down so fast, he thought. Why is this? People were running wildly about the decks while lifeboats dangled grotesquely from the starboard side. As the smoke cleared he could make out the name* Lusitania *in large brass letters on the stern, letters which had been obliterated for wartime, but which were legible again as the sea and the weather wore the paint away. He stood back from the periscope and to the men standing around him in the control room among the tangle of wheels, pumps and diving machines, he exclaimed, 'She's sinking fast!'*

*It was Otto Rikowsky's turn to peer through the patrol*

*periscope. Awestruck, he watched the great liner settling slowly by the bow. Boats were capsizing halfway from the boat deck, tossing their occupants into the water. He saw people leaping overboard, desperate to escape. It's horrible, he thought. He did not want to look again.*

*Schwieger returned to his attack periscope. Like the others, he was fascinated by the sight. People were jumping from the sloping decks and attempting to swim to overturned boats. He could see no destroyers in sight. It would be safe to linger for a few minutes more. Usually he was exasperated when he missed the chance of sinking an enemy ship, and when a ship went down he and his crew shared in the triumph. Now, as he watched helpless women and children trapped on the* Lusitania, *his professional objectivity was shaken. But it was a feeling that passed quickly. He had been given to understand that Allied passenger ships were used to carry arms and contraband for the war. Firing a torpedo was his duty; yet he had not fired a second torpedo, as he often did to finish off a stricken vessel. In his diary he would write later, 'I could not have fired a second torpedo into those throngs of people on board trying to save themselves.'*

*As his men stepped up to look through the periscope they could hardly believe their eyes. Whenever they sank a destroyer or a cruiser they cheered and laughed. Now they stood in silence, incredulous that their G torpedo had wrought such chaos and destruction. Such a great liner should have taken hours to sink, allowing passengers and crew time to get away in the boats. Perhaps he asked himself if he should have given a warning before he attacked. But he knew that the* Lusitania's *wireless room would have sent messages to armed ships giving her exact location. It would have taken at least an hour to get the passengers and crew safely away, and by then other ships would have arrived at the scene and the U-20 would have been in real danger. Perhaps the* Lusitania, *if forewarned, would have zigzagged towards the coast, or steamed directly towards the U-20's periscope to ram the submarine. But if Schwieger had allowed the* Lusitania *to continue her voyage without attempting to attack he would have faced a disciplinary court on his return to Germany.*

*As the seconds ticked away glances were exchanged, but nothing was said. Voegele watched Schwieger, whose eyes were fixed on the periscope. Then without warning the silence was broken as Seaman Ulbricht spun round and, pulling a revolver from his pocket, pointed it at the Commander. Rikowsky, who understood Ulbricht's 'excitable temperament', lunged at the crewman and grabbed his wrist. 'Don't do that!' he warned him.*

*Schwieger seemed scarcely to notice what was happening. He turned briefly from the periscope and ordered, 'Take her down to 60 feet.'*

# 18

# THE LAST WAVE

THE *LUSITANIA* rolled further to starboard as passengers fought desperately to save themselves. Women cried, 'Don't leave us!' When crowded lifeboats could not take them they flung themselves into the sea. The cries from those in the lifts were stifled as water swept through the accommodation on B deck. drowning the trapped occupants.

As though indifferent to the pandemonium Charles Frohman stood with his friends by the sinking starboard rail. He went on smoking a cigar, his bland features betraying no hint of his real feelings. 'Hold on to the rail,' he suggested to Rita Jolivet. 'You will need to save your strength.'

Like a great wounded animal the *Lusitania* again lurched helplessly. Ignoring the terror around him, Frohman remarked, 'To die would be an awfully big adventure.' The words were not his own; he remembered them from a scene in *Peter Pan*, the play by Barrie. (The scene he had incorporated during the play's second run in New York was titled 'Marooner's Rock, or The Mermaid's Lagoon'.) Prevented by his arthritis from becoming a part of the struggling mass, the impresario faced the steadily rising waters like Barrie's character marooned by pirates on a rock in the sea; it was as though he was translating his personal catastrophe into a moment of theatre, himself the hero, the Germans the pirates. Unwilling to abandon him, Rita Jolivet, George Vernon and Alick Scott drew closer to their friend.

Dr. Fisher said to Dorothy Conner and Margaret Mackworth, 'I think we had better jump.' He and Dorothy moved towards a section of the deck from which a lifeboat had been launched and where there was no rail. Margaret followed them, nervous about jumping, but telling herself, 'How silly to be afraid of taking this one step when I am in such danger.' Looking down she saw the water sweeping over the planking and realised they were not now sixty feet above the sea, but already slipping under it.

Vanderbilt emerged from the Grand Entrance with his valet Ronald Denyer. A woman heard him order, 'Find all the kiddies you can.' She was surprised to see him hurrying to the lifeboats with two children in his arms. Dr. Owen Kennan, a first-class passenger from New York, also discovered the millionaire at his rescue work. Later, Vanderbilt's friend, Thomas Slidell saw him remove his life-jacket, place it on a young woman passenger, Alice Middleton, and walk away without a word. Like Frohman and Margaret Mackworth, Vanderbilt was making no attempt to get into a lifeboat. Even when confronted with death he could not bring himself to be part of this demented crowd: men of his standing were not supposed to panic.

When Charles Lauriat went through to the starboard side of the boat deck he was in no doubt that the *Lusitania* was about to make her final plunge. He saw women and children crammed into lifeboats which the men were trying to launch. It only added horror to a situation in which people were packed into boats which simply could not be cleared and would go down with the liner. Why not leave them on deck? he wondered. Why not let them take their chance with a piece of wreckage?

One of the crowded boats was floating flush with the rail; no one had succeeded in releasing it from the davits. Jumping into the stern Lauriat freed his end and swung the ropes clear. In the bow an inexperienced steward hacked frantically at the ropes with a pocket knife. Lauriat tried to reach him, but it was impossible to climb across the mass of people jammed among jars, water kegs, sails and rope ladders. A towering smokestack leaned over them as though about to crush the boat, 'It's hopeless,' Lauriat decided. 'He'll never clear the falls in time.' A blow on the back from the davit knocked him into the crowd. Steadying himself, he urged the women to get out and swim. But they sat petrified. He didn't wait, but jumped straight into the sea. Surfacing, he swam for about thirty yards and then turned to see the lifeboat being pulled down by the bow.

The only passenger to climb to the funnel deck was Oliver Bernard. Below him on the boat deck crazed people were running about to nowhere. A stoker reeled as though drunk, his face a black and scarlet smear, the crown of his head sliced open 'like a bloody sponge pudding'. Safe above the turmoil Bernard found the funnel deck another world. From where he stood the *Lusitania*, save for her starboard list and dipping bow, might have been lying peacefully at anchor in the sunshine off Kinsale, and the shrieks from the lower decks might have been laughter.

Bernard no longer doubted the fate of the liner. It was now a question of how many minutes more she could stay afloat. Some distance out, among the floating wreckage and drowning people, a man was swimming on his back, quite naked, paddling gently and looking up at the liner with a smile. Heartened by the sight, Bernard stood under the third funnel and began to remove some of his clothes. From habit he methodically folded his jacket, waistcoat, collar and tie and placed them at the base of the funnel. Then he put his tiepin in his trouser pocket. 'Death is close,' he thought. 'How insignificant everything seems in retrospect. All one's struggles, hopes and achievements will be wiped out in seconds.' He felt a profound sadness. 'What a fuss I've made about my life. It has amounted to nothing. When I'm dead everybody will say "How sad", and go on fussing until they come to their own silly end.'

He suddenly realised he wasn't alone. At the door of the Marconi room the chief electrician George Hutchinson was talking to the wireless operators. Bernard looked in to find

Robert Leith tapping out a last SOS: SEND HELP QUICKLY AM LISTING BADLY. It was 2.25 pm by the Marconi office clock.

Hutchinson remarked, 'There are plenty of boats around.'

So far as Bernard could see the horizon was empty. He shrugged. 'That doesn't interest me much. I can't swim a stroke.'

Donald McCormick, the young assistant operator, pushed a swivel chair out of the door towards him. 'Here's something for you to hang on to, sir.'

'I'm no good at working waterwheels either,' Bernard joked.

The men laughed as the chair went careering down the slanting deck to crash into the starboard rail. McCormick stepped out of the wireless room with a small camera. Kneeling on the deck he took a photograph of the sinking liner looking towards the bow.

Bernard decided it was time to go. Climbing over the stairway rail, he dropped feet first on to the boat deck with his back to the sea. His rubbersoled shoes gripped the wet planking securely. He recognised No. 11 lifeboat, which earlier he had seen empty its occupants into the sea, floating close to the edge of the deck, held to the liner by the tackle of a single davit. Now it was filling with other passengers, and Bernard helped David Thomas into the boat. He had time to be amused by the 'rather worried and puzzled expression' on the Welshman's face.

'We can beach her,' an officer assured Michael Byrne. The Irish businessman was amazed at such a remark. 'How can you when the engines are dead?' he asked. At that moment the water washed over the tops of his shoes. He dived off the boat deck and swam as fast as he could to get away from the liner. William McMillan Adams and his father sat in a crowded, waterlogged boat which had fallen from the bow davit. If only they could get it away from the liner, a seaman assured them, the boat would float. The father threw off his overcoat and worked feverishly to release the falls. But it was impossible. He shouted to his son, 'Jump!' The two men plunged over the side and swam away from the boat.

Sliding down the deck shipbuilder Fred Gauntlett grabbed a davit to save himself from falling into the sea. He steadied himself, then climbed over the rail and swung by the falls into an empty boat which nobody had attempted to lower. He was congratulating himself on his luck when the davits heeled over and carried him down with the boat.

Warren Pearl and his wife had spent the time since the torpedo struck losing and finding each other as they searched for their four children. Major Pearl had seen the vain efforts to lower the port boats, the passengers crushed to death as boats crashed inwards, the sudden forward plunge by the liner as the sea came rushing over the fo'c's'le head. Still, he continued his search. He did not know that on another part of the decks a seaman had snatched his son Stuart from nurse Alice Lines. The nurse tried to follow, but she was held back by crewmen as the boat was lowered from the davits. 'He's my boy!' she screamed hysterically. 'I must be with him!' She broke free from the men and flung herself over the rail. There had been no time to bind up her flowing hair which she usually wore in a bun; now its length was to save her life. As she floundered in the water, the baby secured around her neck in a shawl, a man grabbed her long hair and pulled her into the boat.

Theodate Pope and Edwin Friend had refused to be separated at the boats. With Theodate's maid they climbed down the port side of the exposed hull and stepped into the water. Dr. Houghton and Marie de Page took to the water together as it washed over their ankles on the starboard side. When the Belgian woman became entangled in floating ropes, the doctor tried to swim to her, but he was carried away from the liner. Josephine Brandell was lowered in a boat. The art dealer Edward Gorer had given her his life-jacket and her luncheon companion Max Schwarz had found her a place in the lifeboat. As the boat hit the water it capsized, but Josephine caught a deck chair as it floated past.

For those who held back from the lifeboats it was now too late for decisions. As Lady Allan clasped her daughters' hands, her maid and a Canadian passenger joined hands with them. Within minutes they were all dragged beneath the sea.

The least-known saloon passenger had sought desperately to reach the German prisoners below decks. Detective Inspector Pierpoint groped his way down the lopsided corridors only to be driven back by a sudden rush of water which swept him towards the stairway to the boat deck. By now he knew the men were lost.

When Ernest Cowper returned with a life-jacket to the second-class promenade deck he found little Helen Smith waiting patiently for him. 'You came back to me,' she exclaimed, 'just like you said you would!' He caught her up in his arms and carried her along the boat deck to a lifeboat which was hanging so far from the starboard side that he had to throw her into the crowd. He jumped in to join her, and helped to push the boat away from the liner's side as the boatswain managed to cut through the lashing on deck with a knife.

Ian Stoughton Holbourn placed Avis Dolphin in a starboard boat with Hilda Ellis and Sarah Smith. The girl and her nurses were trying to find themselves a seat when two men landed heavily in the boat, freeing the falls and toppling everybody into the sea. It seemed to Avis that she was being held by some force beneath the water before she came to the surface. As she floated in her bulky life-jacket her tinted glasses caught in the threads of her woollen cardigan. She brushed them off and let them drift away. She didn't think she would need them again. Holbourn had tucked his precious manuscript into his life-jacket before diving into the water. When he saw Avis Dolphin's boat swamp and capsize he was seized with dread. He tried to swim to the boat, but it was impossible to reach it through the mass of bodies and wreckage.

Nobody offered to help Norah Bretherton as she rushed along the starboard boat deck, dragging Paul with her. Neither did anyone offer to help a woman and baby who fell and slid down the wet deck. Norah pushed through the crowd searching vainly for a place in two of the lifeboats before an officer helped her into a third boat. Looking around her, she was surprised to find more men than women in the boat.

Julia and Flor Sullivan slithered down the slanting deck to the starboard side. Water was lapping over the edge of the deck and Julia saw passengers throwing wooden gratings, deckchairs and tables into the sea to use as rafts. A little man with a shiny leather briefcase strapped to his life-jacket sidled up to the wealthier women. Julia heard him cajole a woman near her, 'Look, lady, I'm from the Bank of New York. You can entrust all your valuables safely to me. I'll give you a signed receipt on the bank's official form.' The woman ignored him, so he moved to the next likely passenger. He didn't waste a second look on Julia as she and Flor held hands and slipped towards the edge. Together they landed in the water, feet first. As they surfaced Julia called to Flor, 'Hold on to me.' He clung to her lifejacket as she struck out, swimming powerfully through the crowd and away from the ship.

Lucy Taylor, very much in love, steadfastly refused to be separated from her husband, weeping, 'I won't go, I won't go.' Harold pulled himself from her fierce embrace and dropped her into a starboard boat. She tried to climb back to him, but the boat fell quickly astern. He had no life-jacket and could not swim. It seemed useless to jump, so he stood at the rail waiting for the end. Lucy could see him from the boat as the *Lusitania*'s starboard deck sank deeper into the water. She gestured wildly to him, convinced they would never meet again.

George Hook persuaded his two children to stay away from the crowded boats and jump into the sea with him. Their shipboard friends Jack Walsh and Gerda Nielson had pledged themselves to 'sink or swim together'. When Walsh saw his fiancée flung from the lifeboat in which he had placed her he climbed onto the rail and dived in, determined to swim to her. Mary Maycock decided to climb as high as she could. With no life-jacket and wearing her high-buttoned shoes she hauled herself slowly up the steel ladder leading to the top of the fourth funnel. She told herself, 'This will be the last part of the ship to go under.'

Apparently indifferent to the danger, some passengers at first made no attempt to leave the liner. Martin Mannion, a curly-haired lad with a lame foot, made for the bar. 'Let's die game,' he called to the startled barman who ignored him and ran out onto the deck. Unperturbed, Mannion weaved his way through the upturned chairs, crossing the tilting floor strewn with small change that had fallen from the till, and uncorked a bottle of beer.

Soren Sorensen was still playing poker and drinking whiskey with a group of other young men in the second-class saloon when the liner lurched heavily, as though about to go under. Sorensen looked at his hand. He held a pair of kings back to back. 'Ten dollars on the last card,' he called. Only one player accepted the challenge: the rest scrambled on deck. His opponent threw down an ace in the hole. 'If only I'd quit before now,' Sorensen thought, 'I'd be 35 dollars ahead.'

Margaret Cox met one of the card players on deck, a young man in a tweed suit. To her surprise he put his arm round her and pulled her close, whispering: 'Think of the One above and hold on.' She was astonished. This young gambler had given her a rule for life.

Leslie Morton found his brother at No. 1 lifeboat at the for'ard end of the boat deck. He took over the after-fall and he and John lowered the crowded boat into the water. As they pushed off with boathooks passengers clung tenaciously to lengths of rope dangling from the rails which were level with the water, believing they would be safer hanging on to the liner than entrusting themselves to a small boat. Leslie shouted angrily, 'Let go!' But they weren't listening. As the liner heeled further, as though settling for her final plunge, John yelled, 'I'm going over the side, Les.' His brother called back at him, 'So am I,' and took the water in a clean shallow dive from the outboard side of the lifeboat.

He surfaced, gulping in air, and looked around for John, recalling that his brother had never learned to swim. It was difficult to see beyond the corpses and the wreckage, so he put his head down and struck out with a double trudgeon to get clear of the debris. Fireman John O'Connell had also dived into the sea. Assistant Cook George Wynne had managed to get into a lifeboat, but he looked in vain for his father.

Bellboy William Holton had been helping to lower No. 7 lifeboat when he saw the liner's great stern rise ominously into the sky. 'Och, but they can't sink a Clyde-built ship,' he heard an engineer boasting. 'Oh, but they can,' thought Holton. An officer snapped at him, 'Boy, where is your life-jacket?' In the excitement Holton had forgotten about it, and now it was too late to return to his stern quarters. Remembering that a number of saloon cabins had not been occupied during the voyage he made for the nearest cabin and took down a jacket from the wardrobe. As he stepped out a frenzied passenger snatched it from him, pushing him back through the doorway. The bellboy slid down the sloping floor under a bunk. Startled, he managed to find another life-jacket and went on deck again.

The starboard side had dipped to the rails. The giant funnels seemed about to topple over. Fastening on the life-jacket Holton dived into the water and swam strongly around the liner under the bridge to the port side. Above him he could see Captain Turner on the bridge wing. He thought, 'I bet the Old Man's going down with his ship.'

Hugh Johnston had been singing out the degree of list to starboard as he watched the indicator swing beneath the compass. 'Eighteen! . . Nineteen! . . Twenty! . .' It seemed pointless to continue. The port windows of the wheelhouse were tilting towards the sky. He read the worst in Turner's face – for Turner had arrived at that moment all Captains dread, the moment, traditionally, when he must go down with his ship.

Water lapped over the starboard wing of the bridge and splashed onto the planking. Turner pulled himself uphill to the port wing. He remembered two possessions now swamped in his cabin: his favourite sextant and the new bowler which

Mabel Every had bought him.

Johnston thought, 'He's as cool as a cucumber.' The indicator was swinging wildly out of control. He looked at his Captain in desperation. 'All right, lad,' Turner called to him, the gruffness gone from his voice. 'Save yourself.' Stepping from the starboard bridge wing Johnston found himself in the sea.

It was just 2.28 pm.

As though by a common impulse Charles Frohman and his companions Rita Jolivet, George Vernon and Alick Scott suddenly joined hands. Frohman began to speak Barrie's line again, 'To die would . . .' He had not finished the quotation when a green cliff of water, carrying a monstrous tide of dead and debris, came thundering down the deck and swept the four friends apart.

The same terrible wave carried Margaret Mackworth into the sea. She had seen the water rising to her knees and after the wave struck she remembered nothing until she was sucked under. Isaac Lehmann was dragging himself painfully across the deck when the wave came, burying him in the sea. It came without warning to Belle Naish as she helped a woman put on a life-jacket; hearing a 'roar and a splintering sound' she threw up her left hand as though to ward off a blow and found the water up to her waist; it felt dreadfully cold when it rose to her shoulders. Then the water pushed her upward and forward until she found herself resting on the pillow of her life-jacket, thinking, 'How beautiful the sunlight and water are from under the surface.' She felt a bump against her head. She put up her hand, saw the blue sky, and found herself clinging to the lifeline of lifeboat No. 22.

As the wave raced up from the vanished fo'c's'le Captain Turner felt the water swirling around his legs. Ramming his Commodore's cap firmly on his head he began to climb the ladder to the halyards, reaching confidently for the rigging as he had done in his sailing days. More than a hundred yards away in the stern he could see people clinging to the decks as to an illusory island of refuge. He felt he was hanging in air, his ship trembling beneath him as if resisting her approaching death. He grabbed a floating oar as the *Lusitania*, her smokestacks almost horizontal, quivered her entire length. He let go the oar, grabbed a chair and held onto it.

Albert Bestic was working at the last of the starboard boats when the roaring sound made him turn to see the wave thundering up the boat deck carrying the wreckage of boats and people on its crest. He flung himself over the side, knowing that if this all-engulfing tide reached him he was lost. He swam as fast and as far as he could, exultant at having cheated the killer wave. He was not expecting the whirlpool that swept him into its vortex, spinning and twisting and turning him over and over. The green turned to darkness and he gave up the struggle. To try to swim was as futile as attempting to climb a waterfall. A rumble sounded in his ears, the water became brighter — he was rising again. Working his arms and legs strongly, he pushed upwards for what seemed minutes before breaking the surface and gulping air in his bursting lungs. It was then he heard a heart-rending wail 'like the despair, anguish and terror of hundreds of souls passing into eternity'.

Charles Lauriat heard 'a long, lingering moan as though the lost were calling from the very depths'. Dr. Carl Foss heard the death wail, 'increasing and growing' as he swam from the liner. He could see the propellers and rudders plainly visible as the liner went into a slow dive by the head. He saw a man dangling from a rope as a revolving propeller hacked off his leg. Hundreds had climbed like trippers on a mountain top to the stern decks. The sight of people clinging desperately to anything that offered a handhold while others fell from the decks into the sea as the stern reared up was 'fantastic and terrifying'. Foss heard an explosion as a boiler blew away a funnel. Steam and smoke poured anew from the liner as the funnel grazed survivors in a waterlogged lifeboat, the stays lashing them amidships.

Two of the huge smokestacks fell forward and aft of the boat in which Mabel Docherty sat with her baby daughter, sweeping the loosely-tied bonnet off the infant's head and covering her with soot. As the smokestacks hit the surface the sea rushed into their openings, as wide as railway tunnels, and those who were floating nearby were sucked through. Margaret Gwyer, the bride of the young clergyman from Edmonton, had started swimming as soon as the boat deck sank in the water, but within seconds she was drawn head first by an inrush of water into the mouth of one of the funnels. The survivors in Mabel Docherty's boat were appalled, and then amazed to see her spewed out again, black with soot. Detective Inspector Pierpoint was also swallowed by a funnel and, just as surprisingly, swept out again by a mixture of escaping air and black water.

The liner's keel upended the boat in which George Kessler and some thirty stokers and passengers sat and tossed them into the water. Kessler reckoned that, despite his life-jacket, he sank to twenty feet before rising to the surface. Charles Lauriat saw the liner settling along her entire length, certain that all the portholes, even those as far down as E deck, were open. When she was almost submerged along her total length the *Lusitania* began to turn over as though righting herself. Then William Holton saw her give a final shudder and slide, almost perpendicular, beneath the surface to hit the bottom of the sea bed, 300 feet below, with a roar like thunder, 'as though the innards of the ship had broken loose'. To James Brooks it sounded like 'the collapse of a great building on fire'. Hundreds who were dragged into that vortex never rose to the surface, yet the sea was black with the figures of struggling people.

Drawing a choking breath Albert Bestic wondered why, although he had surfaced, he couldn't see. Raising an arm he touched the wooden seat of an upturned boat. He was trapped. His heart began thundering with sledgehammer blows. He must make a last effort to free himself. Reaching down he grasped the gunwale and pulled himself under the water again and clear of the boat. A hand caught him by the collar of his uniform and he was dragged across the keel. Slowly he raised his head to see a vast white ring sparkling on the surface in the afternoon sunlight. Within and around this ring a tangle of floating bodies and wreckage was covering the *Lusitania*'s grave.

It was exactly 18 minutes since the torpedo had struck.

# 19

# RING OF FOAM

WESLEY FROST, the United States Consul at Queenstown, was at his desk in his office on the floor above O'Reilly's grocery and bar, revising his annual commercial report on conditions in Cork and adjoining counties. The news that morning of German submarines sighted off the coast had not alarmed him; he did not believe the Germans were equal to the task of sinking a liner the size of the *Lusitania*. It was just after 2.30 pm by his office clock when he heard the footsteps of Lewis Thompson, his Vice-Consul, hurrying up the narrow stairs.

Thompson burst into the room. 'There's a wildfire rumour in the town that the *Lusitania* has been attacked.'

Frost stared at him in amazement. 'Are you quite sure?'

'Quite sure.'

The Consul stepped to the window. In the harbour across Scott's Square he saw tugs steaming from the quay. He crossed to the desk and telephoned Lieutenant Norcock, secretary to Vice-Admiral Coke, at Admiralty House. Almost apologetically, he said, 'I hear there's some sort of street rumour that the *Lusitania* has been attacked.'

'It's no rumour, Mr. Frost,' Norcock replied. 'We fear she has gone.'

He listened mechanically as Norcock told him of the *Lusitania*'s distress calls and the telephoned confirmation by watchers off the coast near Kinsale. Frost hung up like a man in a dream. He started up and for ten minutes paced the floor trying to adjust his mind to the disaster, turning over the

235

possible ways in which he could help. He decided to send Thompson to the post office to telegraph the news to Consul General Skinner and Ambassador Page in London. Then he went down to the Munster and Leinster Bank where he drew out his deposit in gold and borrowed an additional $1000.

Most of the survivors would probably be landed at the harbour nearest to the sinking, so he gave $500 to Thompson and sent him by car to Kinsale, eighteen miles away. Then he telegraphed London to explain that as none of the rescue craft had wireless there could be no further news until they returned. He estimated that the first survivors would be arriving at Queenstown, some 23 miles from where the *Lusitania* was reported to have gone down, at about seven o'clock. Those few hours would give Cunard manager J. J. Murphy and himself time to organise hotels, lodging houses and clothing shops. Finally he sent a telegram direct to Secretary of State William Bryan in Washington:

LUSITANIA SUNK 2.30 TODAY PROBABLY MANY SURVIVORS RESCUE WORK ENERGETICALLY PRO-CEEDING SHALL I CABLE LIST OF SURVIVORS

From the vantage point of his trellised balcony Vice-Admiral Coke saw the trawlers *Brock* and *Bradford* stop coaling and steam from the quay towards the harbour mouth. They were followed by the *Flying Fox* and *Golden Effort* and the three torpedo boats. When the final message from Kinsale, LUSITANIA SUNK, reached him at 2.41 he decided to recall the *Juno*.

The cruiser had slipped her moorings and was already through the harbour mouth and close to Roches Point when he wirelessed her to turn back. The smaller craft would pick up the survivors. The *Lusitania* had gone and he did not want his ageing cruiser to fall yet another victim to the merciless U-boats.

Shortly before three pm in Whitehall Lord Fisher and Admiral Oliver were informed of the sinking.

Oliver was visibly shaken, Fisher was curiously subdued, as though he could not bring himself to accept the full import of the news. Coke reassured them he was doing his utmost to organise the rescue operations.

Winston Churchill, the First Lord, was motoring from Paris to St. Omer, not far from Calais. When he reached Sir John French's headquarters he was handed a telegram from General Sir Ian Hamilton in the Dardanelles informing him that a full-scale battle was raging. It was not until later that he learned of the sinking of the *Lusitania*. Although his mind was occupied with ground battles, he would say in hindsight that he understood the significance of what had happened off Kinsale. An unlimited U-boat war would prove, in his estimation, the cause of Germany's ruin and arm the friends of the Allies in the United States with a weapon against which German influence would be powerless. Nevertheless on this afternoon of 7 May the military-minded First Lord did not think it necessary to return to England and the Admiralty. Sir John French had briefed him on the attack planned in conjunction with the French against the German lines at daybreak on Sunday. The First Lord wanted to stay on to see the fighting.

At Whitehall, however, Admiral Oliver was concerned that Churchill should prepare a special statement on the sinking of the Cunarder. He must placate public opinion, and he must also sympathise with the United States.

In his office on the Cunard Quay at Queenstown J. J. Murphy was not prepared for a disaster of such magnitude. Since the outbreak of war few liners had called at the port as part of their schedule and he was managing his office with a reduced staff of three clerks.

At 3.25 pm he sent his first telegram to Cunard in Liverpool, informing them that the *Lusitania* had been sunk. He followed this with a second cable giving the approximate time and position of the sinking. At four pm he cabled Liverpool with the news from Admiralty House that the *Lusitania* had gone down off the Old Head of Kinsale. He concluded: NO INTELLIGENCE AS TO CREW OR PASSENGERS. Because of the scrutiny of telegraphs by the Admiralty censor the first telegram sent by Murphy from Queenstown did not reach Liverpool until five pm.

At the other end of the town Otto Humbert, the German owner of the 120-room Queen's Hotel, was sifting through a bundle of postcards, each with its halfpenny stamp, on which clients stated their room requirements and time of arrival. The town's leading hotel, which faced the grand harbour opposite the band promenade and saluting cannon and the landing stages, offered special weekend terms at eighteen shillings. The brochure informed guests that their baggage would be conveyed free of charge from steamer or train to the hotel. Visitors arriving by sea were encouraged to look out for the electric beacon on the rooftop which indicated the hotel's position after dark. On Saturday nights a string orchestra played for guests in the ballroom which also served as a banqueting hall for 400 diners.

Humbert looked up from his desk to see crowds gathering along the promenade quay and craft moving out of the harbour. When the news was brought to him he was stunned. For more than twenty years he had been running his hotel, with well-to-do travellers as his main clientele, and he had grown prosperous on the liner trade. The war had reduced his business, but nothing so terrible had happened in Queenstown as this sinking of the great Cunard liner.

He went down the broad staircase from his office to the entrance hall. He must arrange rooms for the survivors and inform the string orchestra that they need not play that evening.

*At 3.15 pm Kapitänleutnant Schwieger ordered his U-20 to thirty feet. Through the periscope he could see in the distance, aft of the submarine, a number of drifting lifeboats. The* Lusitania *had gone. 'Nothing can be seen any more,' he noted in his log. Fourteen miles away the Old Head lighthouse was clearly visible in the afternoon sun. The navigator worked out the approximate position of the wreck: Latitude 51°, 22 minutes, six seconds North, longitude 8°, 34 minutes West.*

*It was time to resume the journey home to Germany.*

His life-jacket fastened securely, Turner drifted slowly away, still clutching the chair. Around him the upturned faces of corpses showed white in the sun. A man rose gasping to the surface and then sank again. As the ship went down, Turner saw the water hump up like a hill above which hung, momentarily, huge globules of white foam; then it flattened out, carrying him away. Seagulls swooped down as though to attack him, but he beat them off with his arm and they wheeled away to drop on the floating corpses.

Albert Bestic had been staring at the great ring of foam when people reached out and grabbed at the capsized boat across which he lay. Fearing that it would be swamped, he slid back into the water. He had no life-jacket and he regretted not having taken off his shoes. He began to swim a slow trudgeon stroke in the direction of land without any real hope of reaching it. Soon he had lost all sense of time and imagined he was a boy again, watching the new four-funnelled liner steaming past a background of warehouses and shipyards. 'Look, lad, yon's the *Lusitania* awa' on her trials.' A wave slipped over his head leaving him spluttering. Was it the wave from the *Lusitania* tumbling across the deck of his apprentice sailing ship? He thought, 'Perhaps it has washed me overboard and that's why I'm swimming . . .' His head bumped against a hard object, his fingers encountered the gunwale of a boat, only an inch or so above the surface. It was stove in, but he knew it could mean the difference between living and drowning. He tested her cautiously with his weight before dragging himself slowly over the gunwale to lie back exhausted in the stern sheets.

Half his body was in the water, but nothing could spoil the

comforting sensation of a solid support against his back. He closed his eyes with relief, letting the afternoon sun revive him. 'Thank you Lord, for saving my life.' He felt the water rising and, dragging himself into a sitting position, saw that his refuge was sinking after all. The possibility of having to swim again filled him with dread. He looked around the wreckage in the water and spotted four watertight tanks, their copper sides reflecting the sun, floating some yards away. He paddled towards them and managed to secure three of them under the thwarts. Working to get the fourth into position he found a bucket tied beneath the thwart. The discovery was almost too good to be true. Five minutes bailing and he was gaining on the water.

As the level fell he noticed that one of the planks had been sprung. With his knife and handkerchief he was able to caulk the leak. Things were looking up. Pausing in his work he saw a man swimming blindly, just as he had been doing, a few yards away. Albert stood up and shouted, waving his arms. The swimmer altered direction towards him and was soon lying gasping in the stern sheets. He was a dark-haired young man who seemed fit despite his violent shivering. 'Thanks, old chap,' he stammered at length. 'I suppose it's no use asking you for a cigarette.'

'Sorry,' Albert told him ruefully. 'Mine have gone rather soggy.'

If they could get enough water out of the boat they could look for other survivors. 'Can you row?' he asked.

'Bank Holiday fashion,' the stranger answered. 'But let me have a go with that bucket. It'll warm me up.'

Taking turns the two men bailed, laughing inanely as though in a secure but artificial world. When the boat was lightened enough for them to paddle seawards they found the body of a young girl. Her life-jacket had not been properly adjusted and she hung face downwards in the water. Further on they saw a woman floating in a life-jacket, her grey eyes staring transfixed at them. She made no cry for help and seemed indifferent whether they saved her or not. It took both of them to lift her, in her heavy, sodden garments, into the boat. She asked mechanically, 'Where is my baby?'

'I'm sorry,' Albert replied. 'We haven't seen any babies.'

The woman moaned despairingly and threw herself into the water again. Albert was aghast. His companion grabbed her, shouting, 'Your baby is safe. I saw it taken into another boat.'

Albert swore quietly. Why hadn't he thought of lying? The woman let herself be pulled into the boat again. They picked up a dozen more survivors, after which they could risk no more. Despite their bailing and the temporary caulking, the water continued to rise. Soon the boat was so heavy they could row no further.

Fireman John O'Connell hung on to a wooden plank and began to drift among the wreckage. Two men swam up and joined him. A lifeboat passed and he was hauled into it. He heard survivors moaning and crying. It was so crowded the injured could not move. George Wynne pulled himself into a lifeboat, but it soon capsized and he was thrown into the sea again. He hung on determinedly to a lifeline. Hugh Johnston swam from the sinking liner, barely escaping ventilators, stay wires and valveheads as he made for a lifeboat. William Holton had learned to take care of himself in the water. But the Atlantic is cold in May and he knew his enemy was exposure. He kicked off his shoes for easier swimming, but soon gave up; there was nowhere to go. A man swam slowly past him, pushing an open life-jacket before him on which lay a small child. Others floated around him, some living, some dead. He began swimming again to keep warm and spotted a large wooden kennel. He hauled himself on to it, thankful to be out of the water. Three other men also swam to it and clambered on, but the kennel capsized. They hung on until one by one they lost their grip and floated away.

Soon Holton was numb in mind and body with the cold. As the afternoon wore on he lost consciousness.

Swimming among the bodies Charles Lauriat helped those he could by pushing pieces of wreckage towards them. A short distance away he saw a collapsible lifeboat floating right side up, and swam to it. He reached it at the same time as Leslie Morton. 'Charles!' He heard his name called and turned to see the shipbuilder Fred Gauntlett. He and Morton helped Gauntlett into the boat and the three men got out their pocket knives and performed a 'can-opening operation', slicing off the canvas cover.

The collapsible was a flat-bottomed, watertight raft floating almost flush with the water. To make it a real boat they had to raise the canvas sides and lash them into place. Gauntlett then helped his friend Samuel Knox on board. James Brooks also swam to the collapsible and climbed aboard. Soon there were more than thirty people in the boat. As they rowed towards the shore Lauriat, at the steering oar, thought, 'At least we have a good crew.'

Other collapsibles fared badly. The one into which George Kessler was helped had eight men, six of them stokers, and was half-filled with water. Although they bailed rapidly they could not get the water out of the boat fast enough and the collapsible sank beneath them. They managed to right the craft, and began bailing, only to have it capsize again. Kessler lost track of the number of times this happened. He had ceased to think about his plight and was acting instinctively.

Margaret Mackworth had grasped a short piece of wood. In her life-jacket she floated among bodies and debris packed so closely together that there was no water noticeable between them. She saw a whitefaced man with a yellow moustache grasp the other end of her board, which was little more than three feet long, and start inching his way around to her side. He frightened her. She forced herself to speak. 'We must be careful,' she said as firmly as she could, 'to keep this board balanced.' He made no reply, but moved away. Nothing would induce her to let go of the board.

As she floated, her legs bitterly cold, she wondered if this was a nightmare from which she would soon awake. Lifting her face to the sun and the pale blue sky, she wondered, 'Have I reached heaven without knowing it?' She looked around her and noticed that the island of people had drifted some distance from the wreckage. A swell had got up and she realised she was a hundred yards away from any other person. She longed for unconsciousness, and within moments she had her wish.

William McMillan Adams found himself in the water after the rear mast of the *Lusitania* crashed down on his collapsible, slicing through it as though it were paper. Under the water he held his breath, remembering that some of the passengers on the *Titanic* had gone down with the liner and had survived. He surfaced, his lungs bursting, found himself a spar and hung on to it. The wreckage was tossing about dangerously in the swell and he decided to swim away from the area. It seemed about an hour before he was helped onto an overturned collapsible.

When Belle Naish found herself clinging to No. 22 lifeboat a man reached down to her saying, 'Give me your hand. My back is hurt. But I'll do what I can.'

'I can hold on,' Belle told him. 'Take somebody else.'

'Come on,' he said. 'There's no one else I can reach.'

She gave him her hand, fearing her weight might overturn the boat and drag those already saved into the water. But he hauled her safely on board, cold and shivering. When Belle got her breath back she remembered that deep intakes of air sharply expelled keep a person warm in cold weather. She suggested they all try it, which they did. Then she informed them it was through divine providence they had been shipwrecked on a clear day with a calm sea, a soft breeze and the sun on their backs.

One man took out his mouth organ and began to play. Cyril Wallace, on his way to Northumberland to join the Army, had bought the mouth organ in Cleveland and could manage even the bass notes. Belle realised he was playing to cheer up the other survivors, but somebody asked, 'Don't you think you should stop playing? Otherwise we won't hear any cries for help?' Wallace replaced the instrument in his pocket. But from another boat they could hear the voices of the survivors of the Welsh choir. Dewi Michael, Gwynn Jones and the pianist Spencer Hill had improvised a raft by stringing together a couple of capsized boats with ropes. With another Welsh survivor, Tom Williams, they sang 'Praise God From Whom All Blessings Flow'. Their resonant voices echoed across the water, and Spencer Hill thought they had never sung the hymn with such feeling. Then they noticed some of the women weeping openly, so they sang, 'Pull For the Shore, Sailor' and people laughed.

In a nearby boat Margaret Cox, holding her boy close to her, remembered her only prayer had been in the moment of greatest danger; as the funnels were about to crash down on them she had begged, 'Oh, God, if I've got to die, let me die in the water.' In another boat Charlotte Pye sat grief-stricken. She had lost her baby. In the liner's final plunge Marjorie had been swept from her arms, and by then she was sure the child was already dead.

Ian Stoughton Holbourn had made for the nearest boat, intending to hold on to it, and took with him a man who was floating. When they reached the boat the man appeared to be dead and the sailors refused to take him in. Holbourn flung his manuscript, pages of which had been washed away, into the lifeboat and held onto a line which was trailing from the stern. More people were rescued and packed into the crowded boat but he could not be sure, as he was towed through the cold water, if they were making progress. 'Are we getting nearer?' he asked. 'Just another five minutes,' they told him. But he was becoming numb and exhausted.

Some of those alone in the water still clung tenaciously to life. Mary Maycock, unable to understand why she hadn't been sucked into the funnel to which she had clung, begged a man wearing a life-jacket and holding a piece of driftwood, 'Will you let me have that wood?' He pushed it towards her and she managed to climb on to it and crouch on its narrow width on her elbows and knees.

Young William Holt had been so close to a funnel when it crashed into the water beside him that when he put his hand out he could feel the rivets. As the liner disappeared he caught an oar; he was such a good swimmer that, after a while, he let go the oar and began stroking strongly again. A man wearing a life-jacket caught hold of him, but he pushed him off and kept swimming.

Alice Middleton, the young nurse who had accepted the life-jacket from Vanderbilt, floated among the bodies, many of them children. A woman screamed as she struggled to give birth to her baby in the water. Alice cried at the sight; even as a nurse she had never seen anything so terrible. Unable to help, she lay back in her life-jacket, sick and horrified, and drifted into unconsciousness.

The crew of the *Wanderer of Peel*, a Manx lugger of 20 tons, had caught about 800 mackerel when Skipper William Ball decided that rather than lose the rest of the day by returning to Kinsale they should put to sea again for another haul.

Ball and four of his crew had gone to their bunks after the day's work, leaving Tom Woods at the wheel. Woods had sent the boy below to brew a mug of tea when he suddenly saw a liner in distress on the horizon. He shouted the alarm and the rest of the crew tumbled on deck just in time to see the vessel going down bows first. None of them knew it was the *Lusitania*, but her four smokestacks meant she was one of the big liners. She was about three miles south east of them.

'Go for her,' skipper Ball told Woods.

They reached the first lifeboats a quarter of a mile from where the liner had gone down. They were appalled at the condition of the survivors, many of them naked. From the first two boats they took more than one hundred people on board. Two other boats were taken in tow. Several survivors had broken arms and legs; one man was dead. The *Wanderer*'s crew handed out jackets, trousers, waistcoats and oilskins, and plied the conscious with tea and their remaining bottle of whiskey. So crammed was the lugger that James Brooks had to sit with his legs over the side.

# 20

# THE *BLUEBELL*

JOHN ROPER, a seaman from the *Lusitania*, had been picked up by the *Bluebell*, a small steamer patrolling between Kinsale and Ballycotton. He was helping the crew rescue other survivors when he caught a glint of gold braid in the water. He called to his skipper, 'There's a ship's officer!' As the steamer manoeuvred close to the man crew members leaned over and hauled him in. He seemed exhausted and in shock.

'Who have we here?' Captain John Thompson asked.

'Captain Turner of the *Lusitania*.' The voice was almost inaudible.

Thompson took the man's hand. 'My sympathy, sir,' he said. He led him down to the mess room and draped a blanket around his shaking shoulders. The only other survivor to recognise him was George Kessler, whose bruised legs had been bandaged by Captain Thompson. Kessler had been taken from a boat in which nine men lay dead in the bilge water. He looked at Turner, a Captain without a ship, and saw his face was shrouded in despair.

'Look, another!' shouted a lookout.

A wicker chair was floating past with a young woman in it. Using a boathook a crewman pulled the chair alongside. More hands hauled it on board. 'I think there's some life in her,' Thompson said. Others were less sure and she was laid on deck among the dead to avoid overcrowding in the cabin.

When Margaret Mackworth came to she found herself naked between blankets. Her entire body was shaking violently and she felt a stabbing pain in the small of her back. She

246

opened her eyes to see a sailor staring into her face. 'That's better,' he said reassuringly. She was annoyed that an unknown sailor should be tending her instead of her own stewardess. The sailor asked her name. She tried to tell him, but her teeth were chattering. Gradually memory returned. She wasn't on the *Lusitania* after all; she was lying on the deck of some little steamer and she had no idea how long she had been there. 'I am Lady Mackworth,' she managed to say.

'I think you had better go below, madam,' he suggested. 'It'll be warmer. We left you here 'cos we thought you were dead.'

When she heard them discussing how to get her down the stairs, she said, 'I think I can walk.' Two sailors supported her on either arm, a third held back her long dripping hair as she stumbled below. They placed her on the captain's bunk, and with the sudden warmth her shivering ceased. Lying back against the pillow she counted about thirty people in the cabin, all talking in excited voices, clearly overjoyed to be alive. She noticed one woman sitting silently in the outer cabin, not joining in the chatter. When she finally spoke it was in a monotonous voice. She recounted how she had lost her child: told to place him in a raft, it had capsized. 'My child's death was not necessary,' she said bitterly. 'It was due to the lack of discipline and organisation aboard your ship.' The woman was addressing her accusation to the man who sat huddled in a blanket, Captain Turner. A sailor who brought her a cup of tea whispered, 'I'm sorry, I'm afraid that lady is hysterical.' Fresh from the chaos on the *Lusitania*'s decks Margaret thought, 'On the contrary, that woman is the one person on board the *Bluebell* who is not hysterical.'

Meanwhile, on the *Wanderer of Peel* it was becoming uncomfortably crowded. Skipper Ball couldn't take any more survivors. Among those rescued was Oliver Bernard who, four hours after the sinking, was decidedly cold and miserable. He asked a fellow survivor, 'An exciting day, Mr. Thomas?'

'Outrageous. Simply outrageous,' David Thomas growled.

'They certainly made a job of it.'

'Didn't you see what happened at the lifeboats? Deplorable. The standard of human efficiency is far below what we are entitled to expect — today it was ghastly.'

Bernard nodded in agreement. 'Of course, it's got to start at the top. You can't expect efficiency from the crew if you don't set an example on the bridge.'

'What,' Thomas asked Bernard, 'do you imagine the percentage of average efficiency to be?'

Bernard thought about it. 'Fifty per cent?'

'Nonsense, young man. Any employer who gets an average of ten per cent efficiency all round is doing extremely well.'

Their conversation was cut short when it was decided to transfer fifty survivors from the *Wanderer* to the *Flying Fox* Bernard was among those transferred.

Twelve men rowed the Courtmacsherry lifeboat away from the slip at three pm. The Reverend Forde was in the stern with a farmer named Longfield who wore a smart tweed suit. There was no wind for the sails and without an engine it took the *Kezia Guilt* three hours to reach the area of the sinking. The first lifeboat they encountered was crowded with survivors. 'We'll take you in!' the Reverend Forde shouted to them.

'No!' a voice called back. 'We're all right. Go further out. There are plenty more alive.'

As the lifeboat sailed further out to sea, bosun John Maloney spotted through his field glasses bodies floating in the water. They were, he said, 'as thick as grass': children, young girls, men, women, ship's officers and crew. Some looked as though they were asleep, others as though they had died violently, choked by their life-jackets. Jerry Murphy and Dan O'Driscoll began to haul them in, but the Reverend Forde insisted they must save the living first. 'Pull in your oars,' ordered coxwain Timothy Keohane. They drifted slowly through the sea of bodies, searching for signs of life. If only we had had a motor, the Reverend Forde thought, we could have got here sooner and saved lives. By the time they handed the survivors over to the rescue boats they had collected more than eighty people, many of them dead with appalling injuries.

Seaman Leslie Morton was among those taken on board the *Indian Empire*, though not his brother John. Another crew member rescued was young William Holton, who had lapsed into unconsciousness in the sea and came to only after lying in the *Indian Empire* for half an hour. He was shocked to find he had been laid out on the ship's hatch among the dead. When George Wynne was rescued he was still hoping to find his father, but there was no trace of him aboard. When they took Carl Foss from a raft he tried to assist the other survivors, but he was too exhausted and the crew had to carry him aboard.

By now a score of rescue boats had reached the area. Belle Naish had been taken on board the examination vessel *Julia* and given tea and a hot brick for warmth. A sailor passed around a box of tea cakes his wife had baked for him that day. Mrs. Naish recognised Theodate Pope as she was pulled out of the water with a boat-hook and laid among the dead. She had been floating across an oar. Belle could not believe she was dead and encouraged the crew to try artificial respiration. Slowly Theodate came round; they wrapped her in a blanket and sat her before the stove in the cabin.

John O'Connell helped Lady Allan to board the *Katrina*, a Greek steamer inward bound from the West Indies. She was in great pain from her injured shoulder, but she thanked him and joined her maids who had been rescued with Howard Fisher, Rita Jolivet and Major Warren Pearl. William Holt, who had tied a handkerchief to an oar, was taken on board from an upturned boat. O'Connell was sitting in the engine room when he saw a stoker, his sweat rag still knotted around his neck, carried in. He felt sick when he looked at the man's arm; it had been torn from the shoulder and was hanging by the tendons almost to his knee. One of the young doctors who was on his way to France prepared to amputate.

They hoisted Joseph Myers on to the *Katrina* by a tackle. His leg was broken and his ribs were smashed. They removed his clothes and laid him in blankets over a grating in the engine room to keep him warm. Myers had been appalled at the way the *Lusitania*'s lifeboats were manned and launched. Few would have drowned, he felt bitterly, if there had been more efficiency and less confusion.

The torpedo boats took more than two hours to reach the first survivors. Ernest Hey, a young engineer on board the *050*, helped to rescue three stewards from the cover of a collapsible. One died on the way back to Queenstown, a dinner napkin still tied around his neck. A man taken from a raft began climbing over the engines in a desperate effort to get warm and burned himself. They took 27 survivors to port. Hey was astonished that boats should have been launched from the liner with their canvas covers still intact.

As their torpedo boat cut engines to drift among the bodies, William Howard, a young rating on the *055*, was ordered by his Captain, 'Forget about the dead. Pick up the ones who are still alive.' They brought 23 survivors into Queenstown, but two died on the way.

After four hours in the water Charles Lauriat was picked up by the *Flying Fox*. Those most seriously injured were laid on the deck. Lauriat gave his sweater, donned that afternoon for his walk on the *Lusitania*'s promenade, to a shivering, near-naked young man. To a woman in a nightgown he gave his jacket. Looking out over the ocean, calm in the still evening, he thought, 'This must be a special dispensation from heaven!'

For a few moments the survivors on board the *Flying Fox* forgot their misery when they saw Margaret Gwyer, still black with soot from the funnel, recognise her husband in the crowd. At first the young clergyman did not know her as she pushed towards him. Then they kissed and hugged each other, crying and laughing at their good fortune.

As the hours passed Albert Bestic feared that darkness would cover the ocean before rescue boats were able to reach them. He had discovered a watertight tin of biscuits; it recalled for him a bitter winter off Cape Horn when he had been six hours at the wheel of a sailing ship with all hands taking in the sails. An old sailor had handed him a quid of tobacco. ' Chew it, son,' he had told him. 'Chewing keeps you warm.' Now Albert turned to the survivors in his lifeboat with the same advice: 'Chew these biscuits,' he told them. 'You'll find that working your jaws will keep you warm.' There was little or no conversation as they chewed. Even though the water was lapping the thwarts the tanks still kept the boat afloat.

After more than four hours the *Bluebell* came alongside and began taking them aboard. In the nick of time, Albert realised — in another while they would not have been found in the dark.

When they were all on board Captain Thompson decided to abandon any further search and return to Queenstown. Albert was given a mug of tea which flooded his body with warmth. Nursing the mug, he sat in the messroom counting the survivors. Then he noticed Turner. The last time he had seen the Captain he was climbing hand over hand up the signal halyards. Now he looked inexpressibly lonely and Albert wondered if he could comfort him in some way. Those around him were probably asking themselves, 'Why should so many have drowned and not the Captain? Why is he still alive?' Albert moved closer to him and said, 'I'm very glad to see you alive, sir.'

Turner's glance was hostile. 'Why should you be? You're not that fond of me.'

Albert swallowed hard. 'Fondness doesn't enter into it, sir. I'm glad to see you alive because I respect you as my Captain and I admire you as a seaman.'

Turner was silent. Albert went and sat in another corner of the messroom. His mind was in turmoil. His belief that the *Lusitania* could escape a German submarine had been shattered like the decks and boats he had seen hurled skywards by the explosion. Even now he could scarcely accept what had happened. For a few moments the messroom and its occupants became blurred. He bit his lip and dug his fingernails into the palms of his hands, cursing inwardly that he and his Captain had been deprived of a liner that was the pride of the world's shipping.

At Kinsale accommodation had been prepared in barracks, convents and houses. But though the people waited on the quay until long after dark few survivors were brought to the harbour.

The *Daniel O'Connell* and the *Elizabeth* had been halted by the *Stormcock* as they returned with survivors. Edward White, the skipper of the *Elizabeth*, was off the harbour mouth of Kinsale when Commander Shee of the *Stormcock* halted him and ordered him to hand over his survivors. White protested, as did Jimmy Hagan of the *Daniel O'Connell*, that there were others waiting for rescue at sea. Some of the women on board, White said, were in a 'bad way'; he wanted to get them to Kinsale as quickly as possible. But Shee threatened, 'If you don't stop we shall sink your boat.'

The *Elizabeth*'s boats from the *Lusitania* were taken in tow and the *Stormcock* headed back for Queenstown. Not only had time been wasted, White reckoned, but lives would be lost by the *Stormcock*'s action.

Constable Jim Speight was on the quayside at Kinsale. He heard the rumours that boats had been turned back and he could not understand why they had not been allowed to land their survivors and their dead at Kinsale.

Ian Stoughton Holbourn was transferred to the *Stormcock* from the *Wanderer of Peel*. He saw survivors huddled together in the hold, some of them dripping wet, many badly injured. A man lay with his leg broken; an expectant mother had her ribs crushed. A woman kept moaning, 'My baby, my baby, my little baby.' She had tied the child to her life-jacket, but when she surfaced after the liner went down the baby was gone.

At Queenstown the police had cordoned off the Cunard wharf from the sightseers crowding the quayside. Just before eight o'clock the *Stormcock* was sighted in the harbour mouth between the forts, the slanting rays of the evening sun lighting her home-coming. At 8.10 she drew alongside the wharf, the first of the rescue craft to return. She was followed by the *Brock*, the *Indian Empire* and the *Flying Fox*. But at the confined wharf there was room for only one boat at a time to come alongside.

Lieutenant Norcock waited at the gangplank with a naval surgeon and officers from the Royal Naval Hospital. Behind them stood soldiers, police constables and bluejackets with stretchers and blankets. Those survivors who could walk were ushered into a back room of the Cunard office where company clerks and Customs officers took their names.

Wesley Frost, whose wife had joined him, had just received a reply to his cable to Secretary of State Bryan in Washington: COMPANY REPORTS ALL PASSENGERS SAVED IF REPORT UNTRUE CABLE NAMES OF AMERICANS LOST OR NOT ACCOUNTED FOR. But when Frost crossed from his office to the wharf he discovered that the 'flustered and disorganised' staff were not recording the nationality of the survivors. He asked them to do so and then referred to their lists of American citizens.

He sent a further cable to Ambassador Page in London informing him that the first rescue boat had arrived. When the cable reached the Ambassador he was dressing for dinner. Despite the news of the sinking he had decided to go ahead with his party. His assistant Clifford Carver, at his desk in Grosvenor Square, sent down the relevant telegrams to his Ambassador who received them at the dinner table. Each gave further news of casualties and survivors. The Embassy guests ate in embarrassed silence.

It was ten pm before the *Bluebell* eased herself alongside the wharf. The Captain was immediately handed instructions to continue the search for more survivors. He went down to Margaret Mackworth's cabin. 'We have to move on again. Do you think, madam, you'll be able to go ashore?'

'Certainly I can,' she replied. 'But not wrapped in this tiny blanket.'

The men around her laughed when she asked for safety pins to fasten the blanket securely. A crew member went ashore and returned with a British Warm overcoat he had borrowed from a soldier on the quayside. With the coat buttoned loosely, the blanket pinned around her waist beneath it, and the Captain's carpet slippers on her feet, she reached the gangway. Here she had to climb a couple of feet, but she found she was so weak she dropped on her hands and knees and crawled up it. When she reached the other end she looked up. There, on the crowded, gaslit quayside, she was astonished to see her father, safe and well, waiting for her.

The last survivor to come ashore from the *Bluebell* was William Turner. Still wrapped in Thompson's blanket he walked slowly up the gangway. He might have been a crewman without rating, for no one on the quayside recognised him. His face was grey and he looked older than his fifty-nine years.

It can be a shameful experience for a Captain to lose his ship. But for Captain Turner the real nightmare was about to begin.

# PART III

# Queenstown

8 May, 1915 and After

*'Let no one mistake the fact,
a wild beast is loose in the
world.'*

*New York Tribune* 11 May 1915

# 21

# TOWN OF THE DEAD

AT SUNRISE on Saturday, 8 May, Oliver Bernard walked down to the harbour again.

Five of the *Lusitania*'s lifeboats were roped together at the slipway below the roadside tea station; boys were already wading barefoot into the water searching for souvenirs. He had sat up all night in the hotel, smoking cigarettes and drinking cup after cup of hot tea, returning to the Cunard wharf several times in the hope of finding Stewart Mason and his bride. In the cold glare of the gaslamps and the glow of furnaces on tugboats and tenders the harvest of stiff bodies merited the pen of a Gustave Doré.

He walked to the temporary morgues which had been set up. The first morgue in a shed on the Cunard wharf held what looked at first glance like a group of bruised and broken dolls. They were infants so discoloured it was difficult to believe they had ever lived. Around the walls of the shed women were laid in their sodden garments, unbelievably the living human beings of the day before. He went into the second morgue where sunlight filtering through the grimy windows threw light on the gold braid of an officer's uniform. The large bulk of Staff Captain Anderson lay on the floor, his bloated features smeared with bloody mucus. He had not died without a struggle.

Bernard retraced his steps to the third morgue in the Town Hall beneath the arch of the market place. The floor was strewn with sawdust and the air heavy with evaporating moisture. Walking among the rows of bodies he saw children

J

clasped in each other's arms and a woman with two infants strapped to her breast. Then he saw Charles Frohman. The impresario's body was not disfigured; he had died without protest before the sea could do its worst. But he could not find William Lindsey's 'little girl' or her husband. He left the Town Hall reflecting that the death masks of these victims would have revealed 'no individualities, nothing but a lifeless uniformity'. People he had known only yesterday were absent from bodies that looked horribly alike, dumped in these sheds like dead cattle.

With flags at half mast and church bells tolling, the town reeked of death. The sight of gold braid on naval uniforms on the streets unnerved him. Officers, he felt, were staring at him in the ill-fitting clothes he had bought, as though he were a tramp. These were the men who had allowed the *Lusitania* to sink ten miles off Kinsale. They had taken hours to send help. They had let those poor creatures in the sheds drown like rats.

It was only at dawn that hotelier Otto Humbert emerged from the wine cellar of the Queen's where he had shut himself in for the night, terrified of the mounting hysteria against the Germans that had swept the town. A woman had challenged him as the first bodies came ashore, 'Where is your German *Kultur* now?' He had no idea where, or how, the survivors had been accommodated, but few of them had complained about their makeshift accommodation except Lady Mackworth and Isaac Lehmann.

The Queen's was not to Margaret Mackworth's liking. Her father gave up his room to her when she came ashore and she climbed the stairs with a struggle, resting after every two steps. Her first visitor in the morning was Dorothy Conner, looking as pretty in her fawn tweed coat and skirt as when Lady Mackworth saw her step off the deck of the *Lusitania* into the sea. She had not fully unhooked her skirt and it had stayed on when she was sucked down with the ship. Another guest at the hotel had offered to travel into Cork to purchase some clothes for her; and while waiting Margaret decided to take a bath.

Four hours in the sea had not washed her clean, only covered her with a brownish dirt, and she was bruised from head to foot. She decided the bath was filthy. 'Really,' she complained to Dorothy Conner, 'I don't know whether I've come out cleaner or dirtier than when I got in.'

Isaac Lehmann also complained about the Queen's, but not so vociferously. He had been asked to share a small room with three other men and had received 'nothing to eat at all' Waiting to be allowed ashore at the Cunard wharf from the *Flying Fox* he found 'just as hard and as difficult as it was to get saved from the *Lusitania*'.

Wearing an assortment of old and newly-purchased clothing the exhausted survivors wandered about the town searching for those who had been closest to them on the voyage — George Wynne, for instance, unable to find his father. Harold Taylor had been pulled, miraculously he thought, into the same lifeboat as his bride. Avis Dolphin had found her benefactor at the Queen's Hotel, but Holbourn, whose limbs had refused to work when he was carried ashore by two soldiers, was confined to bed. After crouching on her floating board for four hours Mary Maycock's legs were so swollen they had to cut off her knee-high boots. Ernest Cowper had brought little Helen Smith to the Rob Roy Hotel, but there was no trace of her parents or her brother; local people tried to cheer the bemused child by giving her a doll and a flowered hat with ribbons. John O'Connell was safe, so were Albert Martin and Eugene McDermott who had escaped from the stokehold. Actresses Josephine Brandell and Rita Jolivet were safe, but Rita's brother-in-law George Vernon was gone.

Where were the Cromptons and their six children? Dr. Houghton had been taken on board the torpedo boat *050*, but Marie de Page was missing. Joseph Myers was in the Naval Hospital where he told Consul Frost there had been 'panic' on the liner. William Holton was so exhausted after his swim he slept in a hotel room for fourteen hours. William McMillan Adams had lost his father. Albert Bestic could not find Second Officer Hefford. George Hutchinson, safely ashore, insisted he had seen Alfred Vanderbilt in the water. And Virginia Loney, the most beautiful girl in saloon, could not be consoled when she learned her parents were dead.

The oldest woman passenger, Mrs. Morell, was recovering, after hours in the sea, in Queenstown Hospital. Theodate Pope was among a small number of first-class passengers brought to a private hospital in Cork, but her companion Edwin Friend was lost. Jane and Grace MacFarquhar and Belle Naish were safe, but Theodore Naish had drowned. Charlotte Pye and Norah Bretherton had both lost their babies in the sea, but Margaret Cox had saved her baby boy. Three of the Welsh choir had been lost, and now George Lane and Dewi Michael went in search of their leader George Davies. Lane remembered him singing 'Down With the Salamander' at the ship's concert on Thursday evening; he could still hear those beautiful bass notes. Robert Cairns, the only passenger not on the liner's official list, was safe. He had bought his ticket and paid Purser McCubbin for it just before the *Lusitania* had sailed. McCubbin himself was lost; he would never farm the land he had bought for his retirement at Golders Green.

Throughout the morning more bodies were carried ashore from trawlers at the quays. Later, when dust sheets had been placed over the bodies in the morgues, Leslie Morton went in search of his brother. At the first shed he saw the covered corpses laid on the floor in rows and people moving slowly from body to body, turning back the sheets to see if they could identify a relative or friend. Morton started on the same grisly task. As he put out his hand to turn back a sheet he noticed a hand on the other side of the corpse, about to do the same. He looked up to see John grinning at him. Tears of relief filled their eyes. Leslie was still in his seaman's jersey and blue serge trousers, but his brother, who had been rescued wearing only a shirt, had bought himself a loud check suit, courtesy of Cunard, a check tie and cap, and a pair of yellow brogues. Leslie laughed with relief at the absurd figure cut by his brother. He whispered, 'We should have a drink on this!' The

Morton brothers had sent similar telegrams to their father in Leeds: AM SAVED. LOOKING FOR JOHN/LOOKING FOR LES.

George Wynne was trembling so much he had to ask another crew member to write a telegram to his mother in Liverpool: BOTH SAVED. HOME LATER. It was untrue, but how could he possibly tell his mother, with six children to care for, that Joseph was probably drowned?

Captain Turner walked through the town in a badly-fitting suit he had been given while his uniform was being dried and pressed, nodding good morning to survivors, even chatting briefly to them. Reporters tried to question him, but he had been advised by Vice-Admiral Coke not to make any statement to the Press. He would only say, 'I stuck to my ship until she went from under me. It's the fortunes of war.'

At half past eleven on Friday evening a large crowd had gathered outside the London offices of Cunard in Cockspur Street. At 11.40 pm a notice was posted: FIRST LIST OF SAVED EXPECTED SHORTLY. NUMBERS NOT YET KNOWN. Merseyside was stunned by the news. Hundreds of people formed queues outside the Cunard office in Water Street, blank disbelief in their faces at the news of the disaster for a company which boasted that it had 'never lost a passenger'. Throughout the night the hundreds grew to thousands as the families of local seamen gathered to await the names of the survivors.

New Yorkers saw the news flashed on the bulletin boards above the newspaper offices. Not since the war began had they been so astonished as by the line announcing, LUSITANIA TORPEDOED. Men and women turned to their neighbours as if seeking a contradiction. Had the *Lusitania* really gone? Had all the passengers been saved? At the Cunard offices, where first rumours of the sinking had been discounted, anxious relatives and friends stormed the counters. Clerks worked overtime answering hundreds of long distance calls.

In Manhattan's smart German Club officers hailed the

262 Queenstown, 8 May 1915 and After

sinking as a masterstroke and toasted *Der Tag* — the day which had sealed the fate of Britain's dominion of the seas. At Lüchow's on 14th Street the restaurant was crowded with Germans celebrating the victory.

Count von Bernstorff had arrived at the Ritz-Carlton on Madison and 46th Street. With the news of the sinking he became a virtual prisoner in his suite. He gave orders that he must not be disturbed by telephone calls or interviewers. He cancelled his visit to the Metropolitan Opera House where a special performance of *Die Fledermaus* was to be given in aid of the German Red Cross. Instead, he asked Captain Boy-Ed, the naval attaché, to take his place.

Fearing trouble between German sympathisers and those of the Allies, the management placed plain-clothes men in all parts of the theatre. They cancelled the singing of 'Deutschland Über Alles' and removed the German flags. During the intervals both Boy-Ed and von Papen were publicly insulted in the lobbies. Many opera-goers were angry that Alfred Gwynne Vanderbilt's private box, which only he and his family occupied, had been sold for the performance; the proceeds were to go to the German cause.

Soon after 5.30 am on Saturday von Bernstorff tried to slip from the Ritz-Carlton unnoticed, but he could not elude the pressmen who surrounded him as he jumped into a taxicab. 'I will not make a statement,' he shouted. A reporter banged his fist on the window and the driver, not wanting to interrupt a conversation, held the cab at the kerb. Bernstorff leaned forward in his seat, shouting at him, 'Go on, damn you, go on!'

Taxicabs packed with reporters chased Bernstorff's cab to Pennsylvania Station where the Ambassador planned to catch the 6.10 am train to Washington. They pursued him down the steep iron stairs to the platform, assailing him with questions. 'I shall not say one word,' he declared angrily, as he made for the train. 'Not one word.'

But his questioners persisted; 'The editorials are saying you provoked this act by the warning in the papers before the *Lusitania* sailed . . . They say you're a murderer.'

Bernstorff was angry. 'I don't care what the papers say,' he fumed, climbing into one of the train's parlour cars. The reporters followed and found him three cars beyond the car he had entered. 'Don't you think,' one reporter asked him, 'it's up to you to say something at this time? The whole world is waiting for an explanation.' But Bernstorff refused.

The newspaper headlines were unanimous as to the enormity of the disaster: LUSITANIA TORPEDOED AND SUNK: WORLD AGHAST AT GERMANY'S BIGGEST CRIME; LUSITANIA'S ENORMOUS DEATH TOLL: HUNS MOST COWARDLY CRIME; LUSITANIA SUNK WITHOUT WARN-ING: 1,300 DIE AS LINER GOES TO THE BOTTOM. As yet the figures were guesswork. Cunard were still counting the survivors and subtracting their total from the numbers on their passenger list. After a strong condemnation of her sinking the London *Times* commented,

> The presumption is that the *Lusitania* received no special naval protection, the principle apparently laid down being that when so many large passenger steamers are constantly approaching or leaving the coasts of Great Britain, no single steamer can be singled out for exceptional protection unless the national interests make such a step imperative.

From the Queen's Hotel in Queenstown Vance Pitney, the *New York Tribune*'s special correspondent, cabled reports in which he assured readers that Consul Wesley Frost was doing his utmost to help American survivors and identify victims. Pitney, the first of the pressmen to arrive at Queenstown, asked 'questions which demand answers'. He listed a number of 'well-defined reports':

> The *Lusitania* had orders to take a mid-channel course which would place her approximately 140 miles off the Irish coast and instead she was within eight miles of land where two vessels had been torpedoed within the previous twenty-four hours . . . The liner approached a

dangerous neighbourhood absolutely unescorted despite the warning issued by the German Embassy . . . There was no patrol of any kind to safeguard her . . . All life-boats were swung out on Thursday, but life-rafts remained securely in their places . . . Many passengers say that even after the explosion Captain Turner declared no danger and said the ship would not sink, while at that moment she was listing more to starboard and rapidly going down by the head.

What would America do?

Even in Germany, where the sinking was hailed as 'a new triumph for Germany's naval policy' and Admiral von Tirpitz was showered with congratulatory telegrams, this question was asked. Among less enthusiastic Germans it was felt the disaster might precipitate America's entry into the war. The outcry was placing President Wilson under strain. Walter Hines Page, his Ambassador in London, who had sat through Friday night's almost silent dinner party until the guests had filed out, advised him, 'The United States must declare war or forfeit European respect.' In Berlin Ambassador James Gerard, already convinced that diplomatic relations would be severed, was packing his bags. But President Wilson had uttered not a word since the sinking.

When he heard the news on Friday he had walked from his room and wandered through the White House into the garden. Lost in thought he strayed into Pennsylvania Avenue, apparently oblivious to the traffic and the passers-by and the raucous cries of the newsboys shouting, '*Lusitania* sunk!' He would battle privately with the problem facing him. He would not be panicked into making a statement until he had studied the facts of the sinking from official sources and turned over in his mind the wisest course to be pursued by his Government. He returned to the White House and shut himself in his study, telling his manservant he wanted no callers, not even members of his family. In the late afternoon he sent for William Jennings Bryan, the Secretary of State.

On Saturday morning Bryan told pressmen who crowded into the White House, 'Of course, the President feels the distress and the gravity of the situation to the utmost and he is considering very earnestly and very calmly the right course of action to pursue. He knows that the people of the country wish him to act with deliberation as well as firmness.'

A full statement could be expected after the weekend. Still, few political pundits anticipated a declaration of war. They read into the word 'deliberation' an effort to calm the incensed feelings of Americans about the deaths of their countrymen, feelings not assuaged by an official statement from Berlin which claimed the *Lusitania* was armed and carried war material in her cargo. 'Her owners, Cunard, therefore knew to what danger the passengers were exposed. They alone bore all the responsibility for what happened . . . Germany, for her part, left nothing undone to repeatedly and strongly warn them. The Imperial Ambassador in Washington even went so far as to make a public warning to draw attention to this danger.'

In Kansas City the actress Maude Adams had arrived at the Grand Theatre for the matinée performance of Barrie's *Quality Street* when she received confirmation of Charles Frohman's death. She collapsed, and the management prepared to call off the performance. But she revived and insisted she would go on.

Others close to Frohman were heartbroken. His partner David Belasco announced, 'My dead, dear old friend. If a long night's vigil and tears could bring him back Charlie would be with us.' Barrie described him as 'a man who never broke his word, a man who loved his schemes. I have never known anyone more modest and no one quite so shy.'

At the military barracks at Kinsale in the afternoon solicitor John Horgan opened an inquest as coroner into the deaths of five victims of the *Lusitania* disaster, three men and two women, whose bodies lay in an adjoining mortuary. At three o'clock a jury of twelve local shopkeepers and fishermen was sworn in.

Horgan addressed the small gathering at the barracks. 'We have come together to investigate what is truly one of the most terrible as well as one of the most inhuman crimes that has ever been perpetrated by people calling themselves a civilised nation.' He seemed convinced that the second explosion on the liner had been caused by a torpedo 'more deadly than the first' because it 'hastened the work of destruction'.

District Inspector Wainsborough, the first witness to be called, stated that on the previous evening the naval patrol boat *Heron* had anchored in the harbour at Kinsale, flying an urgent signal and with her ensign at half-mast. On board he found five bodies, those now in the mortuary. There were also eleven survivors, including a Mrs. Julia Sullivan. The *Heron's* Captain told him he had made for Kinsale because Mrs. Sullivan required immediate medical treatment.

'I hope Mrs. Sullivan is all right?' the coroner enquired.

'She is better,' Wainsborough assured him.

After some further evidence Horgan adjourned the inquest until Monday. He wished to give the authorities time to produce every evidence, including that of the Commander of the *Lusitania*, Captain William Turner, whom he had summoned to attend.

# 22

# THE RIOTS

THE RIOTS FLARED in Liverpool on Saturday night; they continued during Sunday, and by Monday were out of control.

The newspapers referred to them as a 'sequel to the wreck of the *Lusitania*', a tragedy that had 'robbed hundreds of Liverpool homes of their breadwinner and led to a fury of rage among seamen and the docker class'. Shops that were assumed to be German or Austrian were attacked indiscriminately, their windows smashed, their stock and furniture thrown into the streets. Butchers, bakers, barbers, outfitters, jewellers and furniture dealers were the principal victims.

At one shop four men manhandled a piano from the owner's living room and perching it halfway down the stairs began to play *Tipperary*. After just one verse the piano crashed to the bottom of the stairs and the singing ceased. Armed with sticks and stones and other weapons the mob roved from street to street. Outside George Schmetzer's butcher's shop two women fought a tug of war over a leg of boiled ham while children munched at attractive 'polonies'. 'What do you think of this for meat?' a woman cried, waving a leg of pork. 'I'm going to roast some of it tonight and post it to our boys in the trenches.'

Every pork butcher's shop was assumed to be German. Women led the processions, some of them supporting a baby in one arm and flourishing a stick or waving a Union Jack in the other, singing and dancing as they marched. The men smashed windows from top to bottom, hurling hams, pork, brawn and sausages along with chopping blocks, weighing machines and brass fittings into the street. What wasn't

267

carried off was smashed to pieces or burned. Sometimes the women surged through the police lines, shattering windows with heavy sticks and looting the premises.

Riots followed in London and raged from Shepherds Bush to Tooting and from Islington to Stratford. It was a story similar to Liverpool's as shops, principally butchers and bakers, were attacked, windows smashed, stock looted, premises fired and furniture thrown into the streets. Shopkeepers hid under their beds only to be dragged from their premises and have their beds thrown from the upper windows.

The police couldn't cope, so 'specials' were summoned and troops helped voluntarily; when arrests were made these only angered the crowds further and several policemen were in- jured and pulled from their horses.

Even in the City indignation ran high. Two hundred members of the Stock Exchange, waving their silk hats, marched from the steps of the Royal Exchange to Parliament to demand the internment of all Germans. 'No German must be left in the city of London,' was the cry. Members of the public joined the procession which had swollen to large numbers by the time it reached the House of Commons. In Cannon Street an old lady encouraged the marchers by shaking her umbrella and shouting, 'The devils, the devils, round them up!'

The riots spread abroad to South Africa. In Johannesburg more than fifty buildings were wrecked and their contents burned or smashed. In Cape Town the National Anthem was sung and police stood with heads bared before the crowds attacked buildings and set them partially on fire. In Durban the rioters set about their work in 'a most orderly and methodical fashion'; their numbers were so large the police were powerless to stop them.

In Liverpool Lord Derby appealed for public restraint. 'I feel strongly that it is a poor tribute to the memory of those whom the relatives have lost if they try to emulate in any way the deeds of the Germans in the field of brutality.'

While the police charge sheets expressed the time-honoured phraseology of 'insulting conduct', 'threatening behaviour', and 'riotous assembly', the excuses made were extreme and defendants pleaded provocation. One woman defendant explained to a Liverpool magistrate, 'They have killed my brother, so we must kill them.' The fines were modest. At a London court the magistrate bound over the defendants with the reprimand, 'Don't do it again,' to which they shouted, 'Hurrah!'

The widespread rioting convinced the Government that they would have to tackle the problem of the country's aliens. Lord Charles Beresford warned Prime Minister Asquith that unless a clearer policy was adopted the mob would take the law into their own hands. 'People are getting angry,' declared the Unionist peer, 'and disputes as to who is responsible will make them more angry. I want to see these alien enemies put behind barbed wire, not merely the poor waiters, hairdressers, scavengers and chiropodists, but the people in high position who are riding about in their motors and laughing at us.'

Asquith promised a statement. On Thursday he rose, amid cheers in the Commons, to announce a plan which divided aliens into those who were naturalised and those who were not. Already 19,000 non-naturalised aliens were interned, but some 40,000 were at large; all these latter who were of military age would be segregated and interned and those over military age repatriated. Many Germans surrendered voluntarily at the news. Five hundred were escorted to a ship at Southend by a local regiment with fixed bayonets. In Liverpool the police gathered them from their homes in taxi-cabs. There was no further room in the main Bridewell prison, so groups were dispatched to concentration camps near Liverpool or by train to camps in Scotland.

On the day the Prime Minister announced his plan of action Alfred Booth attended a memorial service in Liverpool for the *Lusitania* victims. The riots were almost over. After morning service next day in St. George's Chapel at Windsor the banners, surcoats, swords and other accoutrements of the Kaiser, the Austrian Emperor and other foreign Knights of the Garter were removed without ceremony.

Julia Sullivan awoke in a long, white-walled room filled with single beds. A nurse sitting at the foot of her bed smiled at her. 'You're coming on fine,' she said.

'Where am I?'

'You're in Kinsale. Now I'll just fetch the doctor to have a look at you.'

After the doctor had examined her the nurse tucked in the bedclothes and sent for the priest. 'You're in no danger,' she assured Julia, 'and in no need of the Last Sacraments. But if your mind is troubled he'll do what he can to ease it.' Julia wondered at the nurse's perception. When the priest came she asked him, 'My husband, father. Was he saved?' It was the only thought in her mind.

'What was — is — his name?'

'Sullivan. Flor Sullivan. And he's a fine young man with black curly hair.'

He shook his head and squeezed her hand comfortingly. 'There's no Flor Sullivan in this hospital. But don't give up hope. There are hundreds of survivors in Queenstown and he may be there. I'll get in touch with them and let you know. Get some sleep now, and put your trust in the Mother of God.'

In the evening when the priest returned to the ward his face was expressionless. He had bad news for some patients, good news for others, and he did not want to betray his emotions. When he reached Julia's bed he whispered excitedly to her, 'Your husband is safe and well! He's been told you are here. When you join him in Cork put your heads together and plan some way of giving thanks to God for your deliverance.'

George Hook and his daughter Elsie had spent three days searching the mortuaries for young Frank. To their great surprise and joy they found him in Queenstown Hospital. In jumping from the liner Frank had been struck by a falling lifeboat which broke his leg. He assumed his father and sister had been drowned and a Leeds survivor had offered to 'stand by him through life'.

The charming little Ailsa Booth was missing. A relative arrived at the Imperial Hotel in Cork city and placed an advertisement in the *Cork Examiner*: 'Wanted: any information regarding a girl of eight years, light-golden hair, blue eyes, nice complexion, very pretty, named Ailsa Booth Jones. Also a boy, aged five, short black hair, rather thin face, named Percival Booth Jones; believed to have been rescued from the *Lusitania*.' But Ailsa, her brother and their parents were all drowned.

Avis Dolphin's white sailor skirt and middy blouse were so greasy they had to be washed several times before she could wear them again. Her companion on the voyage, Ian Stoughton Holbourn, had recovered sufficiently to go in search of Avis's two nurses, but they were both lost. On Sunday he and Avis took a train to Dublin and booked rooms at an hotel in Sackville Street. Avis had only to touch her hair and her hands came away filthy with grease. She took a bath and washed her hair and got into bed with the hot water bottle the chambermaid had brought her. Next morning, while Holbourn went shopping, she sat in the residents' writing room and began a long letter to her mother in St. Thomas, Ontario, describing her voyage. 'My dearest Mother,' she began, 'I hope you are well. I am just splendid. I will tell you everything from the time we got on the boat until now . . .'

Warren Pearl and his wife were reunited in Queenstown, but it took Amy some days to recover from her ordeal. The Vice-Admiral's family nursed her while Major Pearl continued his search of the morgues, the hospitals and the railway station for their four children. Then he heard of a nurse answering to the description of Alice Lines in a house where some naval officers were quartered; he dashed round there after midnight and Nurse Lines was awakened by the landlady. She cried tears of relief at seeing Major Pearl again, for young Stuart and baby Audrey were safe with her; however, Amy, Susan and Nurse Greta Lorenson were missing. During the ensuing days Pearl and Nurse Lines continued the grim routine of inspecting the lines of bodies in the morgues; and every day they went to the railway station hoping to find that the nurse and the children were saved. But they never saw them again.

By Saturday afternoon Consul Wesley Frost had compiled a fairly accurate list of the identified bodies and had begun telegraphing relatives for instructions. He decided that the bodies of important Americans, including Frohman, should be embalmed and returned to the United States. But the embalming process was apparently unknown among Irish undertakers, and it was early on Sunday before Frost found a surgeon at University College in Cork and persuaded him to come to Queenstown and set up an improvised operating room at the rear of the Cunard offices. During his visits to the offices Frost looked in occasionally on the surgeon at work. On his second visit he stood mesmerised at the sight of a beautiful girl on the embalmer's table. She lay like a statue 'typifying,' he said later, 'assassinated innocence.'

Frost decided that bodies of the identified first-class passengers should be embalmed, while other identified Americans should be sealed in lead caskets so that they could be shipped to America. But some relatives were so chary of visiting the dimly-lit morgues that Frost or his assistants had to accompany them to make sure they did not shirk the job. The Consul became accustomed to the sight of corpses with expressions on their faces 'as though a friend had played a practical joke the victim didn't understand'. But he was quite unable to control his feelings when he saw the bodies of children, the 'poor little midget corpses' as he later described them.

Although Saturday's newspapers had headlines MR. VANDERBILT'S HEROIC DEATH Margaret Vanderbilt shut herself in her apartment at the Vanderbilt Hotel on Fifth Avenue, refusing to accept that her husband was dead. Alfred's sister Gertrude was more practical. She wired her brother-in-law Almeric Paget in London: CAN OBTAIN NO NEWS OF ALFRED. HAVE INSTRUCTED WEBB WARE

ALFRED'S SECRETARY AND ALSO A REPRESENTATIVE OF
AMERICAN EXPRESS COMPANY MAKE EVERY POSSIBLE
INVESTIGATION WHICH NOW DOING. She believed there
was a slim chance that her brother had either been severely
injured and not identified or picked up by a fishing boat and
landed in some remote harbour along the Irish coast. But she
knew he could not swim and accepted there was little hope of
his survival.

Margaret continued to send cables to friends in England
and Ireland begging them to forward any news of her husband
without delay. On Saturday afternoon she was persuaded to
move into the Vanderbilt family mansion on 57th Street.
She told Gertrude, 'I will not believe Alfred is dead until
I get conclusive proof.' During the weekend a reward of
5,000 dollars was offered for the discovery of Alfred Gwynne
Vanderbilt's body.

As was his custom President Wilson went to Sunday morning
service at the General Presbyterian Church in Washington.
The preacher made no reference to the crisis, but asked for
prayers for the President in his work.

In the afternoon Wilson took a long motor ride in the
countryside with his physician and after dinner retired to his
study. At a late hour the lights in his room, which had been
the Cabinet room of Abraham Lincoln, were still burning.
The *New York Tribune* that morning described Saturday as a
day of 'benumbed and quiescent waiting'. The people wanted
to see Germany compelled to make reparation for 'an act of
savagery of which', the *Tribune* pointed out, 'American
citizens are among the victims'. The President and his men
apparently wanted to 'postpone judgement'.

Wilson was scheduled to address 4,000 newly-naturalised
citizens in Philadelphia the next evening. In his study he
began to prepare his speech. He would have to touch upon the
crisis of the *Lusitania*.

# 23

# 'WILFUL MURDER'

AMBASSADOR PAGE was at Euston Station at eight am on Sunday morning to meet the first of the mail boat trains, searching for American survivors as they stepped onto the platform.

Some survivors were still asleep when the trains pulled into the station; they were allowed to sleep on and their carriages were shunted to another platform. People crowded round the carriage doors greeting relatives and friends in a long embrace. A lone woman in black who had haunted the Cunard offices since the night of the sinking made her way along the platform asking survivors if they had seen Sir Hugh Lane.

Little Helen Smith arrived with her aunt, who had lost both her boys, at Swansea docks. On the journey from Ireland Helen had told well-wishers, 'Everybody is sorry for me because my mummy and daddy have gone. They're coming on another boat.' John O'Connell arrived at Lime Street Station in Liverpool and walked the three and a half miles to Bootle. 'That's John's knock,' he heard someone say as his grandmother and his two aunts came to the door in their night clothes. He ran upstairs to greet his uncle, who made no move to get out of bed, but merely remarked, 'So there you are.' The next morning his grandmother pawned the suit Cunard had paid for in Queenstown.

Among the excited crowds at Lime Street in Liverpool George Wynne saw his mother, holding her youngest child in her arms. He ducked among the crowds, unable to break the news about his father. He crossed to St. George's Hall and sat on the steps until a priest he knew came by. When he told him his story the priest said kindly, 'Come along home, George. We'll both tell your mother what happened.'

At eleven o'clock on Monday morning Captain Turner, wearing a shrunken and faded uniform, arrived by car at the Old Market House in the centre of Kinsale for the resumed hearing of the inquest into five victims of the *Lusitania* sinking. The eyes of the reporters followed him across the crowded courtroom as he took his seat beside the other witnesses. Turner looked hollow-eyed and strained, still suffering from his ordeal.

The court fell silent when District Inspector Wainsborough stood up to announce, 'I now propose, sir, to call the Captain of the *Lusitania*.'

*Coroner*: Captain Turner, please.

Turner took his seat in the witness box.

*Coroner*: When did you leave New York?

*Turner*: On the first of May.

*Coroner*: Had you personally received any warnings?

*Turner*: No, only my papers — that is all.

*Coroner*: Did anything happen on the voyage that you wish to mention?

*Turner*: Nothing whatsoever.

*Coroner*: It was a voyage without incident up to the tragedy?

*Turner*: Quite so.

*Coroner*: You were aware that threats had been made that this ship would be torpedoed?

*Turner*: Fully aware of it.

*Coroner*: Was she armed?

*Turner*: No; sir.

Horgan then asked Turner what special precautions he had taken in connection with the threats.

—I had all the boats served out and bulkheads and doors closed where they were likely to get at them..

--That was when the ship came into the danger zone?

—Yes.

—What time did you pass the Fastnet?

—About eleven o'clock on Friday, I should think, sir.

—Between that time and the time of the accident, did you see any submarines?

—None whatsoever. There was no sign of them.

—I believe, Captain, there was some kind of fog or a haze off the Irish coast when you came to it?

—There was a fog off the Fastnet.

—Did you slow down speed then?

—Yes, I slowed down to 15 knots.

—I take it, Captain, that you were in wireless communication with the shore all the way across?

—Yes, we received, but we did not send, you know.

—Did you receive any message with reference to submarines being off the Irish coast?

—Yes.

—What was the nature of these messages, Captain?

—I respectfully refer you to the Admiralty, sir, about the answering of that question.

Horgan paused, slightly taken aback. Turner who had been answering in a gruff, monotonous voice, seemed weary, and was obviously anxious to get the hearing over as quickly as possible. Horgan changed his line of questioning.

—I will put it to you this way, Captain: Did you receive any message as to the sinking of a ship off Old Kinsale?

—No, sir.

District Inspector Wainsborough interjected, 'The *Earl of Lathom* was the name of that vessel, sir'.

*Coroner*: Did you receive any special instructions?

*Turner*: Yes, sir.

— Are you at liberty to tell us what these instructions are?

— No, sir.

— Did you carry them out?

— Yes, to the best of my ability.

Horgan led Turner through the events leading up to the sinking. Then he asked, 'Was there another explosion after the first?'

— Yes, directly after the first there was another, but that might have been an internal explosion. The order was given to lower all boats down to the rails and to get all the women and children into them.

— Who gave that order, Captain?

— I did and I wanted to stop the ship and could not do so as the engines were out of commission. Therefore it was not safe to lower the boats on account of the speed. It could not be done until the speed was off.

— Was she stopped, as a matter of fact?

— Not altogether. There was a perceptible motion on her when she went down.

Wainsborough asked, 'Where she was struck between the third and fourth engines — was that where the engine room was situated?'

*Turner*: Yes.

*Coroner*: I believe you remained on the bridge all the time?

— Yes, sir, and she went down from under me.

— How long after she was struck did she sink?

— About eighteen minutes, I should imagine. It was a quarter past two by my watch when the explosion took place.

— At the time of the collision was there any warship conveying you?

—None whatever, and I did not see any. In fact there was none reported to me as having been seen.

—Did you pick up any warship at the time that you came to the Irish coast?

—Not that I know of, sir.

—It has been said that the periscope of the submarine was seen?

—It might have been said, but·I did not see it.

—Had you any special reason for only going 18 knots?

—In time of peace we go 25 knots, but in war time that has been reduced to 21 knots. I was going straight ahead to Liverpool for the purpose of arriving at the Bar.

—You wanted to get to Liverpool Bar for high water?

—Not exactly for high water, but two or three hours before full water, without stopping for a pilot.

—Were those your instructions?

—Yes, sir, those were part of my instructions.

—Is it true to say that you were going a zigzag course at the time of the accident?

—No, sir.

Horgan paused, as though surprised to hear this evidence. It was possible, Turner agreed, for a submarine to be in the area without his seeing it. The Coroner asked him if any boats had been launched safely.

—Oh, yes, there were some, and one or two on the portside as well.

—Were your orders promptly carried out according to your instruction, and was there any panic on board?

—Very little panic at all. All was calm.

—All your orders were promptly obeyed and carried out?

—Yes, I could not find fault with anyone.

Horgan thanked the Captain for his co-operation. A member

of the jury of local shopkeepers and fishermen asked, 'Captain Turner, in face of the warnings you heard before you left New York about the vessel being torpedoed before she reached her destination, did you make any particular application to the Admiralty for an escort?'

—No, I did not. I leave that to them. It is their business. I simply carried out my orders to go, and I went. And I would do it again.

*Coroner*: I am glad to hear you express yourself in that way, Captain, and I am sure you would do your duty again.

*Foreman Juror*: Were the watertight compartments closed?

—They were all ordered to be closed, and also the doors previous to this.

—I suppose the explosives opened them up again?

—It opened something, evidently.

—Was any order given approaching the coast about danger?

—There was none.

*Coroner*: Was there any warning given to you before the submarine sent the torpedoes into you?

—None whatever, sir. It was straight and done with, and the whole lot went up in the air. It was straight and done with and finished.

*Coroner*: We all sympathise with you, Captain, and the Cunard company in this terrible crime that was committed against your vessel, and I also desire to express our appreciation of the great courage you have shown; it was worthy of the traditions of the service to which you belong. We realise the deep feelings you must have in the matter.

Turner acknowledged the Coroner's expression of sympathy and bowed his head. Then, overcome with emotion, he broke into sobs. Every eye in the courtroom was on him. Horgan stared at the figure in the witness box. He suddenly realised that from the moment Turner entered his courtroom he was under great strain. When the Captain had composed himself Horgan addressed him again.

— I thank you, Captain, for coming here and giving us such assistance in this inquiry.

Turner raised his head. Slowly he stood up to leave the witness box.

— I was glad to come and help in any way.

He shuffled to his seat, unable to contain his emotions.

Addressing the jurors, Horgan reminded them that 'the whole civilised world stands aghast at this crime'. It was a violation of international law. The *Lusitania* was a non-combatant vessel; she was not armed, and there could be no possible excuse for sinking her. In accordance with his direction, the jury returned their verdict:

'We find that this appalling crime was contrary to international law and the conventions of all civilised nations and we therefore charge the officers of the said submarine and the Emperor and Government of Germany under whose orders they acted, with the crime of wilful and wholesale murder before the tribunal of the civilised world.'

Half an hour later Horgan was about to leave the Old Market House when he was told that Harry Wynne, Crown Solicitor for Cork, wished to see him urgently. Wynne was a friend, and he blurted out, almost apologetically, 'I've got instructions from the Admiralty, John, to stop the inquest. Captain Turner must not give evidence'.

'Too late, Harry,' Horgan told him. 'It's all over.'

The Admiralty had contacted Vice-Admiral Coke during the weekend and Admiral Oliver expressed his anxiety about the holding of an inquest. Coke told him he did not anticipate any problems. Both men evidently assumed that the inquest would be held in Queenstown where they could exercise some control over events. But John Horgan had decided to hold the inquest within his own jurisdiction in Kinsale and bring it forward by a day. Not only had he begun the inquest on

Saturday, but he had summoned Turner to appear on the Monday. The Admiralty had wanted Turner to remain silent until a Board of Trade Inquiry, to which he would be called to give evidence was held in London. They also knew that questions were being asked about the nature of the sinking. Was there an internal explosion? Was the *Lusitania* carrying ammunition? But they moved too late against Horgan. By lunchtime on Monday the jury's verdict in the little town of Kinsale was being telegraphed and telephoned to newspapers and news agencies around the world.

Coroner Horgan was to say later, 'The Admiralty were as belated on this occasion as they had been in protecting the *Lusitania*.'

All day Sunday soldiers had dug huge cellar-like cavities in the Old Church cemetery two miles out of Queenstown. When the undertakers in Queenstown and Cork could supply no more coffins the authorities had them brought by train from Kildare and Dublin. Throughout Monday morning and afternoon the makeshift hearses came and went through the hilly streets, past houses and cottages in which shutters were closed and blinds drawn, carrying their complement of plain wooden coffins. Troops from the Connaught Rangers and the Royal Dublin Fusiliers marched on either side of the hearses and thousands of mourners and local people followed in carriages, motor cars or on foot. In the shallow amphitheatre in the hills, the coffins were lowered, one above the other, into three communal graves, each twenty feet long and thirty wide. Holy water was sprinkled like silver breaths in the sunlight and incense drifted in the still air among the cypress trees. One hundred and fifty four bodies were buried in the three graves; in one there were 65 coffins and 67 bodies because two infants lay with their mothers.

By Cunard's reckoning that Monday afternoon 1,150 passengers and crew were dead and 767 had been saved.

When the First Lord rose to address the House of Commons

that evening there was an ominous gloom among the members not known, according to one parliamentary correspondent, since the days when Britain had confronted Napoleon.

Churchill faced a volley of questions from a group led by Sir Charles Beresford and members leaned forward intently to hear his replies. What was the *Lusitania*'s speed? Had the Admiralty received notice of the warning issued by the German Embassy in New York? What provisions had been made to safeguard the *Lusitania* on her crossing? Was it not known that the *Centurion* and the *Candidate* had been sunk the previous day? Was he aware the Admiralty had provided escorts to meet steamers carrying horses from the United States to Liverpool, and, if so, what arrangements were made to convoy the *Lusitania* to Liverpool?

Churchill made it clear that it was not possible to make public 'the naval dispositions for patrolling the coastal approaches' and that the Admiralty's resources did not allow a destroyer escort for the 200 merchant or passenger ships that reached the shores of England every day.

But Bonar Law intervened in the debate and drew from Churchill the disclosure that messages had been sent to the *Lusitania* by the Admiralty and acknowledged by the liner. 'I will say nothing further,' Churchill added, 'for, pending the inquiry, any discussion might be interpreted as implying blame on the Captain.'

All day Monday Americans had heard rumours that President Wilson had been assassinated. Annoyed by the report, White House officials tried, and failed, to discover where the story had originated. The President, alert though grim-faced, received a tumultuous ovation when he stepped onto the stage of the Convention Hall in Philadelphia on Monday evening before four thousand newly-naturalised Americans. He was interrupted by spontaneous outbursts of applause as he spoke of peace as 'a healing and elevating influence in the world'. He made no direct reference to the sinking of the *Lusitania*, but his audience, and those Americans who opened their newspapers the next morning, interpreted his words as a refusal to declare war. 'There is such a thing,' said Wilson, 'as a man being too proud to fight. There is such a thing as a nation being so right that it does not need to convince others by force that it is right.' For the thousands of new citizens in the Convention Hall that evening this was a cue to wave their miniature Stars and Stripes enthusiastically in their newly-found patriotism. But the words 'too proud to fight' were interpreted by Britain as a refusal by America to enter the war.

That same evening there came an official communique from the German Foreign Office in Berlin expressing the Government's 'deepest sympathy' at the loss of lives on board the *Lusitania*. Responsibility rested, the communique stated, with the British Government which, through its plan of starving the civilian population, had forced Germany to resort to retaliatory measures. Despite the German offer to halt the submarine war if the 'starvation plan' was abandoned, British merchant ships were being armed with guns and had repeatedly tried to ram U-boats, thus making searches impossible.

Dudley Field Malone, the Collector of Taxes at the port of New York, was stung by the German charge that the *Lusitania* had been armed. 'This report is not correct,' he declared. 'She was inspected before sailing, as is customary . . . No guns were found, mounted or unmounted, and the vessel sailed without any armament. No merchant ship would be allowed to arm in this port and leave the harbour.'

Herman Winter, Charles Sumner's assistant at Cunard, who had figured among the British Ambassador's suspects, denied the guns report. He had been on board the liner for some hours before she sailed. It was true, according to Winter, that she had about 4,200 cases of cartridges for small arms, but these did not come within the classification of 'ammunition'. 'There was no explosive of any sort on board. The *Lusitania* was an unarmed passenger steamer.'

On Tuesday morning Consul Wesley Frost sat down in his

office in Queenstown and began a long report to Secretary of
State Bryan. He had decided that the search for floating
bodies had been 'wretchedly mismanaged'. He wrote:

> An Admiralty tug was cruising round the scene until mid-
> night Friday night, rather ineffectively, as she returned
> with neither news nor bodies. No other vessel was sent out
> until Saturday midnight when a Cunard tug was sent out,
> but turned back after a few hours, and, as I understand
> it, did not reach the scene at all. Admiralty patrol boats
> pass not far from the scene and are ordered to look out,
> but not to leave their beats. No other vessel was sent out
> until Monday at four pm when I represented to Cunard
> that diplomatic intervention would result if immediate
> steps were not taken. They then chartered a Dutch tug
> and sent her out. She is due shortly and has some bodies
> on board, but not many — perhaps a dozen.

Frost thought the shipping line and the Admiralty were each
switching responsiblity.

> The Admiralty protests that all their vessels are busy on
> regular patrols, though to my mind the importance of
> searching for the 1,200 bodies would justify some modifi-
> cation of the patrols. Cunard claim that the Admiralty
> has direction of all available vessels and even Liverpool
> could not send an effective boat. I am frankly much dis-
> satisfied with the course of events in this respect, but hope
> that through the Ambassador action may be taken.

He did not want to be abrupt with the Admiralty at Queenstown, but he had given them vigorous hints. What was pre-
venting the search for bodies? Fear? Indifference? Financial
considerations? He simply did not know. There was certainly
goodwill, but mistakes had been made, even by his own
Consulate, he admitted. He drew some conclusions of his own
about the sinking. 'The sinking was in sixty fathoms, and
Turner thinks her nose touched bottom before her stern disappeared, accounting for slight suction. Second torpedo

dubious: probably boiler explosion. Sinking took eighteen minutes; occurred two twenty-three.'

*On the afternoon he sank the* Lusitania *Kapitänleutnant Walther Schwieger shot a stern torpedo from 500 yards at a steamer heading towards the Fastnet, and missed. Weisbach, who had been in the stern torpedo compartment, reported that it had left the tube correctly, but either it had not run at all, or it had run at the wrong angle. Schwieger was not unduly disappointed. He had sunk the* Lusitania. *There could be no bigger prize. He continued his voyage to Germany around the west coast of Ireland and the Hebrides avoiding armed enemy trawlers and patrol boats. He wanted to reach home waters with his remaining torpedo.*

*Early on the morning of Thursday, 13 May, he ordered Rikowsky to resume wireless communication with the German stations. The telegraphist received a message from the Admiral of the Fleet: COMMANDER AND CREW U-20 MY FULLEST RECOGNITION FOR ACHIEVEMENT TO THE PRIDE OF THE HIGH SEAS FLEET CONGRATULATIONS ON YOUR RETURN.*

*At eleven am the* U-20 *sailed into Wilhelmshaven. The order had been sent to naval vessels in the harbour: 'The band and all hands on deck'. As the sea-rusted submarine glided towards her moorings the men from the nearby ships crowded the rails and cheered. Schwieger and his officers and crew assembled on the U-boat's deck, waving and returning the hurrahs. At the sluice gates the Admiral of the Fleet came on board and shook hands with each member of the crew. After nine months' duty they could now go on leave; all except Schwieger, who was ordered by Commodore Bauer to report to Berlin at once.*

*On his arrival at the War Office Schwieger, to his surprise, was reprimanded by Admiral von Müller, the Chief of the Kaiser's War Cabinet. The storm of indignation abroad over the sinking of the* Lusitania *had upset the Kaiser and some members of the Cabinet.*

By the end of the week Consul Frost's complaints had brought results. More than sixty bodies were brought into port. Most of them were found floating with their heads forward and arms down, their life-jackets wrongly adjusted; those floating with their heads back revealed faces from which most of the flesh had been eaten.

For many weeks afterwards bodies were washed ashore as far west as the Aran Islands and as far east as Barry on the Welsh coast. Some of the bodies retrieved within the week were identified: Dr. Pearson and his wife, and Purser McCubbin. The body of Lesley Mason was recovered and shipped to her father in Boston. The bodies of Stephen, John and Peter Crompton were found. Dr. McDermott, the *Lusitania*'s surgeon, was buried in a private grave in Queenstown, as was the body of little Ailsa Booth Jones. Commander Foster Stackhouse's body was buried by relatives in Cork. Gwen Allan's body was sent to London. Norah Bretherton's baby Elizabeth was found and buried in a convent in Cork. Charlotte Pye's baby Marjorie was buried in a private grave at Queenstown. It was the end of June before they found the body of Chief Engineer Bryce.

The last tributes to Charles' Frohman were the most remarkable in the history of the American theatre. At the crowded Temple Emanu-El in New York, a fortnight after the *Lusitania*'s sinking, admission was by ticket only. In Los Angeles at the instigation of Maude Adams, and in San Francisco, Tacoma and Providence, services in his memory were held simultaneously.

Few of the later bodies recovered could be identified. A body found on a beach in July was 'almost a skeleton and unrecognisable'; all that distinguished the cadaver was a new pair of tennis shoes. Throughout the month a grim list was compiled by local police and officials: 'Male body, washed ashore, 20 July. Very decomposed, head and hands missing . . .' 'Male body, recovered on 23 July. Unrecognisable, skull and bones of face bare . . .' 'Male body, 23 July. Portion only from hip to feet . . .' 'Male, unrecognisable, supposed to be a Russian . . .' 'Male, 30 years, apparently fireman, unrecognisable . . .' 'Male, apparently steward, brought ashore, no means of identification; head and arms gone . . .'

Curiously, on 12 July, the remains of a recognisable male were washed ashore in County Kerry. At first the body was taken to be that of a *Lusitania* victim. But a subsequent investigation established the remains as those of Leon Thresher, from the *Falaba*, the first American citizen to lose his life in the U-boat campaign on 28 March.

Until the furore died down Captain von Rintelen halted his operations, issuing a general 'cease fire' to his leading agents and others along the waterfront. All plans to manufacture fire bombs, or 'Scheele's cigars', and plant them on board ships carrying munitions were cancelled. Von Rintelen, who was known as 'Hanson' to his saboteurs, feared that intense anti-German feeling would make sabotage operations impossible.

But his belief that the loss of American lives in the *Lusitania* disaster would halt further shipments of munitions from American ports was proved wrong. The shipments continued, and he directed his agents to resume operations, establishing new cells of saboteurs in Boston, Philadelphia and Baltimore. The Irish, some of whom imagined von Rintelen was connected with Home Rule organisations, remained his enthusiastic supporters.

Suspecting that fire bombs might have been planted on board the *Lusitania*, secret service agents shadowed the German intelligence officer. When incendiary devices discovered on board the steamer *Kirk Oswald* at Marseilles were found to be the type in which Scheele specialised, secret service men were convinced they had been planted on the steamer before she sailed from New York. They intensified their search for the plotters. The leading suspects included Paul Koenig, the Hamburg-Amerika Line's 'special investigator', and his agents Gustav Stahl, Hans Hardenberg and Chester Williams (alias Curt Thummel, alias Charles Thorne). Neal Leach was no longer on their list; he was reported 'drowned on the *Lusitania*'.

Early in June Stahl was arrested. He made a confession stating he was drunk when he went on board the *Lusitania* with Neal Leach the night before the fatal voyage; he had not seen mounted guns on her decks. He was convicted of perjury and sentenced to one year and six months in the Federal Penitentiary in Atlanta. Hardenberg was arrested a few days after Stahl, but the net didn't close on Koenig until an evening in December when detectives arrested him as he left the offices of the Hamburg-Amerika Line. They seized a mass of documents in his office, including a notebook containing the names of almost one hundred Germans living in the United States. Koenig's knowledge of the movements of ships operating out of New York astonished them. Not only did he know what munitions were on board each ship, he knew when they left the factory, by what railroad they were transported, and their hour of arrival at the docks.

On the morning of 6 July Franz von Rintelen was sitting over coffee in the breakfast room of the New York Yacht Club when he was handed a slip of paper bearing a telephone number. He finished his coffee, then called the number. Captain Boy-Ed was at the other end of the line. The naval attaché asked von Rintelen to meet him at the corner of Fifth Avenue and 45th Street at noon. When the intelligence officer arrived at the rendezvous Boy-Ed handed him a telegram. It read:

> TO THE NAVAL ATTACHE AT THE EMBASSY. CAPTAIN VON RINTELEN IS TO BE INFORMED UNOBTRUSIVELY THAT HE IS UNDER INSTRUCTIONS TO RETURN TO GERMANY

Von Rintelen was angry. He had specifically asked Berlin not to use his name in any cable. He could not comprehend his recall. What would his agents think if he left the United States with important business unfinished?

He sailed, nevertheless, early in August on the *Noordam* of the Holland-America Line for Rotterdam, carrying a fake Swiss passport in the name of 'Emile Gache'. Within sight of the chalk cliffs of England the *Noordam* was boarded by British officers. Von Rintelen was taken off the ship and escorted to Ramsgate where his passport was scrutinised. He was then driven to London to be interrogated by a group of officers at Scotland Yard, among them Admiral Sir Reginald Hall, the spy-catcher German Naval Intelligence feared most. Hall asked him, 'Do you know a Captain von Rintelen?'

'I am not obliged to answer you,' von Rintelen replied.

Hall smiled, then pulled a packet of papers from a drawer and passed one to the German. It was a copy of the telegram Boy-Ed had given him in New York ordering him to return to Berlin.

'Where did you get hold of this?' von Rintelen snapped. 'Surely it was in code?'

'It was in code, Captain,' Hall answered. 'But we decoded it.' He added sarcastically, 'We know that you met Captain Boy-Ed at the corner of Fifth Avenue and 45th Street.'

British Intelligence had broken the Germans' 'Most Secret' code. Von Rintelen realised the game was up. He was to spend the next eighteen months in a British prisoner-of-war camp. Afterwards he was shipped to America where he was charged, with thirty other German agents, with having planted fire bombs in the cargo space of ships plying between New York and Allied ports in Europe. He refused to give evidence at his trial or betray his fellow agents. He was sentenced to four years' penal servitude at the Atlanta penitentiary.

Although the secret service had succeeded in breaking the German spy rings in and around the port of New York and netting most of the conspirators, they singularly failed to discover which of these rings had penetrated the security surrounding the *Lusitania*. Some secret service agents believed that von Rintelen, with the help of the Irish, was the only ringleader capable of having incendiaries placed on the liner; but they were unable to produce positive proof.

K

# 24

# THE INQUIRY

FIVE WEEKS AFTER the loss of his ship Captain William Turner faced an ordeal as arduous as the worst Atlantic crossing when he was summoned as the key witness at the Board of Trade Inquiry into the disaster. It was convened at the Admiralty's request at Central Buildings, Westminster, on 15 June; though not a trial as such, Turner was in no doubt that his reputation was at stake.

Heading the inquiry was Lord Mersey, a man experienced in the field of maritime disasters. He had led the inquiries into the sinkings of the *Titanic* and the *Empress of Ireland* and seemed an obvious choice to preside over the *Lusitania* inquiry. At seventy-four he was a redoubtable figure, an expert on maritime and Admiralty law, and a Liberal in politics. He was outspoken, autocratic and sometimes short-tempered, especially when subject to periodic attacks of gout. Members of the legal profession envied him his alert mind and his grip of technicalities, which was surprising since his knowledge of seafaring was minimal.

Turner had reason to fear Lord Mersey. He remembered his handling of the *Titanic* inquiry when, apparently without trial and upon suspect evidence, he had condemned the Master of the *Californian* for his supposed failure to steam to the assistance of the stricken liner. Nor could he expect an easy passage from the Attorney-General, Sir Edward Carson, a master of cross-examination. His oratory was as suited to the courtroom as to the House of Commons of which he was a longtime member. He had been a classmate of Oscar Wilde's

whom he afterwards cross-examined in court when defending
the Marquess of Queensbury in Wilde's action for criminal
libel. 'No doubt,' said Wilde at the time, 'he will perform his
task with all the added bitterness of an old friend.'

Turner was more fortunate in the choice of lawyer representing the Cunard company and himself. Butler
Aspinall, KC, achieved his results by friendly persuasion and a
deceptively mild manner. He may have lacked Carson's Irish
aggression, but witnesses found his chattiness could lead them
into tight corners.

The Board of Trade's case would be put by the Solicitor-
General, Sir Frederick Smith, who had unsuccessfully tried to
halt the Kinsale inquest. Sir Frederick was already inclined to
the view that Captain Turner was guilty of negligence, and
Winston Churchill and Lord Fisher shared this view. Churchill
believed that Turner was to blame on two counts: failure to
zigzag in the danger zone and failure to increase speed when
he knew that submarines were operating in the area. After the
Admiralty's warnings of April, Churchill thought this inex-
cusable. It was perhaps nearer the truth to assume that
Churchill and Fisher were both searching for scapegoats and
hoped to find them in Turner and the Cunard company.

Shortly after ten o'clock on the morning of Tuesday, 15
June, Captain Turner entered Central Hall, accompanied by
Alfred Booth and Butler Aspinall. Thirty witnesses and fifty
survivors of the disaster, their relatives and friends, had
already gathered. Among them was Dr. Warren Pearl and his
wife and Nurse Alice Lines; Pearl was keen to attend the open
sessions (at least two of the six sessions, those relating to the
Captain's handling of his ship, would be held in camera
because the publication of Admiralty instructions on how to
avoid or combat submarines might prove useful information
to the enemy). Walter Webb-Ware arrived to represent the
Vanderbilt family.

Turner and Booth took their seats at one of the tables in the
well of the hall reserved for Cunard officials. At the end of the
hall Lord Mersey and his assessors sat on a raised dais with the

witness box in front of them. No robes or uniforms were worn
and the atmosphere seemed more relaxed than was customary
in judicial courts. The 'Mersey Inquiry', as the Press described
it, was not a regular court of law; nonetheless it had aroused
great interest in legal and maritime circles. Many survivors
and heirs of the victims of the sinking were taking legal action
in the civil courts for damages and their hopes for a generous
settlement depended on the outcome of this inquiry.

Sir Edward Carson opened the proceedings quietly,
describing the design and construction of the *Lusitania*. When
Turner was called to the witness box the reporters, seated
below Lord Mersey and his assessors, showed interest. Having
established that Turner was Master of the *Lusitania* and held
the certificate of Extra Master, Carson asked him if he had not
received Admiralty instructions to pass harbours at full speed
while in the danger zone, steer a mid-channel course, avoid
headlands and take the pilot at the Liverpool Bar. Turner
replied that he had had such instructions.

*Carson*: Why, then, with that information did you come so
close to the Old Head of Kinsale?

*Turner*: To get a fix. We were not quite sure what land it was;
we were so far off.

*Carson*: Is that all you have to say? You say you were warned
specially to avoid the headlands and to stay in mid-channel:
those were the two instructions which were given?

*Turner*: Yes, but I wanted to find out where I was.

*Carson*: Do you mean to say you had no idea where you were?

*Turner*: Yes, I had an approximate idea, but I wanted to be
sure.

*Lord Mersey*: Why?

*Turner*: Well, my Lord, I do not navigate a ship on
guesswork.

*Lord Mersey*: But why did you want to go groping about to try
to find where land was?

*Turner*: So that I could get us a proper course.

*Mersey*: I do not understand this. Do you mean to say it was not possible for you to follow the Admiralty directions which were given to you?

*Turner*: Yes, it was possible.

*Lord Mersey*: Then why did you not do that?

*Turner*: I considered I followed them as well as I could.

*Carson*: I only want to get the facts. You do not suggest for a moment, do you, that when the torpedo struck the *Lusitania* you were in mid-channel?

*Turner*: It is practically what I call mid-channel.

Lord Mersey adjusted his pince-nez as Carson unrolled an Admiralty chart for Turner. 'Do you call that mid-channel?' Turner replied, 'As a seafaring man I would call that mid-channel.'

Carson smiled. There was a heavy irony to his next question. 'Do you not know perfectly well that what the Admiralty instructions were aiming at was that you should be further out from land on the ordinary course?'

*Turner*: So I was. Considerably further out.

*Carson*: At that time not very much?

*Turner*: I wanted to find out the ship's position.

*Carson*: Were you not able to find it out approximately from your navigation?

*Turner*: I do not work on approximation if I can get a proper fix.

*Carson*: But you deemed it of some importance to try and avoid the submarine?

*Turner*: Certainly. Most important.

*Carson*: You had plenty of time in hand, had you not?

*Turner*: Yes. Plenty of time.

*Carson*: I am not at the moment condemning you. You thought it sufficient to be ten miles off Kinsale Head?

*Turner*: Yes.

*Carson*: You knew it was not mid-channel nor anything like it?

*Turner*: No, I thought at the time it was about fifteen miles.

*Carson*: Never mind. Take this from me: you were able for two hours to see the land? I put it to you, whether it was right or wrong, you thought it sufficient to be that ten miles off?

*Turner*: Yes.

*Carson*: And therefore you did not think it necessary to be in mid-channel?

*Turner*: No.

*Carson*: Now why did you disobey the Admiralty instructions You did not try to get to mid-channel: that was not your aim?

*Turner*: My aim was to find land.

*Carson*: What I am putting to you is that you never for a moment tried to carry out what the Admiralty had laid down?

*Turner*: I thought I was trying my best, anyhow.

So far, things had gone against Turner. It was doubtful whether some of his monosyllabic replies under cross-examination had impressed Lord Mersey. Spectators in the gallery and those in the well of the hall could not hear him distinctly while Lord Mersey could be heard only by those close to him. Even Carson's remarks were sometimes unintelligible.

In the afternoon Carson asked Turner whether he had zigzagged his vessel in accordance with Admiralty instructions. Turner replied that he had not.

*Carson*: You were told to do that?

*Turner*: I understood it was only when you saw a submarine that you should zigzag.

*Carson*: You had information that there were submarines about and that the instructions were to zigzag.

*Lord Mersey*: And I think the reason is stated, too.

Carson produced a copy of the Admiralty instructions and read them aloud. Again he asked Turner whether he had zigzagged. Again Turner answered, 'No.'

*Carson*: Why?

*Turner*: Because I didn't think it was necessary until I saw a submarine.

*Carson*: You were told zigzagging was a safeguard; you were told submarines were infesting the southern part of the Irish coast; you had plenty of time in hand, and you did not obey the orders?

*Turner*: I did not.

Butler Aspinall then rose. He returned to the ground already covered by Sir Edward Carson regarding the mid-channel course. He led Turner through the morning events of 7 May and referred to the fog that had made him reduce speed. Lord Mersey interposed to say, 'I think you are leading him rather too much, Mr. Aspinall.'

Aspinall explained, 'I am trying to get at what was in his mind, my Lord.' He turned to Turner. 'You must apply your mind, if you will, and do not answer questions hurriedly or hastily. Just think. Why did you, having knowledge of what the Admiralty instructions were, steer a course which you had intended should take your ship so close to the Coningbeg lightship and not into mid-channel?'

*Turner*: Because there was a submarine in mid-channel, as I understood it, and I wanted to keep clear of him.

*Aspinall*: Is that what weighed with you at the time?

*Turner*: Yes.

*Aspinall*: Did you give the matter consideration?

*Turner*: I did. That is what I am saying.

*Aspinall*: You see, this morning you were asked about this and you did not tell us anything about it?

*Turner*: I forgot it.

Sir Edward Carson later dealt with the measures, if any, taken by Turner after the *Lusitania* was struck to save the lives of those on board. He also referred to two other Board of Trade questions: Were such measures reasonable and proper? Was proper discipline maintained on board the liner after she was struck? He questioned Turner on the difficulty in lowering the boats.

*Turner*: They could not very well lower them on the port side because of the heavy list.

*Carson*: Can you give us a little more information as to the extent of the list?

*Turner*: I should say about 15 degrees.

*Carson*: What happened to the boats on the port side?

*Turner*: They caught on the rail and capsized some of the people out. Some were let go on the run, and some of them fell inboard on the deck and hurt some of the passengers.

Asked at this point by a Mr. Cotter, representing a number of the *Lusitania*'s crew members, if he had held boat drill before leaving Liverpool, Turner replied that he had.

*Cotter*: Was the crew of the *Lusitania* proficient in handling boats, in your estimation?

*Turner*: No, they were not.

*Cotter*: Were the stewards proficient in handling boats?

*Turner*: Just about the same as they all are now, as ships' crews go now.

*Cotter*: Then your contention is that they are incompetent to handle boats?

*Turner*: They are competent enough — they want practice. They do not get practice enough, and they do not get experience.

*Cotter*: When you gave the order to lower the boats to the rail were the crew then attending to the various boats?

*Turner*: Yes, they were.

*Cotter*: Did you notice if they had any difficulty?

*Turner*: Lots of difficulty, owing to the list.

Switching to the subject of life-jackets Cotter asked if the crew had assisted in putting life-jackets on passengers, to which Turner replied, 'I believe so.'

*Cotter*: And your orders were carried out as far as possible?

*Turner*: I understand they were.

When the inquiry resumed next morning Alfred Booth took his place in the witness box. The immaculately-groomed Chairman of Cunard cut an impressive figure. When he spoke it was in a confident and resonant voice. In reply to the Attorney-General he said that his company had decided to run the *Lusitania* at 'three-fourths boiler power', which meant a reduction of speed from an average of about 24 knots to an average of 21 knots.

*Carson*: I take it that you were fully aware of the importance of speed in relation to the journey, so as to avoid submarine attack?

*Booth*: Yes.

*Carson*: Being so alive to that, do you tell his Lordship that you had no consultation of your Board, having regard to the German threats, to increase the speed for the journey by using three-quarter boiler power?

*Booth*: That question, if it had arisen at all, would have arisen in February when the first submarine attacks were made, and the view of my directors was that the *Lusitania*, being in fact the fastest ship that was running, the difference between 21 and 24 knots was not material so far as avoiding submarines was concerned.

*Carson*: Would you say that the difference between 18 and 24 knots was not material?

*Booth*: It is very difficult to say exactly where one would draw the line. No steamer of over 14 knots had ever been caught by a submarine at all.

*Carson*: Did your company give any special directions to your officers with reference to submarines?

*Booth*: We discussed the submarine danger with the individual Captains. I gave no specific instructions to Captain Turner.

*Carson*: At all events you had no communication with Captain Turner with reference to any instructions from the Admiralty?

*Booth*: No.

*Carson*: Was the question of when the ship should arrive at the Bar at Liverpool settled by you or suggested, or how was it left?

*Booth*: We warned Captains that it would not be safe to arrive at certain states of the tide.

*Carson*: Had you any communication whatever with Captain Turner during the voyage from New York?

*Booth*: None whatever. As I understand, the message I asked the Admiralty to send to him was not received.

*Carson:* Had you any communication from him?

*Booth*: He had strict instructions not to use his wireless unless absolutely necessary.

*Carson*: Did you receive anything from your New York office with regard to the threat of destruction of the ship contemplated during the voyage?

*Booth*: No.

When Turner was recalled by the Attorney-General he was asked if the *Lusitania* had been armed or unarmed.

*Turner*: Unarmed.

*Carson*: Had she any weapons of offence or defence against the enemy at all?

Turner replied with an emphatic 'No'.

Lord Mersey referred to the question of zigzagging and

recalled Sir Edward had suggested that Turner should have zigzagged his ship in the dangerous waters off the Coningbeg lightship. Butler Aspinall asked, 'What would it have meant? If off the south coast of Ireland he had remained zigzagging about, it would have meant that whilst he was zigzagging no doubt an admirable manoeuvre for the purpose of avoiding a shot from a submarine he is in fact covering a very large area of ground whilst he is zigzagging. But whilst he is covering that large area of ground he may have been covering the very area he wished to avoid. In truth, and in fact, the submarine that succeeded in getting his ship was the one which had not been reported to him.'

In his final submission Aspinall conceded that Turner had not zigzagged, but he held it was the only Admiralty instruction he had failed to carry out. He wanted to emphasise that Turner, although he may have been a very excellent navigator, was undoubtedly a bad witness.

*Lord Mersey*: No, he was not a bad witness.

*Aspinall*: Well, he was confused, my Lord.

*Lord Mersey*: In my opinion at present he may have been a bad Master during the voyage, but I think he was telling the truth. And I think he is a truthful witness. I think he means to tell the truth. In that sense he did not make a bad witness.

*Aspinall*: No.

*Lord Mersey*: He made a bad witness for you.

*Aspinall*: Well, what I was going to say about him was this, that it was very difficult to get a consecutive story from the man. But I was going to submit that he was an honest man.

*Lord Mersey*: I think he is, and I do not think Sir Edward Carson has suggested otherwise. The impression the man has made upon me is — and I came here prepared to consider his evidence very carefully — but the impression he has made on me is that he was quite straight and honest.

*Aspinall*: Quite. He has gone through naturally the very greatest strain both physical and mental. He lost his ship. He lost his comrades, or many of them. There was a very great loss. And he was in the water for a very long period of time.

On Thursday, 17 July the verdict of the Mersey Inquiry was read at Caxton Hall. Having dealt with such matters as the navigation of the ship and the lifeboat precautions, the report stated, 'The question remains: Was Captain Turner's conduct the conduct of a negligent or of an incompetent man?' Lord Mersey was in no doubt about the answer: 'On this question I have sought the guidance of my assessors, who have rendered me most valuable assistance, and the conclusion at which I have arrived is that blame ought not to be imputed to the Captain. The advice given him, although meant for his most serious and careful consideration, was not intended to deprive him of the exercise of his skilled judgement in the difficult questions that might arise from time to time in the navigation of his ship. His commission to follow the advice in all respects cannot fairly be attributed either to negligence or in-competence.'

He concluded: 'He exercised his judgement for the best. It was the judgement of a skilled and experienced man, and although others might have acted differently and perhaps more successfully, he ought not, in my opinion, to be blamed. The whole blame for the cruel destruction of life in this vast catastrophe must rest solely with those who plotted and with those who committed the crime.'

Outside the hall Alfred Booth and Captain Turner shook hands for the benefit of the Press photographers. The verdict seemed a victory for both of them. Booth had never wavered in his view that the disaster had been unavoidable in the circumstances, although he would admit privately that Turner had made a confused and unconvincing witness. A judgement exonerating the shipping line and the Captain and placing complete responsibility on the German Government was well received in wartime Britain; any other verdict would have embarrassed the State Department and placed Cunard in an awkward position with regard to those undertaking legal action for damages. But among those who disagreed with the verdict was Dr. Warren Pearl; he was convinced that the ship's officers and the Cunard company should have been found guilty of negligence.

That evening Turner and Mabel Every caught the train at Euston for Liverpool. Coming so soon after the disaster the inquiry had left Turner exhausted. But he was relieved: Alfred Booth had kept faith with him, and in the eyes of his seafaring colleagues his name had been cleared. Now he wondered if the Mersey verdict would put an end to the criticism and the innuendoes.

# 25

# TABLE AT LÜCHOW'S

EARLY IN NOVEMBER 1915, Captain Turner was instructed to travel to France to take command of the 10,000-ton freighter *Ultonia* and sail her to Quebec. He was overjoyed and told Booth, 'I'm sick and tired of being idle on shore.'

The Cunard chairman had remained his friend, retaining him on a standby basis as a relief captain. He seemed embarrassed about asking Turner to take command of the *Ultonia*. He admitted he had called him in because the regular Captain had been taken ill and no other Captain was available. 'I'm sorry it's such a small ship after the *Lusitania* and the *Aquitania*.'

'I have no regrets,' Turner replied. 'I would go to sea in a barge if necessary.'

On Friday, 19 November, while the freighter was unloading and being readied for the return voyage to England, Turner travelled to New York and visited his friend, Dr. Edwin Sternberger, who was a prominent physician. To Sternberger he seemed thinner, his hair greyer and his blue eyes not as sharp as they had been. At the doctor's residence he relaxed and even agreed to meet a reporter from the *New York Times*, which surprised his host. Since the British Press had criticised him for his part in the loss of the *Lusitania* he had stubbornly refused to be interviewed. In fact, it turned out to be his first and only newspaper interview.

Wearing his Captain's uniform he allowed himself to be photographed and then sat down to talk with the *Times* reporter. He was anxious to clear the names of his officers and men who had survived and also pay tribute to those who had lost their lives in trying to save many others. But he would not discuss his instructions from the Admiralty. 'After the war everything will be cleared up,' he said confidently.

His praise of the crew's behaviour did not tally with the testimony of the more outspoken among the survivors. He maintained that all hands were drilled in lifeboat duties and knew their stations. He was satisfied that every precaution had been taken and that nothing had been left undone that might have helped to save lives. He had given the order that all bulkhead doors and all side ports from below the water line right up to B deck should be closed. 'If any ports were opened afterwards in the staterooms it was done by the passengers themselves.' On the afternoon of Thursday he had made a round of the ship with Anderson and seen that all the boats were ready for lowering. That was more than 24 hours before the attack and the *Lusitania* was making 21 knots, about average since the after-section of the four boilers had been shut off.

Why had he not reduced the liner's speed so that he would pass the Irish coast at night? 'All I can say is that my instructions from the Cunard company were to arrive at the lightship in the River Mersey at four o'clock on Saturday morning so that I could take the ship over the Bar without stopping for a pilot. I did not slow down on Thursday because there is a good deal of fog off the Irish coast at that season of the year, but all Friday afternoon the *Lusitania* was down to 15 knots and was put up to 18 knots about two hours before she was torpedoed.' Going by night would not have hidden his ship from the lookout on the submarines because in that northern latitude in May the night only lasts two and a half hours; the sun goes down 18 degrees below the horizon and then comes up again.

He emphasised that no matter what he had done or at what speed the liner had been travelling 'the submarines would have got her as they planned. They were just waiting to blow her up with all on board.' He still seemed convinced that there had been two or even three submarines because, after the 'two torpedoes' which struck the ship had been fired, two members of his crew on deck claimed they saw one torpedo shoot under the stern from starboard and another pass at almost the same instant under the stern from port. He admitted that he himself saw only the sheer of one torpedo in the water 'just before it struck the side of the ship between the third and fourth funnels coming from for'ard.'

He denied there was any panic, although just before the liner sank the steerage passengers aft 'started to scream and rush about'. He could not understand this. 'There were plenty of lifebelts in the cabins, and pictures showing how they should be adjusted.'

He was adamant that nothing could have prevented the 'torpedoes' from striking his ship. They were fired, he estimated, from an angle off the starboard bow and they travelled at a speed of 45 knots through the water, so no matter at what speed the *Lusitania* had been travelling she would have been sunk. In hindsight he suggested that if the fog had not lifted that day the 'submarines' might have missed the liner, but 'unfortunately it cleared up at the wrong time'.

Turner was one of the few survivors to contend that more than one submarine had attacked the *Lusitania*, or that the liner had been struck by 'at least two torpedoes'. With a curious fatalism he accepted that no action of his could have saved the *Lusitania* against submarine attack. After the war, he told the *Times* reporter, he expected to be given command of a big Cunarder again, the *Aquitania* perhaps, or some other liner built for the Atlantic trade. 'The directors of Cunard,' he insisted, 'have every confidence in my skill as a navigator.'

At Lüchow's on 14th Street on Saturday night it was like old times. Turner arrived with Dr. Sternberger and was seen as he came through the swing doors by August Lüchow in his up-stairs mirror. A table had been reserved for the Captain and his guest in the Niebelungen area. The music from the eight-piece orchestra rose above the noise of conversation. The war was 3,000 miles away.

Lüchow bustled through the restaurant, arms outstretched, to greet his old friend. He welcomed Turner, nodded sadly, and said, 'I am sorry about your *Lusitania*, Captain. I knew her as well as my own restaurant.' He believed that Turner had 'lost half his life' with the loss of his ship, yet he was certain that the Captain's attitude towards him would not change simply because he was German. And to prove his contention here was the Captain sitting in his restaurant again.

The cosy charm of Lüchow's had always given Turner a glow of contentment. Tonight should have been no different. Yet, as he was to say to Sternberger, it was different from other times. There was no *Lusitania* waiting at the end of the street at Pier 54.

On Sunday he took the train back to Montreal. On Tuesday morning he sailed the *Ultonia* home to England. He was never to see New York again.

That autumn Kapitänleutnant Schwieger was operating the *U-20* off the same area of the Irish coast where he had sunk the *Lusitania*. Like other U-boat commanders he was under new orders to spare passenger ships. Since the sinking of the *Lusitania* the number of ships torpedoed without warning had fallen; the U-boats now used their deck guns. This proved, in fact, to be more effective; the figures for sinkings in August 1915 reached a total of 185,000 tons. The richest pickings were in the south-western approaches to the British Isles, where Britain's answer to the increasing number of attacks by gunfire was to arm her merchantmen with light guns.

However, under the pressure of American opinion, the Kaiser eventually issued an order ending the unrestricted U-boat campaign. His decision angered Admiral von Tirpitz so much that he offered his resignation. It was not accepted, so instead the Admiral began to divert his U-boats to the Mediterranean.

Whether deliberately ignoring the Imperial order or arrogantly pursuing his own ambitions Walther Schwieger went ahead with his own style of warfare. On 14 September he torpedoed the *Hesperian*, a British ship, albeit 'defensively armed', with 600 passengers and crew, off the Irish coast. Thirty-two lives were lost. Schwieger claimed that the *Hesperian* appeared to be an auxiliary cruiser steaming without lights outside the normal shipping lanes. But the incident caused such an outcry that for the second time that year Schwieger was summoned to Berlin and told that henceforth he must follow instructions to the last letter.

Schwieger later claimed that the Kaiser's order to spare large passenger ships had not reached him before he sailed for the Irish coast. He continued, nevertheless, to show a persistent and ruthless pursuit of the enemy that demonstrated a lack of compunction. It was as though he was determined to inflict on the Allies as many casualties as possible.

The following summer the *U-20* ran aground in fog off the Danish coast. Schwieger did not want the British to discover his beached submarine and score a moral victory by torpedoing the U-boat that had sunk the *Lusitania*. He ordered his crew to abandon her, took off the ship's papers and then destroyed her with two bombs.

He was given command of the *U-88*, a better-equipped and more powerful submarine, and took a number of his old crew with him. The reprimand from his superiors had not affected the high regard in which he was held by his U-boat peers. In August 1917 he was awarded the coveted *Pour le Merité*, the highest German decoration a naval officer could receive, not in recognition of his sinking of the *Lusitania*, but for his destruction of the heavily-armed cruiser *Hilary*. The citation praised his 'particularly great courage and circumspection' in the attack.

One month later, on 17 September, Schwieger was dead. The *U-88* had sailed into a British mine cordon.

A number of theories as to how he died have been discounted. One, that he shot himself in a fit of remorse, was disproved in Germany. Another, that the *U-88* was sunk in a fight with the Q-ship *Stonecrop* in the Bay of Biscay, was also discounted, in spite of the fact that in 1921 the British awarded a prize bounty to the *Stonecrop* for the sinking. In a later theory Commander Rehder, a German naval officer, contended that the *U-88* was sunk by the Q-ship *Glenfoyle* off the southwest coast of Ireland on the same date as the alleged *Stonecrop* incident. No such encounter can be traced in the public records. The official theory remains that the *U-88* struck a mine and that Schwieger and all his crew were blown to pieces or asphyxiated in their craft.

Between August 1914 and September 1917, Walther Schweiger had sunk a total of 149 trading ships, an achievement which placed him sixth among the war's top U-boat commanders. Up to the departure of his last patrol Schwieger was adamant that he had received no specific orders to destroy the *Lusitania*; his only instruction on leaving Emden on 30 April 1915, was to 'do as much damage as possible to suspected British troop transports'.

Oberleutnant Werner Furbringer had continued to correspond with his former Commander after Schwieger had presented him with a silver cigar box at the farewell dinner party at Wilhelmshaven in 1915. In September 1917, Furbringer's last letter to Schwieger was returned marked 'Missing'.

Charles Voegele, the crew member of the *U-20* who had disobeyed Schwieger's order, was imprisoned at Kiel. At his court martial in May 1915, he had been sentenced to three years. Already a number of U-boat and other Navy personnel, some of them prisoners of conscience, were serving prison sentences.

In August 1917, the unrest among Navy personnel took a dramatic turn when twenty crew members of the *Heligoland* held a meeting at which, the German naval authorities alleged, they discussed plans for the liberation of their imprisoned comrades. They were promptly arrested.

After the Armistice the German ships were turned over to the British and the mutineers were released, among them Voegele. He left prison at Kiel in October 1918, but his health had suffered. He died at Strasbourg-Cronenbourg in 1920 where the friends who knew of his revolt on the *U-20* laid flowers on his grave every All Saints' Day.

Alfred Booth kept faith with Turner. In the autumn of 1916 he gave him command of the 14,000-ton *Ivernia*, an armed merchant steamer serving as a troop carrier. But, as with the *Ultonia*, this was a last-minute command. Four hours before the *Ivernia* was due to sail her Captain had been taken ill and Booth had to find an immediate replacement.

Just when Turner believed he was getting the feel of the sea again the *Ivernia* was torpedoed without warning about thirty miles off the southern tip of Greece. Again, Turner was lucky to escape with his life. As he swam from the bridge he managed, as he had done when the *Lusitania* went down, to cling to a chair until he was rescued. He later claimed that the *Ivernia* was zigzagging, but he would not elaborate on this. It was his last command.

He remained with Cunard as relief Captain for another year, but he was not allowed to forget the affair of the *Lusitania*. He admitted he was still tormented by the memory. 'I've been trying to forget this thing,' he said, 'and I cannot.'

He was summoned by Judge Julius Mayer as the chief witness in the United States hearings scheduled for October 1917 into the *Lusitania* sinking. Butler Aspinall again represented Cunard and a Mr. Scanlan, who represented the Americans, cross-examined Turner in London. In cross-examination Turner was asked about his instructions from the Admiralty regarding the *Lusitania*'s last voyage.

*Turner*: I could paper the walls with them all.

*Scanlan*: Can I have those instructions?

*Turner*: I am afraid you can't.

*Scanlan*: Do you refuse?

*Turner*: All I can do is to respectfully refer you to the Admiralty.

*Scanlan*: Had you received before the *Lusitania* sailed from

New York on May the first any Admiralty instructions in addition to those which were mentioned at the Lord Mersey inquiry?

*Turner*: I cannot remember anything about them at all.

*Scanlan*: Were they instructions regarding the navigation of the *Lusitania*?

*Turner*: Yes, they tell which course to take.

It was as far as Scanlan got. Turner persistently refused to divulge his orders. When the Mayer verdict was announced more than a year later Turner was exonerated from blame. Mayer declared: 'The cause of the sinking of the *Lusitania* was the illegal act of the Imperial German Government, acting through its instrument, the submarine commander, and violating a cherished and human rule observed, until this war, by even the bitterest antagonist.'

It was a popular verdict. The United States was now at war with Germany.

Even the award of the Order of the British Empire could not erase from Turner's memory the disaster of that May afternoon in 1915. Mabel Every tried to cheer him, but he developed a fixation that Liverpool people believed he was to blame for the loss of the liner. In November 1919 at the retirement age of sixty-three, he resigned as a Cunard Commodore after forty-one years' service. 'All I want now,' he told Mabel, 'is a quiet life.'

The couple retired to the small, scattered moorland village of Yelverton, close to Dartmoor where Mabel had grown up. This was the countryside she knew and loved and to which she introduced Turner. They bought a large detached house in a quiet treelined roadway. 'Newholme' was a double-fronted residence with a tennis court, a vegetable garden and Sir Francis Drake's original stream, which had brought water from Dartmoor to Plymouth, running parallel with the house; the view pleased Turner when he looked out across the lawn from the french windows of the drawing room.

But even in this Devon backwater people soon discovered that the Captain of the *Lusitania* was living among them. Captain Nicholson, RN, later Lord Carnock, who lived nearby, had disapproved of the Admiralty's wartime policy of ordering merchant ships to economise on fuel. He believed the *Lusitania* had carried 'arms and ammunition' and was surprised that Turner had not sailed at full speed through the danger zone. 'Why didn't the man light up his boilers?' he demanded.

Turner spent most of his summers in the garden and neighbours found they had to call on the Captain; he apparently wasn't going to call on them. They were surprised when his housekeeper brought in the tea things and then sat down to join them. But it was not long before the journalists found their way to Westella Road: William Turner could not escape the *Lusitania*.

# 26

# SURVIVORS

AS AN INTENSE SUN scorched the sidewalks of New York in early July 1915, a curious little scene was enacted at the Cunard offices on State Street. In a shaded corner of the main office a group of people gathered round a table examining photographs in the hope of identifying relatives or friends lost on the *Lusitania*.

They were not concerned with the war raging in Europe, nor with the diplomatic notes passing between Washington and Berlin concerning the German submarine offensive; they sat, unnoticed by customers filing in and out of the building, intent on scrutinising the photographs of the 120 *Lusitania* dead who had not been identified before burial in Ireland. The Cunard company was hopeful that this inspection might lead to positive identification.

The photographed victims included two children covered with lilies placed in their coffins by Queenstown people; another photograph showed a small girl hugging a teddy bear, another a mother clasping her baby in her arms. With the exception of the infants the expression on each face was one of agony. Suddenly an old man began to weep. He had recognised the body of a woman relative. Sometimes one of the group stared endlessly at a photograph as though reliving the disaster. It was not as though identification gave these people any hope of seeing their loved ones again; they knew they were buried in a mass grave in Ireland. But it seemed they needed this final proof.

Some survivors were still critical about the loss of lives. Fred

Gauntlett, who returned to New York on the American liner *Philadelphia* with the body of Albert Lloyd Hopkins, was angry because destroyers had not been sent by the Admiralty to rescue the drowning passengers. Oliver Bernard continued to be

> amazed and morbidly suspicious of some callous motive behind the occurrence and contemptuous of the seamanship displayed on the voyage which made the handling of the liner appear as deliberate treachery on the part of all who were responsible for the safety of her passengers, to say nothing of the crew.

A year after the sinking Theodate Pope was awarded 25,000 dollars for her 'suffering and discomfort' in the tragedy and another five thousand dollars for the loss of her jewels and personal property. On his return to Boston Charles Lauriat became president of one of the largest book importing firms in New England and was paid a thousand dollars for the baggage he lost in the sinking. William Holt, the sixteen-year-old heir of Canada's richest man, became one of the foremost figures in Canadian finance. But Sir Montague and Lady Allan never recovered from the shock of losing their daughters Gwen and Anna. Two years later their only son was killed flying over the German lines.

When the Viscounty of Rhondda and Llanwern was created for David Thomas in 1916 the Welsh coal king became one of Britain's most powerful figures, with appointments as Food Controller and Minister for Health. At his death in 1918 Lady Mackworth was allowed by special dispensation to succeed to his title. As Lady Rhondda she took over her father's interests with such enthusiasm that she became the controller of huge coal estates and chairman of 26 companies.

The body of Alfred Gwynne Vanderbilt was never found and no one claimed the reward of 5,000 dollars. For months Alfred's sister Gertrude mourned his death, brooding alone, filling a scrapbook with clippings and letters about his travels. Margaret Vanderbilt resigned herself to a life without Alfred.

His estate was valued at 26,375,000 dollars. His eldest son William inherited five million dollars and his father's effects, including the gold medal voted by Congress to his great-great-grandfather, Commodore Cornelius Vanderbilt. Margaret received eight million dollars in properties, comprising houses in America and England. Her sons, Alfred Gwynne junior and George, each received the residuary estate, estimated at about ten million dollars.

Charles Frohman's brother Daniel ensured that the impresario's name would be remembered by forming a company to manage Frohman's theatrical stars. Maude Adams, the actress rumoured to have secretly married Frohman, voluntarily ended her career with his death. She made occasional reappearances in the thirties, but never relinquished the mantle of aloofness Frohman had encouraged her to wear. She never married, and died in 1953 at the age of eighty.

A year after she had stood with Frohman on the tilting boat deck of the *Lusitania* the actress Rita Jolivet married a wealthy Venetian, Count Giuseppe de Cippico. Two years later she and her husband made a Hollywood film, *Lest We Forget*, in memory of the impresario. Rita stayed on to play the lead in a Goldwyn film, *Theodora*, but she never achieved success in the movies; her career declined and she retired into obscurity.

Her sister Inez decided she could not go on living without her husband George Vernon. Two months after he had drowned she dressed herself in an elegant black evening gown enhanced by a jewelled necklace. Sitting in front of the mirror at the dressing table in her New York apartment, she took a pistol from the drawer and put a bullet through her head.

Second-class passenger Julia Sullivan sent the bundle of bank notes her husband Flor had pushed into her bodice on the liner to a little girl who had lost her parents, brothers and sisters in the sinking. On reaching the Sullivan farm in Kerry she had a novena of Masses offered for 'all the souls that went down in the *Lusitania*'. Life on the remote mountainy farm bound the couple together. They had three children. Their eldest, a girl, trained as a nurse in London and in the early days of the Second World War was killed when a bomb struck her hospital. 'Maybe,' Julia thought, 'the Germans wanted to finish from the sky what they had failed to do from the sea.' Her husband died soon afterwards and she lived on with her sorrows to raise her two young boys. Her golden days with the Branders, skating on the Great Lakes and swimming in Florida, faded to a distant memory.

Ian Stoughton Holbourn had lost the manuscript representing his life's work, but he had saved Avis Dolphin. He wrote the story he had promised her, an adventure book for girls, *The Child of the Moat*, published in the United States in 1916. In 1926 Avis married a journalist, Thomas Foley, whom she had met at the Holbourns' in Edinburgh. He lectured on socialism and, like Holbourn, was a pacifist. The mesmeric Holbourn died in 1933. He had continued to cross the Atlantic, dividing his time between universities in Britain and the United States. He was said to be the only professor who could pack a hall to the doors with a lecture on Greek thought.

Margaret Cox and her baby Desmond, who had survived the sinking, narrowly escaped death again in the Phoenix Park in Dublin during the Easter Rising of 1916. A man who went to help them was killed by machine-gun fire. Margaret Cox died in 1978 at ninety, her husband a year later. In her last years she had begun to write her personal account of the voyage of the *Lusitania*, a subject which until then she had been unable to confront.

Mary Maycock returned from a second stay with the Astor family in America to marry her Yorkshire fiancé Arthur Wood. The four hours she had spent crouching on her elbows and knees on a floating piece of driftwood left her permanently disabled; she was never able to walk any distance afterwards. But she led a full life and before her death at the age of seventy-five she made her first journey by air to revisit America.

George Wynne retired in the 1970's to a sailors' home in suburban Liverpool, where he kept a photograph of his father by his bedside together with one of himself wearing a black armband on his jacket taken the day after his return from Queenstown. Hugh Johnston went to sea again and was on board the *Lancastria* in World War Two when it was torpedoed at St. Nazaire by the Germans. Thousands of soldiers and airmen were drowned, but Johnston climbed to the top of a mast as the ship settled and swam away from his second shipwreck.

Fireman John O'Connell was one of the surviving crew members who never lost his suspicions about the circumstances surrounding the sinking of the *Lusitania*. He remained convinced that Winston Churchill wanted the liner sunk to bring the United States into the war. Some surviving crew members believed that the *Lusitania* had carried two defensive guns mounted in passenger cabins on each side of the ship. The doors of these cabins were reportedly locked throughout the voyage. Others talked of American aircraft engine parts among the cargo. Seven years after the sinking there was a claim that two American submarines had been carried in the liner's hold, a claim, that, although unusual, might have explained the presence on board of Hopkins, Gauntlett, Knox and other American shipbuilders.

Bellboy William Holton, too, had his misgivings. In later years, after he had left the sea and gone into business, he was to write of the economy in coal consumption as 'a predisposing contribution to the ultimate tragedy . . . It would seem that Cunard were guilty of contributory negligence which placed ship, passengers and crew at risk for financial considerations. I have always felt that I could not agree with the Queenstown coroner's verdict in which the owners and the Captain were absolved of blame and the guilt placed "with those who plotted and with those by whom the crime was committed".' Lord Mersey's opinion at the inquiry that the reduction in the liner's speed was 'of no significance and was proper under the circumstances' was 'an exercise in whitewashing Cunard with a very large brush'. Holton recalled that during World War Two the Cunard liners *Queen Mary* and

*Queen Elizabeth* had evaded successful submarine attack by the 'use of their high speed'. With her capablities fully utilised the *Lusitania* was 'not very much behind the *Queens*' in the matter of speed. He also believed that the gravity of the situation had not been accurately evaluated and that there was 'some ineptitude on the bridge in spite of the information radioed to the ship regarding submarine activity in the area'.

Fred Smyth of the *Candidate* was changing trains at Shrewsbury on his way from Milford Haven to Liverpool on the evening of 7 May 1915, when he heard the newsboys running along the platform shouting, '*Lusitania* torpedoed!' He thought then, and was still to maintain sixty-five years later, that his report to the Admiralty should have resulted in the *Lusitania* being diverted from her original course.

The most mysterious figure in the *Lusitania* story is Liverpool's Detective Inspector William Pierpoint. His real identity as a first-class passenger was known perhaps only to Turner and Anderson; his presence on board was a secret. Journalists had no knowledge of his identity when he slipped back into Liverpool among the survivors. In 1919, following a police strike in Liverpool, many members of the force were dismissed; Pierpoint, however, was promoted to Governor of the city's main Bridewell, a rank equal to that of police superintendent. In 1929 he retired, still a mysterious figure, still concealing the fact that he had been on board the ill-fated liner. Following his death in a private nursing home in 1950 there was no official recognition from his former colleagues; it was as though his name was an embarrassment to the force.

Even in their Devonshire backwater Turner and Mabel could not escape the gossip or the newspapers. They sold the house and returned to suburban Liverpool. At least Turner was near the sea and at night he could hear the ships' sirens at the mouth of the Mersey. In the late twenties he went to Australia in the hope of tracing his two sons, but never found them.

Kinsale, the sleepy fishing village of 1915, became 'an Irish Portofino' in the sixties with brightly-painted period houses, sophisticated bars, bistros, tourist hotels, and a harbour filled with smart yachts. Jane Deasy, who had seen the commotion at the harbour when the liner was sinking off the Old Head, lived on until 1980. She related the following phenomenon: A group who sailed out on an anniversary of the sinking to recite prayers and cast flowers over the waters where the *Lusitania* lay, 315 feet deep, saw 'a circle of light covering the sea where she went down, from one end of the ship to the other'.

The official analysis of missing and survivors issued by the Cunard Steamship Company on 1 March 1916, listed 1,195 missing (178 first class, 374 second and 239 third, and 404 crew members), and 764 survivors (113 first class, 227 second and 134 third, and 290 crew members).

# 27

# 'IS THAT YOU, BISSET?'

IN THE AUTUMN of 1932 Albert Bestic learned that William Turner was in failing health. He called to see him at De Villiers Avenue, in a quiet suburb on the outskirts of Liverpool. The door of the semi-detached house was opened by a woman of character and charm.

'May I see the Captain?' he asked. 'I'm a former officer of his. The name is Bestic.'

'I shall have to ask him,' Mabel Every said, motioning him into the hall. 'The Captain is not in the best of health. It isn't everyone he wants to see these days.' She went away, and returned almost immediately with the unexpected reply, 'He says he never heard of you.'

Albert was hurt. True, he had been only a junior officer on the *Lusitania*, but the refusal seemed discourteous. Then he remembered Turner's words to him on board the *Bluebell*. 'Why should you be glad I'm saved? You're not that fond of me.' He thanked the woman. 'It doesn't matter, really. Just give him my compliments. Tell him I hope he'll soon be better.'

As he stepped outside he suddenly recalled that Turner had never called him Bestic; it was always 'Bisset'. Mabel was about to close the door when he turned back. 'Just a moment. Would you be kind enough to tell the Captain that my name is really Bisset.' Mabel looked at him suspiciously. After a moment's hesitation she went to deliver his message. When she returned she was smiling. 'You can see him,' she said.

'What did he say?'

'He said — ,' she gave an apologetic cough. 'He said, Why the hell didn't he say so in the first place?' She ushered him into the drawing-room. Sitting near the window, lost in a large armchair, was a shrunken, pathetic figure. Bestic compared him to the brisk Commodore he had known, resplendent in his gold-encrusted uniform. Now a cardigan hung loosely on his emaciated frame. The old man was in his seventy-sixth year and racked with stomach cancer. The blue eyes, sunken now, looked directly at him and Albert suddenly felt an instinctive compulsion to whip his cap under his left arm and snap his heels to attention.

'Is that you, Bisset? Yes, of course. I remember now. That woman got your name mixed up. Sit down.'

'Thank you, sir.'

'What certificates have you got now, Bisset?' He rapped out the question like an examiner.

'A square-rigged Master's, sir.'

'Good.' The reply evidently pleased him. A 'steamship only' ticket was a back door into the profession. 'That's the *Grasmere*.' He nodded towards a photograph. 'Ran away to join her because my father wanted me to be a devil dodger. Grounded off the Antrim coast. Swam ashore.'

Albert listened as the old man reeled off the names of sailing ships in which he had crossed the world, elaborating on his adventures, recalling the times he was shipwrecked or washed overboard. He droned on, 'Good days, Bisset. I was the quickest man aloft. Except for a Greek. Blighter must have had a monkey for an ancestor, and not so remote either.' With distant eyes he looked out of the bay window as though his memories had conjured up billowing canvas and reeling masts beneath the dull Liverpool skies. Suddenly he looked at the officer with a rueful smile. 'Look at me now,' he said. 'Only fit for the breakers' yard.' Bestic saw his opportunity. 'The *Lusitania*, sir ,' he began hesitantly. 'Did you think she was going to be torpedoed?'

Turner paused to knock out his pipe. Even his hands were feeble. 'I was worried, Bisset. Naturally I was. What Master wouldn't be? I thought we had an odds-on chance of escaping, you know.' He shook his head slowly. 'I didn't get a fair deal. I mean to say, no escort to meet us, despite the signals about submarines. Gave me a false confidence. If the Admiralty didn't think it necessary to worry about a ship worth millions, not to mention hundreds of passengers, I reasoned they must think there's not much danger.' He tried to fill his pipe. 'No, I didn't get a fair deal. A good two years went by before they started issuing definite orders. What courses ships should take. The distance they should keep off headlands. I was told I should have taken a mid-Channel course. And my ship in the Atlantic?' He snapped his finger and thumb in irritation. 'They didn't even explain to me about zigzagging.'

Mabel entered. 'It's time for your medicine, Captain.' Looking at Bestic, she said, 'Don't you think you've talked enough for one afternoon?'

Turner growled. 'Medicine?' He muttered to his visitor, 'Damned petticoat government.'

Albert took the hint and rose. He shook Turner's extended hand and left the room.

During the months that followed Mabel continued to care for Turner. On special days the Captain flew the Union Jack from the tall flagstaff in his garden. When summer came he would sit outdoors in a deckchair, his mind wandering, his cat and dog close beside him, while Mabel tended the beehive by the potting shed.

His condition worsened until he could not leave his bed. He died peacefully on 23 June 1933.

Mabel knew William Turner had died an unhappy man. After his retirement he had suffered from deep depressions and lived as a recluse, convinced that people were avoiding him because they thought he should have gone down with his ship. It was a conviction he carried to his grave. It embittered him to think that others could condemn him for his actions without full knowledge of the facts. He never forgave Churchill for implying that his negligence was in part responsible for the loss of the *Lusitania*.

Whenever people raised the subject of the *Lusitania* Mabel

Every became defensive. Were they still blaming Will Turner for the loss of those lives? To her mind it was not his fault that his 'unsinkable' ship had taken such a heavy list or that the lifeboats could not be safely lowered. She refused to be drawn on whether he had told her about any secret Admiralty instructions. 'It's no good asking me,' she would say. 'All I can tell you is that the Captain followed his instructions.'

Turner's estranged wife took her sons to Australia, where she died. Norman Turner, who worked as a liaison officer between the British and Australian forces in World War Two, died from war injuries in 1968. Captain Turner's other son, Percy, who served as an intelligence officer in World War Two, was killed when the ship in which he was travelling was torpedoed off the southern Irish coast, just a mile from where the *Lusitania* went down.

Mabel Every sold Turner's house and moved to Moor Drive nearby to live with her brother.

In the early 1970's, when her health began to fail, Mabel moved into a private nursing home in Liverpool. In her nineties, she was the home's oldest resident. Outside the window of her small room overlooking the garden she had a special ledge built so that she could feed the birds. Her sense of humour made her popular with the patients and staff, although it could be biting when she was confronted by pretension.

Before she died in 1978 Mabel would occasionally take from the safe by her bedside a silver tray on which she kept her mementoes of Will Turner. Adjusting her spectacles she would remove one of a handful of medals and read the inscription, 'W. T. Turner, Fourth Officer, *City of Chester*, who jumped into the sea to rescue a drowning boy, April 1883.' Engraved on the tray was the Cunard Steamship Company's acknowledgement that Captain W. T. Turner had broken a transatlantic record for a round voyage in the *Mauretania* in December 1910.

But it was on his performance as Commodore of the *Lusitania* that history would judge William Turner.

# ACKNOWLEDGEMENTS

*Britain*:

British Museum Newspaper Library, Colindale. *Liverpool Echo* Library (Neil Williams). Liverpool University: Cunard Archives (Michael Cooke). Manx Public Library, Douglas, Isle of Man. Naval History Library, Ministry of Defence, London. Public Record Office, Kew. Quest Research and Information Services, Liverpool. Somerset House, London.

*Canada*:

Canadian Broadcasting Service, Toronto.

*Ireland*:

Bray Library, Co. Wicklow. British Embassy. Cork County Library (Padraig Ó Maidín). German Embassy (Rüdiger von Lukowitz). National Library, Dublin. Royal Dublin Society Library. United States Embassy (Robin Berrington).

*Germany*:

Bibliothek für Zeitgeschiele, Stuttgart (Professor Rohwer). Bundesarchiv (Abteilung Militärarchiv), Freiburg (Dr. Fleischer). Bundesarchiv, Koblenz. Staatsbibliothek Prussischer Kulturbesitz, Marburg.

*United States*:

British Consulate, New York. Hoover Institution, Stanford, Calif. National Archive and Record Services (Ronald E. Swerczek) and Department of State Library (Mrs. Larsen), Washington. New York Community Trust. New York Museum. New York Public Library. Pierpoint Morgan Library, New York. *Washington Post* Library, Washington.

# SPECIAL THANKS

*Australia*:

Ashton, Adrian; Auld, Annie H.; Barden, May; Burgoyne, L.A.; Comtesse, W. C.; Cain, W.; Caldwell, G.; Cavanaugh, John; Cusack, Mary; Danagher, V.P.; Evans, P.; Grimshaw, April; Hey, Frances D.; Hadland, Elsie; Hook, Frank; Hyde, Lynette; Kennedy, L.M.; McDermott, Barbara Anderson; Marshall, Marion; O'Connell, Max; Pope, Margaret; Preston, M.; Smyth, Frederick; Swanson, K. G.; Tranter, E.; Turner, Rita Edna;

*Britain*:

Adams, Heather; Baty, K. L.; Bestic, Alan; Bonner, Paul; Browning, Helen Campbell; Carnock, Lord; Carter, Craig J. M.; Collard, Frances; Cooke, Michael; Coppock, R. M.; Craddock, M.; Davis, Aubrey; Davies, E. James; Davies, Else; Drury, Alice; Eames, Peter; Every, Lord; Fenton, Kate; Fleet, Elia and Terry; Foley, Avis G.; Galbraith, Alistair; Gwyer, E. M.; Henry, Margaret; Holbourn, P. R. H. S.; Holton, Mini; James, Peggy; Jenkins, W. J.; Johnston, Hugh; Jones, Ellen; Joynson, Irene W.; Ladd, Oliver; Lewis, H. Elwyn; Morris, Evan J.; Murphy, G.; O'Connell, G. J.; O'Connell, John; O'Neill, John; Pidgeon, C.; Pierson, H. M.; Rees, Glyn; Sandilands, John; Shannon, Arthur; Simmons, Dave; Stephens, Marjorie; Thomas, Barbara; Thomas, Helen; Thomas, J. H.; Whelan, Brian & Maureen; Williams, Kendrick; Williams, Neil; Wynne, George.

## Canada:

Chappell, Len; Cox, snr., Richard; Marshall, J. Desmond; Danagher, V. J.; G.; Nickerson, Crowell M.; Evans, Earl L.; Griffin, Paterson, Gladys A.; H. G.; Liberty, Kaye; Lord, Paul, J.

## France:

Hanning, Jack; Ricklin, M. A.

## W. Germany:

Cornelius-Wagenführ, Bodo; Hildebrand, Hans R.; Yvonne; Falke, Barbara; Weisbach, Christian-Rainer; Herbertz, Claudia; Herzog, Weisbach-Zerning, Annelott.

## Ireland:

Alberry, Hilda; Albius, Charles; O'Brien, Bob; Mother; Barker, T. G.; O'Brien, Amelia; O'Connor, Boyer, Capt. Francis; Casey, Michael; O Dulaing, Michael; Clancy, John G.; Donncha; O'Dwyer, Edward; Clarke, Thomas; Deasy, O'Mahony, A. M.; Jane; Gruson, Norman; Ó Maidín, Padraig; Hannigan, Robert; Hughes, O'Malley, Jim; O'Neill, Jim; Margaret; Ireland, John de O'Neill, Seamus; O'Shea, Courcy; Jordan, Danny; Frank; O'Shea, Paul; Kelly, Joan; Lukowitz, O'Sullivan, Mary; Rüdiger von; Lynch, Robertson, Ian & Helga; Charles; Lyons, Larry; Speight, Jim; Thompson, McCarthy, Helen; Martin, Patrick; Walshe, Frances; Grace; Mulcahy, Michael; Wilcox, Edward; Lecky- Murphy, Jerry; Nash, Watson, Mrs.

## Northern Ireland:

Bishop, Bob; Ginty, Peacock, E.; Stewart, Dolly; Elizabeth; Henderson, Anna; Weeks, Frederick.

## United States:

Daniels, David; Galffy, Ortiz, Manuel; Pessin, Adorjan I de; Glynn, George; Ross, Leon; Michael; Mitchell, Jan; Swerczek, Ronald E.

# BIBLIOGRAPHY

*Books*:

Bailey, Thomas A. and Ryan, Paul B. *The Lusitania Disaster.* The Free Press, New York, 1975.

Baldwin, Hanson W. *Sea Flights and Shipwrecks.* Hanover House, New York, 1955.

Baylay, Admiral Sir Leslie. *Pull Together.* Harrap, London, 1939.

Bergen, Klaus. *U-Boat Stories.* Constable, London.

Bernard, Oliver P. *Cock Sparrow.* Jonathan Cape, London, 1936.

Bernstorff, Count Johann von. *My Three Years in America.* Skeffington & Son, London, 1920.

Bestic, Albert. *Kicking Canvas.* Evans Brothers, London, 1957.

Bestic, Albert. *The Waveswept Years.* In manuscript.

Blood-Ryan, H. W. *Franz von Papen, His Life and Times.* Rich & Cowan Ltd., London, 1940.

Briggs, Asa (ed.) *They Saw It Happen.* Basil Blackwell, 1962.

Chandler, George (introduction). *Victorian and Edwardian Liverpool and the North West.* Batsford Ltd., London, 1972.

Chatterton, E. Keble. *Danger Zone.* Rich & Cowan Ltd., London, 1934.

Churchill, Winston S. *The World Crisis.* Thornton Butterworth Ltd., London, 1923.

Coleman, Terry. *The Liners.* Allen Lane, London, 1976.

Corbett, Sir Julian S. *Naval Operations.* Longmans, London, 1921.

Croall, James. *Fourteen Minutes; The Last Voyage of the Empress of Ireland.* Michael Joseph, London, 1974.

Cronin, Sean. *The McGarrity Papers*. Anvil Books, Tralee, 1973.

Davidson, Marshall B. *New York: A Pictorial History*. Charles Scribner's Sons, New York, 1952.

Dönitz, Karl. *Zehn Jahre und Zwanzig Tage*. Athenaum-Verlag Junker and Dunnhaupt KG, Bonn, 1958.

Droste, C. L. & W. H. Tantum. *The Lusitania Case*. Riverside, Conn., 1972.

Dunbar, Janet. *J. M. Barrie: The Man Behind the Image*. Collins, 1970.

Ellis, Captain Frederick D. *The Tragedy of the Lusitania*. Privately printed, 1915.

Endle, Rufus. *Dartmoor Prison*. Bossiney Books, 1979.

Fitzgibbon, Constantine. *Denazification*. Michael Joseph, London, 1969.

Friedman, B. L. *Gertrude Vanderbilt Whitney*. Doubleday and Co. Inc., New York, 1978.

Frost, Wesley. *German Submarine Warfare*. Appleton and Co., New York, 1918.

Furbringer, Werner. *Alarm! Tauchen!* Berlin, 1933.

Garrett, Richard. *Submarines*. Weidenfeld and Nicolson, London, 1977.

Garrett, Richard. *Stories of Famous Ships*. Arthur Barker Ltd., 1972.

Gerard, James. W. *My Four Years in Germany*. New York, 1917.

Gibson, R. H. and Prendergast, M. *The German Submarine War*. Constable, London, 1931.

Goldberger, Paul. *The City Observed: New York*. Vintage Books, New York, 1979.

Grant, Robert M. *U-Boats Destroyed*. Putnam, London, 1964.

Gray, Edwyn A. *The Killing Time*. Seeley Service & Co. Ltd., 1972.

Hashagen, Ernst. *U-Boats Westwards!* Putnam, London, 1931.

Hendricks, Burton J. *The Life and Letters of Walter Hines Page*. Doubleday, New York, 1922.

Herzog, Bodo and Schomaekers, Gunter. *Ritter Der Tiefe-Graue Wolfe*. München-Wels, 1965.

Hoehling, A. A. and Hoehling, Mary. *The Last Voyage of the Lusitania*. Longmans, Green & Co., London, 1956.

Holbourn, Professor Ian Stoughton. *The Isle of Foula*. Edited with a memoir by Marian Constance Holbourn, 1936.

Horgan, John J. *Parnell to Pearse*. Browne and Nolan Ltd., Dublin, 1949.

Hoyt, Edwin. *The Vanderbilts and Their Fortunes*. Frederick Muller, London, 1962.

Hyde, Francis E. *Cunard and the North Atlantic 1940–1973*. Macmillan, 1975.

James, Admiral Sir William. *The Eyes of the Navy*. Methuen and Co., London, 1955.

James, Admiral Sir William. *The Code Breakers of Room 40*. New York, 1956.

Jones, John Price. *America Entangled*. A. C. Laut, New York, 1917.

Langsdorff, Walter von. *U-Boote Am Feind*. Gütersloh, 1941.

Lauriat, Charles E. *The Lusitania's Last Voyage*. Houghton Mifflin and Co., Boston, 1915.

Longford, Elizabeth. *Winston S. Churchill*. Sidgwick and Jackson, 1974.

Lord, Walter. *A Night to Remember*. Longmans Green and Co., 1956.

Maddocks, Melvin and the Editors of *Time-Life* Books. *The Great Liners*. Time-Life Books. Amsterdam, 1978.

Marder, Arthur J. *From the Dreadnought to Scapa Flow*. Oxford University Press, 1965.

Marcossan, Isaac and Frohman, Daniel. *Charles Frohman, Manager and Man*. Harper, New York, 1916.

Maurois, Andre. *A History of the USA.* Weidenfeld and Nicolson, London, 1964.

Midwinter, Eric. *Old Liverpool.* David and Charles Newton Abbot, 1971.

Mitchell, Jan. *Lüchow's Cookbook.* Doubleday and Co., New York, 1952.

Morton, Leslie. *The Long Wake.* Routledge and Keegan Paul, London, 1968.

O'Connor, Joseph. *Hostage to Fortune.* Michael F. Moynihan Publishing Co., Dublin, 1951.

Papen, Franz von. *Memoirs.* Translated by Brian Connell. Andre Deutsch, London, 1952.

Pratt, F. *Secret and Urgent.* New York, 1939.

Preston, Anthony. *U-Boats.* Bison Books, 1978.

Radfield, Peter. *The Titanic and Californian.* Hodder and Stoughton, 1965.

Rhondda, Viscountess. *This Was My World.* Macmillan, London, 1933.

Rintelen, Ranz von. *The Dark Invader.* Peter Davies, London, 1933.

Roskill, Stephen. *Churchill and the Admirals.* Collins, 1978.

Rowan, Richard Wilmer. *The Story of Secret Service.* Doubleday and Co., New York, 1937.

Schaeffer, Heinz. *U-Boat 977.* William Kimber, London, 1952.

Schuschnigg, Kurt von. *Farewell Austria.* Cassell and Co., 1952.

Seymour, Charles (ed.) *Intimate Papers of Colonel House.* Houghton Mifflin and Co., Boston, 1926.

Silver, Nathan. *Lost New York.* Schocken Books, New York, 1971.

Simon, Kate. *Fifth Avenue.* Harcourt Brace Jovanovich, New York and London, 1978.

Simpson, Colin. *Lusitania.* Longman, London, 1972.

Spiegel, E. F. von. *U-Boote im Fegenfeuer.* Preetz, 1963.

Strother, French. *Fighting Germany's Spies.* Doubleday, New York, 1918.

Stumpf. Richard. *War, Mutiny and Revolution in the German Navy.* Edited, translated and with an introduction by Daniel Horn. Rutgers University Press, New Brunswick, 1967.

Thomas, Lowell. *Raiders of the Deep.* William Heineman Ltd., London, 1929.

Ward, Maisie. *Father Maturin.* Longmans, Green, London, 1920.

Vanderbilt, Cornelius Jr. *The Vanderbilt Feud.* Hutchinson, London, 1957.

*Magazines and Periodicals*:

*The Beacon*, Ontario; *Cunard Magazine*; *Illustrated London News*; *Journal of Commerce*, 1913; *The Listener*, 26 October and 14 December 1972; *Lloyd's Weekly*; *Saturday Evening Post*; *The Shipbuilder*, June 1914; *Sports Illustrated* ('Was There a Gun?'), 24 December 1962; *Sunday Press* ('Lusitania Guns Probe'), December 1972; *Sunday Times Magazine* ('Samuel Cunard's Floating Palaces'); *The Times Engineering Supplement*, 6 and 13 June 1906.

*Newspapers*:

Ireland: *Cork Examiner, Clare Journal, Evening Echo* (Cork), *Irish Independent, Irish Weekly Independent, Irish Times.*

Britain: *Daily Express, Daily News, Daily Sketch, Evening News, Glasgow Daily Record, Glasgow Herald, Glasgow Weekly News, Liverpool Echo, Liverpool Post, Nottingham Guardian, The Star, Sunday Herald, Sunday Pictorial.*

France: *Le Monde.*

330  Bibliography

Germany:  *Berliner Tageblatt, Frankfurter-Zeitung, Köl- nische Rundschau, Kölnische Zeitung, Neue Prussische Zeitung.*

United States:  *Chicago Daily Tribune, New York Daily Tribune, The Fatherland, New York Herald, New York Sun, New York Times, New York World, Washington Post.*

Canada:  *Toronto Star, Winnipeg Free Press.*

Australia:  *Sydney Herald.*

*Correspondence, Diaries, Documents, Private Papers, Statements:*

*Lusitania* documents, Public Record Office, Kew, and Navy Library, Ministry of Defence, Earls Court (including Admiralty correspondence, telegrams and signals).

*Lusitania* documents, National Archives, Washington (in- cluding consular despatches of Wesley Frost, reports of Captains Miller and Castle and diplomatic correspondence between London and Washington).

*Lusitania* archives at the Hoover Institution, Stanford, California (including Frank Mason version of the *War Diary* of Walther Schwieger).

*U-20* log book and *War Diary* of Walter Schwieger, Bun- desarchiv, Freiburg, Germany.

*Lusitania* documents, Cunard Archives, Liverpool University.

Documents relating to the construction of the *Lusitania* and depositions at the Mersey Inquiry from the private collection of Alistair Galbraith, Wallasey.

Unpublished account of the *Lusitania* voyage by William Holton, 1965.

Log of the *Wanderer of Peel*, Manx Historical Society.

Log of the *Kezia Guilt*, Courtmacsherry, Co. Cork.

*Aftermath of the Lusitania Catastrophe* by Patrick Thompson.

*The Lusitania in Folklore.* A paper by Michael Mulcahy, B.E.

*R.M.S. Lusitania*, Cunard Brochure.

*The Bridge*, Verolme Dockyard, Cork.

*The Cunard Line and the War* (Supplement to *The Syren and Shipping*), 9 April, 1919.

*Mercantile Marine Service Association Notes*


*Television and Radio*:

*Who Sank the Lusitania?* BBC Television, 1972.

*Rendezvous with Death*. CBC Radio Canada, 1968.

# INDEX

IRELAND

Dungarva

CORK
Queenstown
(Cobh)
Cor
Kinsale

Old Head of Ki

Valentia
Island

Seven Head
Galley
Head
SUNK

U-20

Fastnet
Rock

Cape
Clear

U-20

LUSITANIA'S COURSE

from
New
York

— *Lusitania's* course, 7 May
-- Course of *U-20*, 5-7 May

Sea Miles

| 0 | 5 | 10 | 20 | 30 | 40 | 50 |